PRAISE FOR
CORE Leadership

"In a world that often prioritizes hustle over reflection, this book is a refreshing guide to leading with clarity and intention. Miki Feldman Simon has created a smart, accessible roadmap for anyone ready to lead from the inside out."

DORIE CLARK, *Wall Street Journal* bestselling author of *The Long Game* and executive education faculty at Columbia Business School

"Whether you are a seasoned executive or just beginning your leadership journey, this book will meet you where you are and help you move forward with greater clarity and purpose. I'm honored to support this work and the kind of leadership it represents. As you turn these pages, I hope you will not only think differently, but lead differently."

DR. MARSHALL GOLDSMITH, Thinkers50 #1 Executive Coach and *New York Times* bestselling author of *The Earned Life*, *Triggers*, and *What Got You Here Won't Get You There*

"The CORE framework is a powerful reminder that true leadership starts from within. This work helped several leaders on my team lead with greater clarity, purpose, and authenticity, and I've seen the ripple effects firsthand."

ADRIEN NUSSENBAUM, Co-founder and Co-CEO, MIRAKL

"What makes *CORE Leadership* special is how it invites leaders into reflection without losing sight of results. Get ready for an engaging conversation based on wisdom from life and from Miki Feldman Simon's professional journey. Beyond this, her interviews and the evidence-based practices that underlie her interventions weave together to form an honest and skillful approach to growing as a leader and a person."

CAROL KAUFFMAN, Assistant Professor at Harvard Medical School and Founder/Executive Director of Harvard's Institute of Coaching

"As a former CEO and now executive coach, I've read countless books on leadership. *CORE Leadership* stands out as both a deeply practical and inspiring guide. Whether you're a professional coach or someone simply looking to lead with more intention and impact, this book delivers. It's filled with illustrative stories, insights from top leadership thinkers, and actionable tools that make personal growth feel achievable. Miki Feldman Simon has created a framework that not only helps you lead others—but live a more grounded, fulfilling life. It's the kind of book that stays with you long after the final page."

SHIRA GOODMAN, former CEO, Staples, and Executive Coach

"Miki Feldman Simon reminds us that the hardest person you'll ever lead is yourself. Her CORE framework is a clear, practical guide to doing just that—with purpose, presence, and heart. A valuable read for any leader."

GARRY RIDGE, bestselling author of *Any Dumb-Ass Can Do It* and Chairman Emeritus, WD-40 Company

"I've worked closely with Miki for years, and her impact on how I show up as a leader, and as a person, has been profound. *CORE Leadership* distills her wisdom, clarity, and emotional intelligence into a framework that's both actionable and deeply human. This book isn't just about leadership; it's about learning to lead yourself with intention, and in doing so, amplifying your impact on those around you. If you're ready to grow from the inside out, this book is the guide you've been looking for."

RON ZALKIND, Founding General Partner, Lama Partners

"*CORE Leadership* is a mirror and a map for modern leaders. Miki Feldman Simon shows you how to uncover the blind spots between your intentions and your impact, then gives you the tools to close the gap. Her CORE framework is practical, powerful, and profoundly human—helping leaders clarify, act, reflect, and grow. If you want to lead with clarity, courage, and authenticity in a world that demands all three, start here."

DR. KIRSTIN FERGUSON AM, Winner of the Thinkers50 Distinguished Award for Leadership, top-ranked Thinkers50 management thinker, and bestselling author of *Women Kind*, *Head & Heart*, and *Blindspotting*

"*CORE Leadership* is more than a framework—it's a roadmap for becoming the leader you were meant to be. Miki Feldman Simon moves beyond theory, offering a clear, actionable process to lead yourself with clarity, purpose, and integrity. This book will not only elevate how you lead, it will transform how you live."

DR. RUTH GOTIAN, Thinkers50 #1 Emerging Management Thinker in the world, top 50 global executive coach, and author of *The Success Factor* and *The Financial Times Guide to Mentoring*

"Miki Feldman Simon has written a leadership playbook that actually starts where real leadership begins—with you. The CORE framework is clear, compelling, and immediately usable. If you want to lead with greater purpose, consistency, and impact, start here."

RHETT POWER, CEO of Accountability Inc. and *Forbes* Columnist

"Founders and executives often focus on building the business but real, sustainable growth starts with the person leading it. Miki Feldman Simon's four-step framework helps leaders strengthen their self-awareness, align their actions, and lead with clarity through complexity. It's the kind of guidance I wish more leaders embraced early on."

IZHAR ARMONY, Managing General Partner, CRV

"We all want to lead with more purpose, gratitude, and impact. The question is, 'How do we do that?' In this gem of a book, Miki provides the framework that turns self-awareness into everyday leadership wins. I love this book, and you will too!"

CHESTER ELTON, bestselling author of *The Carrot Principle*, *All In*, and *Leading with Gratitude*

"*CORE Leadership* provides a powerful system for translating inner clarity into better decision-making and organizational performance. Miki's framework is practical yet grounded in behavioral science—exactly the kind of leadership approach we need to close the gap between intention and impact."

JAMES R. LANGABEER II, PhD, MBA, Executive Director and Professor of Behavioral and Data Sciences, The University of Texas Health Science Center

"In my organizations, we've long referred to working with Miki Feldman Simon as 'The Gift of Miki,' and for good reason. Her coaching has shaped the way I lead and the way our teams grow. This book captures that same transformative experience and makes it accessible to anyone willing to do the work. I've seen firsthand the power of the CORE framework to spark meaningful change. If you're ready to lead with greater clarity, focus, and intention, this book will guide the way."

GUY YEHIAV, President, SmartSense by Digi

"What sets *CORE Leadership* apart is how seamlessly it blends strategy with humanity. Miki Feldman Simon doesn't just offer a leadership framework, she provides a compass for navigating both professional challenges and personal growth. Through her stories and tools, she makes the inner work of self-leadership accessible, practical, and deeply inspiring. This is the rare book that helps leaders succeed in their careers and thrive in their lives."

SHARON KAN, Entrepreneur in Residence, Yale University, and CEO, Fifty Five Creative

A four-step framework to
Lead Yourself,
Grow Your Influence,
and
Amplify Your Impact

CORE
leadership

Miki Feldman Simon

BONDI
WAVE
PRESS

CORE Leadership: A Four-Step Framework to Lead Yourself, Grow Your Influence, and Amplify Your Impact

Copyright © 2026 Miki (Michal) Feldman Simon
All rights reserved.

No part of this publication may be reproduced, stored in a retrieval system, or transmitted in any form or by any means (electronic, mechanical, photocopying, recording, or otherwise), without the prior written permission of the copyright holder, except in the case of brief quotations embodied in critical articles or reviews. For permissions or inquiries, contact: www.mikifeldmansimon.com

Edited by Ruth-Anne Eisler
Proofread by Plotwise Editorial Inc.
Indexed by Lisa Stumpf
Cover and interior design by Andrew Welyczko, AbandonedWest Creative, Inc.

Hardcover ISBN: 979-8-9931904-0-2
Paperback ISBN: 979-8-9931904-1-9
eBook ISBN: 979-8-9931904-2-6

Library of Congress Control Number: 2025920405

Published by Bondi Wave Press, Boston, Massachusetts

To Bart, Arden, and Sean

You have helped me become a better human, a more present mother, and a more loving partner. Your love, support, and the space you gave me shaped this book and the journey behind it.

Contents

Foreword by Dr. Marshall Goldsmith   xi

Introduction   1

CORE FOUR-STEP FRAMEWORK

1 CLARIFY   9

    Clarity is the Keystone of Success   12

    Defining Your Values: Your Inner Compass   15

    Identifying and Leveraging Your Strengths   31

    Navigating Life's Priorities   42

    Defining Success in Your Terms   46

    Summary   53

2 OPERATIONALIZE   55

    The Shift from Clarity to Action   57

    Aligning Actions with Values and Priorities   59

    Living Your Values Through Action   66

    Building Habits and Routines That Stick   77

    Leveraging Your Strengths   87

    Accountability   92

    Staying Motivated on the Journey   97

    Summary   105

3 REFLECT 109
- Slowing Down to Speed Up 113
- Triggers 130
- The Stories We Tell Ourselves 134
- What We Think, We Become 140
- Nurture a Growth Mindset 170
- Letting Go 177
- Trekking Up Kilimanjaro 179
- Summary 181

4 EVALUATE 185
- Mind the Gap 188
- From Feedback to Impact 208
- Time to Self-Evaluate 216
- Summary 222

THE RIPPLE EFFECT OF CORE 225

What's Next? 231
Acknowledgments 235
Notes 237
Index 243
About The Author 249

Foreword

By Dr. Marshall Goldsmith

OVER THE COURSE of my career, I've worked with some of the world's most successful leaders, and the most surprising truth I've learned is this: the hardest person you will ever lead is yourself.

It's not strategy or vision that holds most leaders back. It's not skill or intelligence. It's the daily challenge of aligning our behavior with our intentions of showing up consistently as the person we most want to be.

That's what makes this book so valuable.

In *Core Leadership: A Four-Step Framework to Lead Yourself, Grow Your Influence, and Amplify Your Impact*, Miki Feldman Simon introduces a simple yet powerful framework that helps you do the hard work of self-leadership. Her framework CORE: Clarify, Operationalize, Reflect, Evaluate, is not just a model. It's a daily practice that supports leaders in turning self-awareness into consistent, values-driven action.

In *The Earned Life*, I wrote that fulfillment isn't something we achieve once, it is something we earn every day by aligning our efforts with our values and aspirations. That belief runs through every page of this book.

This book is about being intentional. It is not filled with empty inspiration or abstract theory. It is grounded in the real challenges of leading in complex, fast-moving environments. It offers practical tools for doing the work day in and day out to show up as the kind of leader others want to follow. It helps close the gap between what you mean to do and how others experience you. And it challenges you to look inward as a starting point for meaningful, lasting change.

I have long believed that leadership is not about what you know—it is about what you do. Miki's book honors that principle beautifully. It is filled with honest questions, compelling stories, and tools that actually work. She brings deep wisdom and clarity to the often-messy process of growth.

Whether you are a seasoned executive or just beginning your leadership journey, this book will meet you where you are and help you move forward with greater clarity and purpose.

I'm honored to support this work and the kind of leadership it represents. As you turn these pages, I hope you will not only think differently, but lead differently.

> Dr. Marshall Goldsmith is the Thinkers50 #1 Executive Coach and *New York Times* bestselling author of *The Earned Life*, *Triggers*, and *What Got You Here Won't Get You There*.

Introduction

LEADERSHIP is an inner journey before it becomes an outward expression. It is about being the kind of person others will willingly follow, not because of a role or rank, but because of the example you set through how you live.

Leadership isn't limited to the corner office. It happens everywhere: in classrooms, across dinner tables, and in day-to-day encounters.

Leadership begins with self-leadership, with a commitment to self-mastery. It is the conscious decision to take responsibility for your life, to lead with intention rather than reacting passively to what life throws at you. If you don't lead yourself, you will inevitably be led by others, by their expectations, their priorities, their values, and their vision. Leadership will happen in some way, but the question is: Will you actively shape it, or will you allow it to be shaped for you? Wouldn't you prefer to be the leader of your own life, shaping your destiny with clarity and purpose, rather than being swept along by the tides of circumstance or dictated by the agendas of others?

Self-leadership isn't just about controlling your actions; it's about deeply understanding yourself, your values, strengths, and areas for growth. It is about aligning your decisions with your goals and principles, even when it's difficult. It's about mastering your thoughts and emotions so that they serve you rather than sabotage you. This inner mastery builds a steady foundation that allows you to face challenges with resilience and grace. It's the quiet, unshakable strength that comes from knowing who you are and what you stand for.

When you embrace self-leadership, you claim ownership over your choices and, by extension, your future. Instead of waiting for permission or external validation, you chart your course based on what matters most to you. This doesn't mean ignoring others or being selfish, it means honoring your own voice while respecting and valuing the perspectives of others.

Leadership can be about grand gestures or public accolades, yet more often leadership lies in the smallest, most personal acts. It's in the way you approach your day, the courage to say no to distractions, and the determination to stay aligned with your priorities. It's choosing to grow, even when growth is uncomfortable. It's recognizing that the world around you will always pull at your attention, but the power to choose your direction ultimately lies within you.

In a world full of noise and competing priorities, self-leadership is an anchor. It allows you to stay grounded in your purpose and vision, even as circumstances change or challenges arise. By leading yourself first, you not only take control of your own life, but also radiate outwards, creating a ripple effect and empowering those around you.

In a refreshing departure from traditional leadership narratives that often focus on controlling or directing others, this take on leadership centers on self-direction. The premise of this book is that leadership at its core isn't just about managing others, it's about mastering yourself and, in doing so, unlocking the potential to lead with impact and genuine influence. Leadership is, therefore, a universal concept, not reserved for a select few, but accessible to anyone willing to take responsibility for their own life. It is an open invitation for everyone to lead, in big moments and small ones, by being the best version of themselves. When we navigate our lives with self-awareness, clarity, and accountability, we not only steer our own ship but light the way for others.

In my own leadership journey, I was once on a mission to prove that I was capable and worthy, driven to achieve success in defiance of limiting beliefs and negative perceptions instilled in me. But true fulfillment came when I embraced self-leadership, when my values, vision, and mission crystallized with glaring clarity. When I realized that I could always choose how to respond to life's challenges. It was then that I began leading with intention, authenticity, and integrity. I started thriving, feeling more content, relaxed, and impactful.

This book is deeply personal for me. It is the guide I wish someone had given me earlier in my life and career. It is the advice, and formalized process,

I want to pass on to my kids and the generations to come, to help them be happy and succeed in the world. It is a framework for making intentional choices, navigating challenges, and leading with clarity and confidence. The lessons and strategies in this book are ones I have seen transform not only my own personal and professional life but also the lives of the leaders I coach. I have watched clients step into their full potential, align their actions with their values, and find the fulfillment they were seeking, not by waiting for circumstances to change, but by leading themselves first. That is the message of this book, and it is one I deeply believe in.

Over my thirty-year career, I've had the unique experience of leading across different countries, functions, and industries. My leadership journey has taken me through roles in marketing, operations, and human resources, across the United States, Israel, and Australia. I've worked in sectors ranging from high-tech and communications to education and supply chain. Two of the companies I helped lead, Profitect and Phonetic Systems, were successfully acquired. I enjoyed overcoming the challenges faced by fast-moving start-ups and scale-ups, and helping organizations grow and build strong, intentional cultures.

Beyond my corporate career, I also founded *IamBackatWork*, a platform dedicated to supporting women in reentering the workforce, and my successful Executive Coaching business. Through this work, I've seen firsthand how powerful it is when individuals take charge of their own growth and careers.

But leadership isn't just about work; it's about how we show up in all aspects of our lives. I have been married to a wonderful guy for thirty-two years, and I am the proud mother of two incredible children. My greatest fulfillment comes from the relationships I've built and the growth I've experienced alongside my family. I know firsthand how important it is to balance ambition with presence, and to align personal and professional values to live a meaningful, impactful life.

I also know what it means to push past discomfort in the pursuit of growth. At fifty, I ventured to summit Mount Kilimanjaro, a personal milestone that reinforced my belief that true transformation happens outside of our comfort zones. More recently, my recovery from long COVID has deepened my perspective on resilience, adaptation, and self-compassion, lessons that apply just as much to leadership as they do to personal well-being.

Through my experience as both an executive and an executive coach, I've seen how powerful self-leadership can be. My academic background [a bachelor's in psychology and education, a master of science in organizational behavior, professional coach certification (ICF PCC), and senior professional in human resources certification] has deepened this insight. Drawing on the research, writing, and lived experience of global leaders, I recognized that leadership truly begins with leading oneself.

I've identified four key steps that anyone can take to become their best selves and lead with purpose. These steps form the CORE framework: Clarify, Operationalize, Reflect, and Evaluate.

Leadership is a lifelong journey of self-discovery and growth, and through the CORE framework, you will unlock the tools, insights, and confidence to take the reins of your life, becoming not just the leader you aspire to be, but the person you were always meant to become.

Welcome to Your CORE Journey of Self-Leadership

Hello, and welcome. This journey promises to be both enlightening and empowering.

If you've picked up this book, it's likely because you're seeking something more. You want a deeper understanding of yourself, a clearer vision for your life, and a stronger ability to lead—both personally and professionally.

You might be wondering, What exactly is the CORE framework? Simply put, it's your new compass for personal and leadership development, a tool kit designed to help you engage deeply with the fundamental aspects of who you are and who you aspire to be. There are many strategies for leading others. CORE is a strategy for leading yourself. CORE stands for Clarify, Operationalize, Reflect, and Evaluate—four pillars that together support a robust structure for growth and fulfillment.

The book is divided into four parts; each section is dedicated to one aspect of CORE. In each part, I will share stories and tools to help you implement the strategies you will learn. In the **Clarify** chapter, we will explore your values, identify the principles guiding you today, recognize your strengths, and define what success means to you.

In the **Operationalize** chapter, we'll work on how to put this into action. We'll assess how well your current life aligns with your goals, leverage your strengths, and build supportive habits.

In the **Reflect** chapter, we delve into understanding your thought processes and the obstacles you create for yourself, enhancing your self-awareness and equipping you with strategies to consistently present your best self.

In the **Evaluate** chapter, we examine if your behaviors align with your intentions, introduce tools to discover your blind spots, and open up to feedback.

You might be arriving at this book from any point in the CORE journey.

- Perhaps you received feedback that didn't land well or uncovered a disconnect between your intent and your impact—this falls within the realm of "Evaluate."
- Maybe you've become aware of limiting beliefs, recurring doubts, or negative thought patterns that are holding you back, the work we do in "Reflect."
- Or you might simply feel stuck or unclear about what really matters to you; this is what we address in "Clarify."
- Perhaps you know what you want but are struggling to turn intention into consistent behavior. That's where "Operationalize" comes in, helping you align your daily actions with your values and goals.

Your starting point doesn't have to be linear. As an executive coach, I often begin with 360° interviews to gather feedback, which means starting with "Evaluate" and then weaving in the rest of the framework. The beauty of CORE is that it's cyclical. Wherever you begin, CORE will meet you there and support your growth.

Following the CORE framework will transform personal insights into actionable changes in both your personal and professional life. You'll develop a structured approach to growth by integrating clarity, operationalization, reflection, and evaluation, each section building upon the last.

FIGURE 1: The CORE Framework

CORE Step	What You Do	Guiding Question
Clarify Define what matters most	Clarify your values, identify your priorities, recognize your strengths, and define success	Who do you want to be?
Operationalize Turn clarity into action	Translate intentions into consistent habits and practices	What habits and behaviors will demonstrate your values and priorities?
Reflect Grow from the inside out	Notice patterns, recognize self-sabotage, and adjust your approach	How are you getting in your own way?
Evaluate Assess your impact	Measure progress and ensure your actions align with your intentions	Are you walking the talk?

Engage and Transform

This book is more than something to read. It's something to engage with. Think of it as your guide and companion—a space for reflection, growth, and action.

The "Clarify" chapter is foundational. It will help you define who you are, what matters to you most, and where you want to go. I highly recommend completing at least one of the exercises in each section in the "Clarify" chapter to vividly envision the leader you want to be. In the "Operationalize" and "Reflect" chapters, choose the exercises that best match what you're working on or struggling with right now. Don't skip the "Evaluate" chapter; it's helpful for all of us to get out of our own heads and gain other perspectives.

As we embark on this journey together, I invite you to bring an open heart and a curious mind. Reflect on the insights shared, engage with the exercises, and allow yourself to be both challenged and inspired. This book is not just about reading, it's about doing, reflecting, and transforming.

It's about taking charge of your personal narrative and crafting a life that resonates with the deepest parts of your being.

So, grab your favorite pen, a fresh notebook, your laptop or your iPad, and perhaps a comforting cup of tea, or my favorite, coffee, and let's dive into the essence of "Clarity." It's time to clear the fog, sharpen your focus, and light up your path to personal and leadership mastery. Your CORE journey begins now.

A Note About This Work

To protect the privacy and confidentiality of clients, all names and identifying details in the stories and examples throughout this book have been changed. In some cases, stories represent a composite of multiple clients, woven together to illustrate common patterns or insights without revealing any individual's identity.

1
CLARIFY

Knowing yourself is the beginning of all wisdom.

Aristotle

AND YOU know what? He was onto something. As kids, we were bombarded with questions about what we wanted to do when we grew up. But rarely did anyone ask us WHO we wanted to be, or why that mattered. Yet, who you are shapes what you do. Your values, character, and sense of purpose drive your decisions, actions, and ultimately, your impact on others.

Who you become isn't just about career—it's about character. And that begins with understanding yourself.

Character is the invisible force that drives how we show up, especially when no one is watching. It's built in moments of choice: Do you speak up or stay silent? Do you cut corners or stand by your principles? Character is revealed not in what you say, but in what you do when things are hard, uncertain, or uncomfortable.

In the CORE framework, "Clarify" offers a practical starting point for building character and deepening self-awareness. This chapter will help you explore essential questions: What do I stand for? What are my strengths? What mission drives me? You'll examine your values, priorities, personal definition of success, and sense of purpose. These are not just abstract ideas, they are the building blocks of who you are and who you want to become. By understanding these foundational elements, you can make more deliberate choices, show up with integrity, and lead yourself in a way that aligns with the kind of person and leader you aspire to be.

Clarity is the Keystone of Success

In our fast-paced lives, we're constantly caught up in a whirlwind of activities. From back-to-back meetings to the perpetual chase of deadlines, it often feels like we're running a marathon every day. Many of my clients share how the essentials—lunch breaks, catching their breath, a quick trip to the restroom—can feel like luxuries.

That's where our coaching sessions become a haven, a pause from the hustle. It's a chance for them to step back, reflect, and breathe. This isn't just about slowing down; it's about gaining the clarity needed to move forward with intention.

Embracing clarity involves taking a step back to reflect, a strategic pause that's not about losing time but investing it wisely to make your actions more impactful when you accelerate again.

I interviewed Dorie Clark, an accomplished author, speaker, and expert in strategic thinking, for this book. She shared a powerful insight about taking the time to pause that struck at the heart of intentional living:

> No one at any point in your career is going to make this easy for you. This is not anything that your boss or anybody else is going to hand to you where they say, "Oh, please do this. You know, this is the top of the list." It's never going to be top of the list, because it is always in other people's self-interest for you to be immediately responsive to their needs. Even if they claim they want strategic thinking from you, in reality, what they want is for you to return their email very quickly.[1]

It's a hard truth: No one will give you permission to pause. The immediate demands of others will always compete for your time and attention. But true clarity requires intention. It demands that *you* take charge.

Dorie also shared a metaphor from her book *The Long Game* that captures the power of clarity:

> We're all in life, in our careers, basically floating in the ocean, buffeted by forces larger than us. If you don't have any preferences about where you end up, you're like a jellyfish, drifting wherever the waves take you. But most of us do have preferences, a vision of what we want our lives or careers to look like. That's why we need to be more like a speedboat. A speedboat, even in regular conditions, can chart a course, take initiative, and move deliberately toward its destination… by having that clarity, by having that initiative and propulsion, you are much more likely to achieve the outcome that you want to have…. You have to be the driver. You have to be the person that is carving time out… It will never, ever happen unless you are proactively making it happen.[2]

This metaphor highlights the essence of clarity: Without it, you're subject to external forces, passively drifting through your days. Carve out the time to gain clarity. It may feel more gratifying to clear five emails from your inbox than to spend fifteen minutes reviewing your goals and priorities. The dopamine hit of instant productivity can feel more satisfying in the moment. But the real work of intentional living is a discipline, one that involves making deliberate choices.

This is your invitation to become the driver of your life. To define your values, priorities, and goals, to identify your North Star, to become the speedboat.

Schedule the time with yourself to gain clarity. Treat that time as sacred. Because in slowing down, you're not just hitting pause, you're making room to move forward with focus, strategy, and intention.

The words of Frances Hesselbein, CEO of the Girl Scouts of America for more than twenty years, have stayed with me. "Leadership is a matter of how to be, not how to do."[3]

This idea challenged the way I thought about leadership, not as a set of skills or strategies, but as a reflection of who we are at our core. It's not just about executing tasks or making decisions; it's about embodying authenticity, integrity, and purpose.

When I reflect on the most impactful leaders I've encountered, they weren't necessarily the ones with the perfect strategy or flawless execution. They were the ones whose presence inspired trust, whose values were evident in their actions, and who led with a deep sense of purpose. Their leadership wasn't performative; it was a natural extension of who they were.

When you focus on *how to be* rather than just *what to do*, you create a foundation for lasting impact. Clarifying your values and purpose provides that foundation. It ensures that your actions reflect who you are, not just what's expected.

Clarity is not just a buzzword. It is the thread that connects your intentions with your actions, your goals with your daily choices. Without it, we tend to react to life instead of shaping it with purpose.

Clarity simplifies decision-making and sharpens your focus. When you are grounded in your priorities, distractions fall away, and you can direct your time and energy toward what will make the greatest difference.

Clarity extends beyond individual growth, it enhances communication and relationships as well. When you understand your own goals and values, you articulate them more effectively to others, whether in personal relationships or leadership roles. Clear communication fosters trust, alignment, and collaboration in all settings and, as a result, increases your influence.

It also plays a powerful role in reducing stress. Uncertainty often breeds anxiety, but when you have a clear roadmap, you can navigate challenges with greater ease. Instead of feeling stuck or unsure, you move forward with confidence. Even in moments of conflict, it serves as an anchor. It helps you stay true to your values and seek solutions that reflect who you want to be. It also shapes how you show up in those moments, guiding how you respond, how you treat others, and how you expect to be treated yourself. Instead of reacting impulsively, you can approach conflict with intentionality.

Ultimately, clarity turns ambitions into action. Lofty goals can feel overwhelming, but when broken down into clear, tangible steps, they become achievable.

The more clarity you cultivate, the more intentional and fulfilling your life becomes. It is the foundation that allows you to lead with purpose, navigate challenges with confidence, and shape a future that aligns with who you truly are.

Think of clarity as your personal GPS in life's journey, guiding your decisions and helping you stay true to your principles.

To understand your principles, to gain clarity, we will explore your values, understand their impact and how they were formed, identify your strengths and priorities, and craft your personal definition of success. Each of these elements shapes the foundation of how you lead yourself and others. Without this foundation, success can feel hollow, and leadership can be reactive rather than intentional. Let's start with values, the core of who you are.

Defining Your Values: Your Inner Compass

What Values Are and Why They Matter

Values aren't just abstract concepts; they're the underlying motivations for our actions and reactions. They influence how we interpret the world and how we respond to it, shaping both our perspective and our behavior. To understand values, think of them as the principles that you live by, almost like a personal code of conduct that guides you through life's maze.

Understanding your values isn't just an intellectual exercise, it's about reflection and intentional choice. In this section, we'll explore how values shape your leadership and life, to give you the tools to clarify your own values so you can make more aligned decisions. Because your values are expressed through your actions, they play a central role in shaping your character over time.

Values are rooted in our experiences. They often start with our upbringing, embedded in the advice we receive, the stories we're told, and the behaviors we observe. They're shaped by the cultural context we grow up in, from the community norms we absorb to the education we receive. But they don't stop there. Values grow and adapt as we encounter new experiences and as our understanding of the world, and ourselves, evolves.

Think about a time when you had to make a difficult decision. What factors did you consider? Did you prioritize honesty, even when it was hard to tell the truth? Did you strive for excellence, no matter the effort required? Or did you choose kindness, aiming to support others even if it meant setting aside your own needs? These considerations are a reflection of your values.

But values do more than just guide decisions; they shape our goals and aspirations. They're the measuring sticks we use to determine our success. Someone who values creativity might measure success by the ability to innovate and express original ideas. Another person who values stability might focus on long-term planning and security.

Remember the last time you felt truly upset? Think back to that moment when frustration bubbled up inside you. Can you recall what ignited it? Can you recall what was happening? That frustration might be another clue to understanding your values.

In practice, values are like a compass that helps us navigate every aspect of our lives. They show up in the way we communicate with others, the integrity with which we perform our work, and the compassion we show to those around us. They're at play when we're faced with societal issues, influencing our stance and our willingness to act.

How Values Are Shaped: Childhood, Culture, and Experience

Childhood Echoes

Consider the old adages that echo from your childhood. "Don't cry over spilt milk," one of my mum's favorite sayings, isn't just about dairy mishaps, it's a lesson on not lamenting about what has already happened and wasting time and energy on what is done and you cannot change. And "Laughter is the best medicine" does more than summon smiles; it reminds us that optimism is a choice. These snippets of wisdom weave the initial fabric of our value system, but as we grow, so too do our values, sometimes outgrowing the very maxims we once embraced.

My clients often echo phrases that have been ingrained in them:

- Family comes first.
- Work hard and you will succeed.
- If you don't like your environment, change it.
- Use your time efficiently.

Why bring these up? These sayings often reflect values that have been so deeply embedded in us that we might not even realize they're guiding our actions. They're like the background music to the movie of our lives, always playing, even if we're not consciously listening.

Not all values are spoken aloud. Take my father, for example. He never said outright that men were superior to women, but his actions spoke volumes of a chauvinistic belief, a belief I could not subscribe to. It's not a value I choose to carry forward. For others, values may be revealed in what their family did or didn't do for money, work, community, etc., or in the way they treated others.

Some values demand attention, like my father's evident chauvinism. Others are subtler, hiding in the shadows of our choices. Both types, however, shape the contours of our lives.

It's essential to sift through these influences to uncover which values truly belong to you. What resonates with you, as opposed to what's been passed down from friends, family, or society. It's about discerning *your* authentic values from the noise and letting go of the ones that no longer serve you. One that I chose to let go of is one of my father's favorites: Men like women who keep quiet. My client Joe still believes "It doesn't matter what others are doing, it matters what you are doing." Trisha has decided to let go of "Just try to be like the other kids."

Remember, values are dynamic; they shift as we navigate through life's unpredictable waters. Consider the profound impact of the pandemic. It was an unexpected storm that compelled many to seek shelter in the form of introspection and reassessment of what truly matters. During those long months of isolation, priorities shifted for countless individuals. Connections with loved ones took precedence, personal health and well-being climbed to the top of the list, and the concept of work-life balance was redefined, spurring movements like the Great Resignation. People sought careers that not only paid the bills but also brought satisfaction and a sense of purpose.

Such significant external events, or a new love, or the birth of a child, have the power to rearrange our values hierarchy dramatically. Family, once important, may become paramount; financial stability, always a consideration, could emerge as crucial in the face of economic uncertainty.

That's why it's essential to revisit your values periodically. Your current values and priorities paint the most accurate picture of who you are today, illuminated by the lens of your experiences and the broader context of the world around you.

Cultural Values

During a trip to Missoula, Montana, to see my son, I found myself in a moment of cultural introspection amidst the aisles of the Good Food Store. In search of breakfast, I arrived just before the 11:00 a.m. breakfast cutoff, relieved to find precisely four sandwiches that could accommodate our intricate dietary needs, I being the most problematic of the bunch. I hastily reached for the egg and tofu sandwiches, aware of a woman who had been browsing before me. Though she ended up selecting other options, a pang of discomfort accompanied my supposed victory.

Back home, announcing my successful haul, the triumph felt hollow. It prompted me to revisit a deeply ingrained value from my early years in Israel: the aversion to being a 'frier,' someone who is taken advantage of, a sucker. For Israelis, the 'frier' is a negative label that should be avoided. "Don't be a frier" is more than just a colloquialism, it's a cultural emblem woven into the very fabric of assertiveness and survival in Israel.

However, standing there in Montana, with the sandwiches in hand, I questioned this value. Adam Grant's teachings from his book *Think Again* came to mind. His wisdom on reassessing our beliefs, the act of learning to unlearn, and the challenge of changing our core values resonated with me.[4] I had acted on an old belief, that to avoid being a 'frier,' being taken advantage of, one must act quickly, even preemptively. But now, confronted with a woman whose choice I had preempted, I questioned the value of this particular belief.

"Don't be a frier" had served me once, but did it represent who I am now? I decided it didn't. The value of courteous patience, of giving precedence to those before me, felt more congruent with the person I had evolved into. It's a change I've come to embrace, as I demonstrated months later in the supermarket, pausing before the last loaf of bread on the shelf. I let the shopper ahead of me choose first, stepping away from a cultural imprint that no longer aligned with my personal ethos.

Grant suggests that when new information challenges our core beliefs, our natural reaction might be to resist because these beliefs are part of our identity.[5] Yet, it is in these moments that we have the greatest opportunity for growth. By consciously deciding to prioritize respect and patience over the fear of missing out, I was detaching my present from my past. Letting go of old values allowed me to reshape my identity into one that better reflected my current beliefs.

As you engage with the exercises below, consider the values you hold. Ask yourself: Which beliefs have I outgrown? What values no longer resonate with the life I am leading now? By identifying and releasing the values and beliefs that no longer serve you, you create space for new, more aligned ways of being. This is not just about learning; it's about evolving as an individual.

When you know your values, you start creating clarity. This clarity empowers you to make choices that bring a sense of fulfillment and purpose. It enables you to live authentically and to build a life that resonates with your true self.

Living Your Values

Leading at Home and Work: One Authentic Self

Our values don't live in silos. They guide us in every aspect of our lives, from our boardrooms to our living rooms. Leadership, too, isn't confined to a title or workspace. It thrives wherever we show up fully as ourselves, at home, at work, and in our communities. Chester Elton, the globally recognized leadership expert, puts it succinctly: "Don't leave leadership principles at work, bring them home."[6]

It's tempting to compartmentalize leadership, to bring our best selves to work but leave those principles behind when we come home, or vice versa. Yet leadership is not a coat you take off at the office door.

True leadership transcends roles. The clarity, compassion, and integrity you demonstrate at work can, and should, be mirrored at home. Likewise, the care, empathy, and patience you offer loved ones can become strengths in the workplace. Take compassion, for example. At home, you might show patience with a child learning something new or offer support to a partner after a hard day. That same compassion, listening to a struggling team member, giving feedback constructively, or recognizing someone's effort, can transform workplace dynamics, fostering trust and connection. When you embrace consistency in who you are across all areas of life, you lead not just as a professional but as a whole, authentic human being.

Recent research backs this up. A study published in *Organizational Behavior and Human Decision Processes* found that individuals who perceive a low overlap between their work and personal identities, what researchers call *low identity integration*, feel significantly less authentic and are more likely to behave unethically. In contrast, those with *high identity integration*, who see consistency in how they show up across roles, experience a stronger sense of authenticity and are less likely to engage in dishonest behavior.[7]

This means that trying to be one person at work and a completely different person at home isn't just exhausting, it can also chip away at your integrity. The more aligned you feel across roles, the more you access your true self, and the more ethically grounded your decisions become.

The Ripple Effect

When you lead with authenticity, when who you are at home and at work is rooted in the same values, people notice. That internal alignment doesn't just feel better; it has a powerful external impact. It shapes how others experience you and what they believe is possible for themselves. Imagine the example you set for your children or loved ones when they see you act with integrity, respect, and purpose. Now, imagine the impact when those same qualities are brought to your team or organization.

Marshall Goldsmith, the renowned executive coach, often tells leaders, "The behaviors you demonstrate influence those around you more than you realize."[8]

As a leader, you are always on stage. Your actions, big and small, send signals about what is valued, acceptable, and expected. People watch you closely, even when you don't realize it, and your behavior sets the tone for the entire team, at work and at home.

When you show up calm under pressure, take accountability, or celebrate others' efforts, you inspire trust and encourage the same behaviors. Conversely, inconsistency, dismissiveness, or failing to honor commitments can erode morale and trust faster than you think. Leadership is not about telling others what to do; it's about modeling the behavior you want to see.

Your actions create ripples. Be intentional, because as a leader, you're not just influencing outcomes, you're shaping people, culture, and the future of your team and family.

To put leadership into practice in all areas of life, try these strategies:

1. **Reflect on your values:** Ask yourself: What values guide me as a leader at work? How do they show up at home? Are there areas where I can align these more closely?
2. **Bring compassion to work:** Treat colleagues as you would family: Listen, empathize, and lead with care.
3. **Bring discipline and clarity home:** Leadership principles like clear communication, accountability, and planning apply to your personal life as well. For example, family meetings or shared goal setting can create cohesion and clarity.
4. **Set boundaries and role-model balance:** As a leader, prioritize self-care and work-life balance, showing both teams and loved ones that success is about thriving, not just achieving.

Leadership principles are not confined to the workplace, they are universal and apply to every aspect of life. Whether you are leading a team at work, guiding your family at home, or contributing to your community, the core values of leadership, like trust, accountability, empathy, and being true to your word, remain the same.

When you embody these principles authentically, you create alignment between your personal and professional lives. At work, you foster thriving, engaged organizations where people feel seen and valued. At home, those same behaviors nurture deeper, more fulfilling relationships built on respect, trust, and care.

True leadership isn't something you switch on and off; it's a lifelong practice that starts with who you are, how you show up, and the example you set in every environment. The stronger you are as a leader in your personal life, the greater your impact will be at work, and vice versa.

Living Your Mandate

In writing this book, I had the privilege of interviewing Dr. Carol Kauffman, a world-renowned executive coach and leadership thinker. Carol has spent decades coaching leaders across industries, helping them align their lives and leadership with purpose.

Carol shared a pivotal moment that changed the trajectory of her life. One afternoon, sitting at her desk, she felt a strong sense that something important was happening. After winning a free spot in a coaching program, she paused, turned to face a blank wall, closed her eyes, and asked herself, "If there's a life lesson for me right now, what is it?" The answer came clearly: "Don't hold back." That phrase became a personal mandate. It wasn't about suddenly feeling confident. It was about choosing to act. The next time she had an impulse to reach out to someone, like writing to Martin Seligman or voicing her desire to keynote at a global conference, she followed through. What began as a quiet moment of reflection led to opportunities she had never imagined. She went on to co-found the Institute of Coaching at Harvard, deliver keynote speeches, and form transformational professional relationships. That simple but powerful commitment, to not hold back, became a guiding value that opened unexpected doors and helped shape her legacy.[9]

Carol's story underscores that values are not just abstract ideals, they can be mandates we choose to live by. Identifying your own mandate can provide clarity and direction during moments of doubt or hesitation.

I know this firsthand. I remember a time when I wasn't living by my mandate, and how frustrated it made me feel.

Over twenty years ago, I was the Director of HR at Phonetic Systems, a pioneer in speech recognition technology. As the head of HR and a member of the Executive Management team, I had the title, the status, and even the flexibility I desired while raising young children. On paper, everything looked right. And yet, I felt stagnant.

Phonetic Systems was leading innovation, developing automated systems that would answer calls and direct people to the right person. In our executive meetings, there were endless discussions about telephone switches and speech recognition advancements; topics that, to be honest, held no interest for me. I found myself tuning out, disengaging.

Then, leadership changed. Not long after I joined, the CEO was let go, and for the next few years, I worked under an interim CEO whose leadership style didn't resonate with me. Though the company was ultimately acquired successfully, I spent years feeling stuck. I had the position, but I wasn't growing. I had stability, but I wasn't engaged. I wasn't living my mandate.

If I had been clearer on my personal values, on what fuels me as a professional, I would have recognized the warning signs sooner. I was no longer learning, no longer passionate, and no longer making the kind of impact that energized me. I should have left earlier.

That experience became a turning point. After I left, I made a commitment to myself: Pay attention. Be aware of when you stop growing. Recognize when you no longer feel passion for your work. And never settle for just going through the motions.

Ask yourself: What is one principle or value I could commit to living by? Once you have it, don't just state it, *live it*. Let it guide your actions, decisions, and leadership.

Reflect on Your Values Periodically

It's important to periodically reflect on your values. Are they still serving you well, or are they holding you back? Are they helping you grow, or do they need adjusting? This reflection is not just an exercise in self-awareness; it's a way to ensure that your actions are aligned with the person you want to be. It leads to greater fulfillment and authenticity, and is your path to finding your purpose. I have often heard both young and older professionals talk about a lack of purpose in their lives. At times, this lack of purpose is debilitating, causing them to leave their careers without a clear path forward. Start by clarifying your values, then find a career, aspects of your role, or an organization that aligns with them.

Understanding your values will help you prioritize your time and resources, make choices that resonate with your true self, and navigate challenges with integrity.

When your actions are aligned with your values, you build trust with others. People are more likely to follow and engage with leaders who are consistent and whose actions match their words. In essence, clarity in your values is the foundation for living a purpose-driven life and leading with conviction.

In my conversations with Marshall Goldsmith, he emphasized the transformative impact of gaining clarity on one's values, both in his own life and in the lives of his clients:

> Gaining clarity on my values has been foundational for both my life and career. It enables me to make decisions that align with what I truly believe in and stand for. For example, one of my core values is helping others achieve their goals. This principle guided me toward a career in executive coaching, where I can make a meaningful difference in the lives and careers of others.
>
> In my personal life, understanding my values helps me prioritize my time and energy on activities and relationships that are truly meaningful. Equally important, it has taught me to say 'no' to opportunities and commitments that don't align with my values, a skill as critical as saying 'yes' to the right ones.
>
> Professionally, value clarity has shaped how I interact with clients and approach my coaching practice. It has anchored me in ethical decision-making, a commitment to continuous learning, and a dedication to giving back. For instance, through my '15 Coaches' project, I provide free coaching to emerging leaders, helping to develop the next generation of talent.
>
> Ultimately, knowing my values has served as a compass for both my actions and decisions. This alignment ensures that I live and work with integrity and congruence, key elements in achieving fulfillment and success.

Aligning Your Values with Your Actions: Paul's Story

Paul was an executive, leading a high-performing team in a fast-paced industry. He was sharp, ambitious, and relentlessly focused on results, qualities that had propelled him up the corporate ladder. But behind closed doors, his leadership was causing cracks in his team's performance and morale.

Paul's team avoided coming to him with challenges unless absolutely necessary. Meetings were tense and transactional, with little open discussion. High-potential employees were quitting or disengaging, and feedback from his peers indicated that his reputation as a leader was more intimidating than inspiring.

Paul was confused. He prided himself on his commitment to excellence, so why was his team struggling?

During our coaching sessions, I introduced Paul to the values clarification exercise. As we worked through it, he identified his top four core values: Excellence, Respectfulness, Teamwork, and Integrity. At first, this seemed validating; he had always believed in pushing for excellence and integrity.

But when I asked him to define these values in behavioral terms, something shifted.

For Excellence, he wrote: *Delivering high-quality work, leading by example, and pushing for the best results without compromising my team's well-being.*

For Respectfulness, he hesitated before writing: *Listening to others, valuing input, and treating colleagues as partners, not just executors of tasks.*

For Teamwork, he defined: *Building trust, fostering open dialogue, and creating an environment where people feel heard and supported.*

And then came the realization.

Paul had been living by one of his values, Excellence, but at the expense of the others. In his relentless pursuit of results, he had neglected Respectfulness and Teamwork. He wasn't listening. He wasn't building trust. And as a result, his team wasn't engaged.

This was a turning point.

Paul committed to aligning his leadership style with his full set of values. He started by:

- Actively soliciting input from his team before making major decisions.
- Shifting his approach in meetings, from rapid-fire problem-solving to facilitating discussions that invited ideas.
- Making space for acknowledgment, celebrating wins, recognizing individual contributions, and reinforcing a sense of shared success.
- Practicing transparency, sharing not just what needed to be done, but why it mattered, giving his team a greater sense of ownership.

It wasn't a sudden overnight shift, but over the next few months, the transformation was undeniable. His team became more engaged, more proactive, and more willing to challenge ideas, something he had once seen as a threat but now recognized as a sign of a strong, dynamic team.

Paul's relationships with his peers also improved. Instead of being seen as demanding and dismissive, he was now regarded as a leader who balanced high expectations with genuine respect and collaboration.

His biggest takeaway? That clarity isn't just about knowing what you stand for, it's about ensuring your actions align with your values. Leadership isn't just about pushing for results; it's about how you achieve them.

In my experience as a coach, I've seen countless leaders experience profound transformation once they gain clarity on their values and align their actions accordingly. It impacts not only their leadership effectiveness but also their sense of fulfillment.

Leadership and Organizational Values

When we lead, our values extend beyond us, like shadows cast at sunset. They form the heart of our organizations, influencing culture in silent but profound ways. The core values of key people, particularly founders, are often transferred to their organizations, shaping the culture. Being clear about your values allows you to intentionally create a culture that leads to success and aligns with your leadership style.

Garry Ridge was the CEO of WD-40 from 1997–2022. During his tenure, the market cap of the company increased from US$250 million to US$3 billion. While achieving these incredible financial results, what many see as most impressive is the organizational culture he created; one where a company selling lubricants and rust removal products has consistently had over 90 percent of its employees highly engaged and very happy. (For comparison, according to the Gallup 2024 report, the overall engagement of US employees is at 31 percent.)[10]

I interviewed Garry for this book. Garry shared that at WD-40, they had very clear organizational values, set in a hierarchical order. Garry explained that if you have a set of values that are hierarchical, it really does stop people within the organization from cherry-picking the value that would be aligned with the outcome they really want. Having the most important value as number 1, and then going down the scale to still important, but less so, really provides people with the priorities they should consider.

Garry shared this example:

> The number one value at WD-40 was we value doing the right thing. The number 6th value was we value sustaining the WD-40 economy, which means we want to be continually profitable to be able to fuel the growth of the company. Now, if we didn't have them hierarchically, people might choose a decision that enhances profitability against doing the right thing, and we didn't want that to happen. So we wanted to guide people in their thinking around how they made decisions by making them hierarchical.

According to Garry, values in an organization are absolutely, without doubt, the very foundation. Values are meant to protect people, but also set them free. Many people think values are restrictive. They're not. Garry thinks of them a little bit like the banks of a river. If you think about a river running from the mountains to the sea, it is the banks of the river that allows the river to flow to the destination. And without those banks, that water would become a cesspool, if you will. Values are there to guide us to our destination; the one we've already determined we want to arrive at.[11]

Knowing your values is not a passive act; it is an intentional practice of sculpting the very ethos of your leadership. Now it's your turn. The following exercises will help you gain clarity on your personal values, those you've inherited, those you wish to keep, and those you may need to let go. By working through the exercises, you'll create a personalized values compass to guide your decisions, leadership, and life.

→ YOUR TURN: Identify Your Values

Clarifying your values at this moment in your life can aid you in shaping your purpose and vision.

Below, you'll find a few exercises to help you gain clarity around your values right now. In embracing these exercises, you're not just listing values;

you're engaging in a dialogue with your inner compass, ensuring it points toward the True North of your aspirations.

By sitting down and writing your values you can:

1. Identify what values have influenced your life.
2. Decide what values are important to you now.
3. Assess what values you would like to let go.
4. Evaluate what new values you may want to adopt to help you become the person you want to be.

Your Childhood Values

Grab a pen, and let's journey back. Reflect on the sayings that were repeated in your home when you were younger. (Remember the examples of "Don't cry over spilled milk" or "Just try to be like the other kids.")

Write them down. How do they resonate with you now? Explore whether they still resonate with your present self or if they clash with the person you've become.

What values are no longer serving you? What values would you like to let go?

Who Are Your Heroes?

Warren Buffett once said, "If you can tell me who your heroes are, I can tell you how you're going to turn out."[12] Who inspires you? Whom do you admire?

For a long time, I struggled with this question. Growing up, I didn't feel like I had heroes. The idea of putting someone on a pedestal, of calling someone a role model, felt foreign to me. No one seemed perfect enough, and the thought of having a hero felt unrealistic.

What helped me shift was realizing that heroes don't have to be flawless. Instead of seeking perfection, I started looking for specific qualities, attributes, and actions that I admired in different people. Some stood out for their courage, others for their kindness or resilience. Once I let go of the idea that a hero had to be an idealized figure, I found that I could learn from and be inspired by many people, in different ways.

Take, for example, my admiration for Ruth Bader Ginsburg, the U.S. Supreme Court Justice. She was a woman ahead of her time, relentlessly fighting for women's rights and equality. I respect her commitment to justice, her intellect, and her perseverance. Those are the qualities that resonate with me, and they reflect values I strive to embody in my own work.

Take a moment to think about your heroes. They can be dead or alive, fictional or real, people you know, or ones you have never met. They don't need to be perfect, nobody is. Instead, focus on what they represent to you.

Ask yourself:

- Whom do I admire, and why?
- What qualities do they have that I respect?

Write down the names of a few people who inspire you. Under each name, list what it is about them, their personality, their characteristics, their presence, that you respect.

Now, take it one step further. Cross out their name and write your own.

These qualities are your qualities. The values you admire in others are already part of you, or they are qualities you are striving to strengthen. How does it feel? What would it look like to embody those values more fully in your own life?

The Heroes Exercise, created by Ayse Birsel, taps into an unexpected but powerful truth: The qualities we admire in others are often a mirror of the values we hold ourselves. As Ayse explained when I interviewed her, "What you see in others are actually your own qualities and values. That's why you notice them."[13]

This insight is what makes the exercise so powerful. It's not just about who inspires you, it's about what that says about who you are, and who you want to become. The Heroes Exercise is adapted from the book *Design the Life You Love* by my friend Ayse Birsel.[14]

Your Value Pantheon

Select 10–15 values that resonate with you at this very moment from the list in Figure 2. Try to group them together in relevant topics.

Now, from this list of 10–15 values, identify the three to five that, if absent, would leave your life's painting incomplete. Narrow down the list to the top five values that hold the greatest significance for you at this stage of your life.

FIGURE 2: List of values

Achievement	Focus	Participation
Accuracy	Free spirit	Partnership
Acknowledgment	Free time	Peace
Advancement	Freedom	Performance
Adventure	Friendship	Personal power
Aesthetics	Fun	Pleasure
Affection	Growth	Power
Authenticity	Harmony	Precision
Autonomy	Health	Productivity
Beauty	Help others	Recognition
Caring	Help society	Responsibility
Challenge	Honesty	Risk-taking
Change	Humor	Romance
Collaboration	Independence	Self-expression
Community	Integrity	Service
Comradeship	Intellectual status	Spirituality
Connectedness	Joy	Stability
Contribution	Knowledge	Success
Creativity	Lack of pretense	Time Freedom
Directness	Leadership	Tradition
Economic security	Leisure	Trust
Elegance	Lightness	Vitality
Empowerment	Location	Wealth
Excellence	Loyalty	Wisdom
Excitement	Nurturing	Zest
Family happiness	Orderliness	*(Or, add your own)*

If you have a long list of values and you are struggling to narrow the list down you can match the values in pairs and for each pair decide which one is more important to you, until you have narrowed down the list.

Another helpful approach is to group related values into themes. For example, "honesty," "integrity," and "authenticity" might fall under a broader theme of "truth." "Kindness," "compassion," and "generosity" could be grouped as "caring." Grouping by theme can help you identify the core idea behind multiple values and clarify what matters most to you.

Portions of this exercise were adapted from *Co-Active Coaching*.[15]

Congratulations! After completing these exercises you should have a clearer picture of your values, the principles that you live by (or want to live by); your personal code of conduct to guide you. Is there a hierarchy to your values? Are some more important to you than others?

How does it feel?

You have completed the first step in gaining clarity! Keep your values top-of-mind as you continue to gain clarity and consider who you want to be. We will also go back to this list in the "Operationalize" chapter, where we identify specific steps to make your values part of your daily life.

Identifying and Leveraging Your Strengths

Playing to Your Strengths: The Trail to Excellence

We're often taught that growth means fixing what's lacking, turning weaknesses into strengths. And while improvement has its place, real breakthroughs come from amplifying what already makes us strong. When we fully embrace and develop our natural strengths, we move beyond adequacy into excellence.

Psychologist Martin Seligman's Positive Psychology emphasizes the power of recognizing and cultivating our strengths. He suggests that applying them not only leads to greater success but also to what he defines as a "good life," one where we channel our unique abilities to contribute meaningfully to our own well-being and that of others.[16] By leveraging what we do best, we unlock both personal fulfillment and professional achievement.

Rather than striving for adequacy by fixing every weakness, what if we focused on mastery? Polishing what we naturally excel at transforms competence into brilliance. It's the difference between being good at something or being truly exceptional.

Recognizing your strengths is like finding steady ground beneath your feet. It gives you confidence, clarity, and direction. But what does this look like in practice?

Let me take you on a trail, a literal one.

During a recent hike in the White Mountains in New Hampshire, I became acutely aware of my pace. Yes, I am a slow hiker, and no, physical strength is not my forte. As my husband swiftly scaled Mount Lafayette and my son completed the ambitious 29.5-mile Pemi Loop hike, I trekked at my own measured pace. I could have drowned in comparison, feeling overshadowed by their abilities and those of every hiker who passed me by. But there was a choice to be made, and it was one that stemmed from understanding where my true power lies.

I chose to lean into my enduring determination, my unwavering 'can-do' attitude that has been my anchor throughout life. This mindset, this intangible yet forceful strength, has guided me through not just trails but life's intricate challenges. It's what led me to the summit of Mount Kilimanjaro, not by negating my slower pace, but by embracing the relentless spirit within.

When we harness our strengths, we don't just traverse trails; we conquer mountains.

So, as we ponder our personal and professional journeys, it's pivotal to ask: What are your strengths?

Strengths in Action: Personal and Professional Growth

Identifying your strengths isn't an act of vanity; it's an act of clarity.

It bolsters your confidence and shines a light on what you bring to the world. When you understand your strengths, you position yourself to tackle tasks and roles that not only align with these attributes but also enhance your effectiveness and job satisfaction. This isn't merely an exercise in self-assessment, it's a strategy for empowerment. Building upon these strengths is a path to not just growth, but to achieving your version of greatness. It allows you to operate from a position of competence and excellence, which naturally inspires and motivates both you and those around you. With each task that plays to your strengths, your performance improves, leading to greater productivity and innovation. This realization fosters a deeper engagement with your work, enhances your resilience against stress and burnout, and significantly boosts your overall well-being.

Leveraging Strengths to Build High-Performing Teams

Great leaders don't just recognize their own strengths; they use them strategically to build teams that bring different capabilities to the table. By surrounding yourself with people who offer diverse skills and perspectives, you create a more dynamic, high-performing team. You foster a collaborative environment ripe for innovative solutions and collective success. This approach doesn't just benefit individual career paths, it enhances the entire organizational culture.

When I took the reins of Kurzweil Education's marketing department, my marketing experience was modest, but my strengths were clear. I had a deep understanding of the industry, a knack for viewing challenges from the customer's perspective, and a creative flair that brought fresh ideas to the table. My organizational skills were top-notch, and my openness to learning and experimenting with new strategies was boundless. However, I was acutely aware of my limitations in digital marketing, which was crucial for our success.

Acknowledging this gap, I made a strategic move to hire a seasoned digital marketer whose skills complemented my own. This decision wasn't just about filling a gap; it was about creating a balanced team where each member could shine in their area of expertise. As for organizing conferences, a task within my wheelhouse, I chose to bring on a novice whom I could mentor. This not only allowed me to play to my strengths but also provided an opportunity to cultivate new talent within our team.

By mapping out my strengths and acknowledging areas where I needed support, I was able to assemble a team with diverse levels of experience and expertise. This not only enriched our department with a range of skills but also ensured that our collective efforts were both innovative and effectively aligned with our long-term goals.

Leaders and managers, consider this: while it's easy to zero in on where your team falls short, the magic happens when you spot and cultivate their natural talents. When you enable your team to thrive in their strengths, you're not just fostering individual growth; you're elevating the collective prowess.

So, let's not only focus on the hurdles, but also on where we naturally excel. Can you identify your core strengths? How can you utilize these talents to overcome challenges and reach new heights?

Uncovering What Sets You Apart

Sarah's Leap from Technical Expert to Strategic Leader

Sarah had built a reputation as a top-performing technical leader at a fast-growing technology firm. She was known for her sharp problem-solving skills, deep technical knowledge, and ability to execute complex projects flawlessly. If there was a crisis, Sarah was the one leadership turned to. But despite her expertise, she was beginning to feel stuck.

The company was growing rapidly, and while she had mastered the technical and operational side of her role, she knew that simply being the go-to problem solver wasn't enough to move her forward. She saw peers getting promoted into strategic roles, roles where they were shaping the direction of the company, not just delivering projects. Why not her?

During our coaching sessions, we explored this question deeply. What was holding her back? Through 360° feedback, leadership assessments, and self-reflection, Sarah began to uncover something surprising: her strategic thinking and leadership potential had been recognized by others, but she hadn't fully embraced it herself.

She had always been comfortable proving her value through execution and technical expertise, but the next step required something different, a shift from being the expert in the room to being the leader who shapes the bigger picture.

At first, this realization was unsettling. Sarah felt a deep loyalty to her team and worried that stepping away from the details meant she was abandoning them. She also feared that if she spent less time troubleshooting, she might lose credibility as the hands-on expert she had always been.

But the more we discussed it, the clearer it became: Her real value wasn't just in fixing problems, it was in helping her team solve them independently.

By holding on to the execution work, she was inadvertently limiting both her team's growth and her own.

So, she took a leap.

Sarah began delegating key technical responsibilities to her team, not because she didn't care, but because she cared too much to let them remain dependent on her. She blocked time on her calendar for strategic thinking, setting aside space for innovation rather than just crisis management. She started speaking up in leadership meetings, not just about ongoing projects, but about where the company was headed, the industry shifts she foresaw, and the opportunities they weren't yet capitalizing on.

At first, stepping into this new role felt uncomfortable. She caught herself gravitating back to technical details, wanting to double-check every decision her team made. But with coaching and conscious effort, she stayed the course. And then, something remarkable happened.

Her team became more confident and proactive, taking full ownership of their work and anticipating challenges before she even needed to step in. Instead of being the sole problem-solver, Sarah became a thought partner, helping her team refine their ideas and align their work with broader business goals. As she shifted her focus, senior executives began to recognize her impact beyond technical execution—they saw her as someone who could shape strategy, drive innovation, and contribute to the company's long-term vision.

Over time, Sarah's influence expanded. She found herself leading discussions on bigger-picture challenges, guiding cross-functional teams, and helping the organization navigate change. Her role had evolved, not because she had acquired an entirely new set of skills, but because she had fully stepped into her strengths.

Looking back, Sarah realized her breakthrough wasn't about letting go of her expertise; it was about embracing it differently. She had always been strategic, innovative, and capable of inspiring others, but now she was owning those strengths in a new way. By leaning into what she did best, she had not only grown as a leader but had also elevated the people around her.

Unleashing Your Innate Talents

Gavin, a seasoned CEO of innovative tech companies, has a gift for gazing into the future. His strategic foresight is like a beacon, illuminating the path for his companies. His vision extends beyond the horizon, crafting new products and exploring uncharted markets with an instinctive grace. Gavin's thought process is not just a skill; it's his second nature, a way of being that defines his leadership and success.

Fiona's talent lies in the art of connection. In the competitive world of sales, she possesses a rare charm, a superpower of rapport. Her peers watch in awe as she navigates through a sea of potential clients, leaving an indelible mark on each encounter. It's as if every handshake and smile is infused with a magnetic memory, binding her name to their minds. Fiona's knack for remembering names and details turns brief introductions into memorable interactions, transforming prospects into long-lost friends in mere moments. Her talent is more than just a technique for networking; it's a masterstroke of personal branding that distinguishes her in her field.

Everyone has their own palette of colors that they bring to their work, a unique blend of strengths that sets them apart.

Discovering Your Strengths

Unwrapping the Gift of Compliments

Think about the compliments that come your way, the ones you brush aside as though they were mere pleasantries, not reflections of your true talents. For me, it was my friend Martha's casual remark that sparked a moment of self-discovery. "Miki," she'd say with a mix of wonder and admiration, "I can't believe how effortlessly you bring these dinner parties to life." To me, her words felt like an everyday observation, not a testament to skill. After all, wasn't this something anyone could do?

Yet, as I pondered the ease with which I could wrap up my workday and, within a mere two hours, welcome a group of friends to a dinner spread, I began to see it through a different lens. I wasn't a culinary maestro by any means, but what I lacked in gastronomic flair, I made up for with meticulous planning.

The real recipe for those evenings wasn't just in the food, it was in the foresight. The market runs done a day ahead, the marination timed just right, and the mental choreography of what to cook when, all danced in my head with clarity and precision. It wasn't the cooking, it was the orchestrating where my true strength lay.

A similar realization struck me in my professional life. In my leadership roles, particularly in HR, I was often met with a familiar reaction after conducting interviews: "How did you get them to tell you that?"

I had conducted thousands of interviews over the years, and time and time again, candidates would open up to me in ways they wouldn't with others. You would be surprised what people have shared with me in job interviews. There were moments when candidates revealed struggles they had never voiced before, personal insights about their motivations, and challenges they hadn't even articulated to themselves.

At first, I dismissed this as something anyone could do. Wasn't it just a matter of asking the right questions? But as the pattern repeated itself, and I kept hearing the same remark, "People open up to you in a way they don't with others," I started to recognize this wasn't just about asking questions. It was about how I asked, how I listened, and how I made people feel.

So what was really happening? I was creating psychological safety, making people feel at ease and instinctively knowing when to soften my approach or when to gently press further. I practiced active listening, not just waiting for my turn to speak but fully engaging, picking up on subtle cues and responding in a way that made people feel truly heard. My nonverbal communication played a role too, through eye contact, an encouraging nod, or an open posture, I signaled that it was safe to be honest. Beyond that, I had an intuitive sense of asking the right questions at the right time, knowing how to sequence them, when to pause, and how to frame things in a way that invited deeper sharing. Most importantly, I led with empathy and emotional intelligence. People weren't just answering interview questions; they were engaging in a conversation where they felt seen, not evaluated.

This is a core skill I use in my executive coaching today. Whether I'm leading a 360° feedback session or holding space for a difficult reflection, I draw on the same skills, creating trust, noticing what's unsaid, and helping leaders feel safe enough to look inward with honesty and courage. Looking back, I realize this was a strength I had taken for granted. It wasn't just about interviewing, it was about connection. And just like with my dinner parties, where I had assumed that organizing everything seamlessly was just something "anyone could do," I now saw that this ability to disarm people and create space for real conversations was something unique to me.

Strengths don't always look like hard skills on a résumé. Sometimes, they are the things we do so naturally that we don't even recognize them as skills at all.

What are the compliments you've dismissed? What do people repeatedly tell you you're good at? The answers may just reveal a strength you never fully acknowledged.

Finding Your Strengths: Dorie Clark's Advice

In our interview, Dorie Clark points out that identifying your strengths can be challenging: "Since we're all our own point of reference, everything about us feels normal. It's only through interactions with others that we begin to notice what sets us apart."

Dorie explains that your strengths often lie in what feels effortless to you but is remarkable to others. You may think it's normal to run a metaphorical three-minute mile, but when you look around and realize others aren't keeping the same pace, you uncover a strength.

To find your strengths, Dorie recommends paying close attention to the following:

- What people come to you for. What kinds of help or advice do others seek from you disproportionately?
- Where you excel effortlessly. What tasks seem to come naturally to you but feel like a struggle for others?
- Where you feel uniquely capable. In what areas do you find yourself working faster, solving problems more easily, or feeling in the flow compared to those around you?[17]

By observing these patterns over time, you can begin to see your strengths emerge clearly. It's about listening to the feedback you're already receiving but may not have fully recognized.

Seeing Ourselves Through Others' Eyes

It's peculiar how the strengths we carry can be invisible to our own eyes, yet stand out so clearly to others. We're so immersed in our daily lives that what feels effortless to us often goes unnoticed, mistaken for, as Dorie Clark said, "normal." Yet, to those around us, these very abilities can seem exceptional. Seeking the viewpoints of those around us can be like looking into a mirror that reflects not our image, but the essence of our capabilities.

I recall the enlightening moment when my daughter, at the cusp of her twenties, offered me an unexpected insight: "You have simple solutions to complicated issues." Her words were a revelation. To me, simplifying and solving was as natural as breathing, so much so that I hadn't recognized it as a unique strength.

Imagine the wealth of insight we can uncover by turning to those who know us best. Consider asking three people in your circle, be they colleagues, friends, or family, to hold up a mirror to your talents. What reflections of your strengths will they reveal?

Through this exercise, you may discover facets of your abilities that you've overlooked or undervalued. Their perspectives can not only affirm the strengths you possess but can also illuminate the hidden corners of your potential, giving you new avenues to explore and embrace.

→ YOUR TURN: Identify Your Strengths

- What compliments do you receive and easily dismiss?
- What are the skills you use in that strength?
- What strengths set your work apart?
- What are the innate abilities that have fueled your ascent in your career?
- What are the characteristics that contribute to your success at work?
- What differentiates you from your colleagues performing the same or similar role?
- Think about a time when you solved a problem. What were the skills you used to solve it? What do they tell you about your strengths?

- Reach out to at least three people who know you well and ask them what they think your strengths are.

Now, let's connect the threads and reflect on what makes you distinct from your peers who may share your role but not your particular flair. Think about what it is that you naturally do. Your unique strengths are not just tools for your trade; they're the signatures of your professional identity. Recognize them, refine them, and let them guide you to your own definition of success.

Structured Reflections through Self-Assessments

To further identify your strengths, you could turn to self-assessments. Self-assessments are vital tools that provide structured reflections, helping us unearth our innate talents. Among these, the VIA Character Strengths assessment[18] and Clifton Strengths[19] are incredibly insightful, revealing our inherent capabilities. I've found Patrick Lencioni's new assessment, *The 6 Types of Working Genius*,[20] to be especially interesting, both for individual reflection and team dynamics. This assessment doesn't just reveal what we're good at; it pinpoints what energizes and fulfills us, transforming how we engage with our work.

Lencioni describes six types of working genius: Wonder, Invention, Discernment, Galvanizing, Enablement, and Tenacity.[21] Each type highlights a unique contribution style. For instance, my geniuses, Wonder and Discernment, allow me to perceive the potential within individuals and organizations alike, seeing beyond the present to what could be possible. In tandem, my discerning nature offers a balanced view that evaluates these possibilities, ensuring they're not just inspirational but actionable. This combination drives my ability to help leaders and organizations not just survive but thrive by turning complex challenges into opportunities for growth.

Understanding your geniuses and frustrations is more than self-knowledge; it's a strategy for aligning your professional life with tasks that truly resonate with your natural inclinations. This alignment leads to work that is not only productive but also joyous, reducing frustration and enhancing satisfaction.

I often recommend that leadership teams take *The 6 Types of Working Genius* assessment to better understand their dynamics. Recently, I facilitated this assessment with a management team, and while their individual geniuses were affirming, they uncovered surprising insights about their collective dynamics. The CEO, known for his Galvanizing prowess, confessed he found no joy in these activities; in fact, they were a source of significant frustration. This revelation prompted a reevaluation of roles within the team and at the same time highlighted a crucial gap in Tenacity as they realized they were faltering in driving projects to completion.

So, what does your genius look like? And how do the geniuses within your team interlock to create a dynamic and effective unit? Engaging with these assessments not only illuminates the strengths you bring to your work but also how they blend with those of your colleagues to forge a high-performing team.

By pinpointing everyone's geniuses and frustrations, you empower your team to thrive in their strengths and address areas where you collectively lack. This strategy not only enhances individual job satisfaction and effectiveness but also elevates the entire team's performance, fostering a workplace culture rooted in mutual understanding and optimized collaboration.

Embracing your genius transforms work from mere duty to a vibrant expression of your deepest capabilities, turning leadership into an art form. This approach doesn't just benefit you; it inspires your entire team, propelling everyone towards a shared vision of success.

As our exploration of strengths draws to a close, hopefully it has become evident that this journey of introspection is not merely about self-knowledge; it's a pathway to harnessing our true potential. Recognizing and embracing your unique strengths is akin to unlocking a personal superpower, one that bolsters confidence and provides the fortitude to overcome challenges.

It is easy to flick through the book and not pause to actually do the exercises. I admit I've done that too. If asked about your strengths and values, do you have a clear answer? If you have reached this point and you do not, take the time to complete at least one of the exercises for each section.

My hope for you is that the clarity you find in recognizing your strengths goes beyond mere acknowledgment; it empowers you, steering you towards utilizing those skills to effectively meet and overcome the hurdles you encounter. You stand poised to lean into your strengths, making them the cornerstone of your approach to both work and life's hurdles. It is here, in the embracing of our innate talents, that we transition from merely enduring to thriving, from competence to excellence.

With this newfound understanding, ask yourself again: How can you focus more on your strengths to overcome challenges? As you ponder this, remember that embracing one's strengths is not just about self-fulfillment; it's about embodying your greatest self in all aspects of life.

Navigating Life's Priorities

The Shifting Nature of Priorities

At twelve years old, I embarked on a transformative journey, moving from Israel to Sydney, Australia, with my family. Despite the scenic surroundings, I felt like an outsider. Longing for a sense of belonging, I made a bold decision after high school: I returned to Israel on my own, determined to reconnect with my roots.

Then, at twenty-two, life presented another crossroads. I had completed my service in the Israeli army and was preparing to start university in Israel. Before diving into my studies, I decided to return to Sydney for a few months to see family, work, and save money. But as life often does, it surprised me. I met a guy. A brilliant, kind, and handsome one, who would later become my husband.

At the time, I was fiercely focused on my education. Many of my Australian peers had already completed their bachelor's degrees, some even starting their master's. I felt behind. My priority was clear: I would return to Israel and earn my degree. I made my intentions clear, if he wanted to be with me, he'd have to follow.

Love, as it turns out, has its own gravitational pull. He moved to Israel, and together, we built our future.

Fast forward eight years, married and nurturing a young family, my husband and I found ourselves at a crossroads, wrestling with a decision that many families face but few find easy. With my husband's entrepreneurial ventures frequently taking him to the United States, I often found myself solo parenting, juggling the demands of our young family with my own career ambitions. His trips were long, often three weeks at a stretch, and even when he was in Israel, the time differences meant that on a good night, he'd be home by 11:00 p.m., though more often not until the early hours of 3:00 a.m. This wasn't the family life I had envisioned; I felt more like a single mom than a partner in a shared journey.

At this juncture, we encountered an opportunity that promised to bring us back to the family life we both valued: moving to the United States. Such a move meant my husband would travel less, and we could finally enjoy more quality time together as a family. Yet, the decision weighed heavily on me. I had established a successful consulting business in Israel and was on the cusp of a significant partnership with the country's largest HR organization. The professional stakes were high.

After much reflection on what mattered most to us—our family's unity and well-being—we decided to relocate to the United States in 1998, planning initially for our stay to last just one year. Little did we know this move would redefine our lives, transforming what was meant to be a temporary arrangement into our new home base. This pivotal decision, driven by our quest for a stable and cohesive family life, not only brought us closer together but also opened new doors and opportunities that have since shaped our lives in ways we couldn't have anticipated.

How Priorities Evolve Over Time

Looking back, these pivotal moments highlight a truth we often forget: priorities shift with life's seasons. It underscores the importance of identifying priorities at various life stages. Whether single or with a family, financially secure or seeking stability, our priorities ebb and flow, guided by evolving circumstances and personal aspirations. During the early years of motherhood, flexibility became paramount as I sought to balance career goals with nurturing a growing family. Yet, as circumstances shifted and my children grew older, my focus transitioned again towards career advancement, fueled by newfound opportunities and personal ambition.

Life's priorities are not fixed; they adapt and transform in tandem with our experiences and aspirations. The journey of self-discovery often prompts introspection, challenging us to realign our actions with our values and aspirations.

I interviewed entrepreneurship thought leader Rhett Power, who, reflecting on his journey, offers a powerful reminder of the importance of maintaining balance and living in alignment with our values. Early in his career, Rhett was all in, working eighteen-hour days to keep his first business afloat. But the relentless focus on work came at a cost: "I lost sight of friends, I lost sight of my kids, and I lost sight of my spouse. ... When you love what you do, it's so easy to get absorbed."[22]

Rhett underscores the need to pause, take stock, and ensure that your priorities align with what truly matters. He emphasizes that the most successful people he knows have "a lot of clarity around who they are, what's important to them, and what values drive them."[23] By anchoring yourself in your values, you make decisions that, while sometimes painful, remain clear and unwavering. Living by your priorities, even when faced with competing demands, allows you to achieve success not just in your career, but in the relationships and moments that define a fulfilling life.

Redefining Priorities in Leadership

David, one of my coaching clients, was soaring up the corporate ranks. He had recently been promoted to lead a division. At home, his two young children were brightening his world and a third was just a whisper away. David's home brimmed with the vibrant chaos of early parenthood.

Despite his efforts to be present, work always followed him home, turning family time into fragmented moments between calls and emails. Even Saturdays, meant for family, were filled with urgent customer calls, a testament to the company's rapid expansion.

David loved his work, but he also loved his family. He felt the tension growing between his career aspirations and his deep-seated values of being present for his family. The fulfillment he gleaned from his work was overshadowed by the growing realization that his presence was needed elsewhere, anchored at home, alongside his partner, in the heart of his family. He felt his priorities shifting.

The company admired David for his work ethic, but it was evident that he needed a more sustainable work-life balance. Recognizing this imbalance, David and I collaborated to refine his priorities. We implemented boundaries that afforded him time away from work on evenings and weekends. By enhancing his delegation skills, David learned to trust his team with greater responsibilities, aligning his actions with his values of personal and professional development for himself and his colleagues.

With newfound boundaries and a commitment to disconnect, David's evenings and weekends were reclaimed for his loved ones. This deliberate realignment allowed David to live more harmoniously with his values and priorities. It ensured that he did not miss out on being an integral part of his growing family's life while still fostering his division's success.

Reevaluating Priorities: A Continuous Process

There is fluidity to our priorities. They aren't fixed. They evolve as we do. What mattered deeply five years ago may no longer hold the same weight today. Regular reevaluation of our priorities is crucial, as they can shift with life's various stages and demands. That's why it's essential to pause, reflect, and realign.

Take the time to pause and ponder: What are your priorities now? How do they align with your values and aspirations? Embracing clarity on your priorities enables you to chart a course aligned with your deepest desires, fostering a sense of fulfillment and purpose along the way.

→ YOUR TURN: Clarify Your Priorities

- What are your top priorities at this stage of your life?
- Do they align with your values, or do they need adjustment?
- What is one small shift you can make today to bring your life into greater alignment?

Getting clear on your priorities allows you to make better decisions about where to spend your time, energy, and attention. It helps you align your actions with what you genuinely value.

But clarity around priorities is only part of the equation. Once you've named what you care about and where you want to focus, a deeper question follows: What does success look like when it reflects those choices?

Too often, our definitions of success are shaped by external expectations—status, achievement, perfection. But real success is personal. It starts with you. Let's take a closer look at how you define success—and whether that definition supports the life and leadership you actually want.

Defining Success in Your Terms

Success is a concept that carries many meanings, yet is often narrowly defined by society's standards, wealth, status, titles, and material possessions. The pursuit of these external markers can be relentless, leading many to chase the next promotion, the next milestone, or the next big purchase. But true success is deeply personal, shaped by our experiences, values, and aspirations. Success, in its purest form, is the alignment of life's work with inner joy.

In conversations with accomplished CEOs, I have often heard about their financial success and their pursuit of more: more money, a bigger house, a fancier car. Yet, for many, the joy of reaching the next goal was fleeting. As soon as one milestone was achieved, another took its place, keeping them in an endless loop of striving but never truly arriving at fulfillment.

Success is not simply the accumulation of things; it is the realization of what truly matters. It is about crafting a life not shaped by external accolades but by the internal compass of fulfillment.

It is not about meeting external expectations but about aligning your life with what genuinely brings you joy and fulfillment.

It's the quiet satisfaction of work that resonates with your soul. It's the peace that comes from living in harmony with your values. It's the warmth of family, the strength of relationships, and the contentment of being true to yourself. Success is about enjoying the journey and not just the end goal.

Perspectives from Visionary Leaders

Many visionary thinkers and influential leaders have challenged the traditional definitions of success. Rather than measuring it by status or wealth, they offer deeper, more expansive views grounded in purpose, resilience, and impact. Their insights invite us to see success not as a destination, but as a meaningful journey shaped by our values, contributions, and growth.

Albert Einstein: *"Try not to become a person of success, but rather try to become a person of value."*

Michelle Obama: *"Success isn't about how much money you make. It's about the difference you make in people's lives."*

Michael Jordan: *"I've failed over and over and over again in my life, and that is why I succeed."*

Arianna Huffington: *"We need to accept that we won't always make the right decisions, that we'll screw up royally sometimes, understanding that failure is not the opposite of success, it's part of success."*

Nelson Mandela: *"Do not judge me by my successes; judge me by how many times I fell down and got back up again."*

Marshall Goldsmith believes success is living a life consistent with your values, one where fulfillment comes from making a meaningful impact on others.

Maya Angelou: *"Success is liking yourself, liking what you do, and liking how you do it."*

Dorie Clark sees success as self-actualization, fully realizing one's potential and ensuring that regrets of "what could have been" don't overshadow the present.

Carol Kauffman defines success through the impact she has on others, asking herself, *"Is this leader a better human as a result of my coaching?"*

Chester Elton finds success in happiness, relationships, and integrity, rather than chasing external validation.

Garry Ridge believes success is about helping others step into the best version of themselves, creating an environment where people feel they belong and contribute to something greater than themselves.

Ayse Birsel defines success as living an original life, *"not doing what others tell you to do, but doing what you believe in... being true to yourself and putting it into action."*

These perspectives offer a wider, richer lens through which to view success, not as a static achievement but as a journey shaped by resilience, impact, and purpose.

At its core, success is about living with clarity and intention. It's not a fixed endpoint, but an evolving reflection of your values, choices, and impact. There is no one-size-fits-all definition—only the one that aligns with who you are and the life you want to lead.

→ YOUR TURN: Define Success

Success is unique to each of us. There's no universal formula, it's a reflection of what truly matters to you.

What does success mean for you? Is it the serenity found in daily meditation? The fulfillment of making a difference? The joy of deep connections?

Consider the questions below to shape your own definition:

- What truly brings you a sense of fulfillment?
- Does your definition of success align with your values?
- Are you pursuing success on your terms, or are you influenced by external expectations?

Imagine your life as a canvas. What picture do you want to paint on it? What colors, shapes, textures and scenes make you feel alive? What elements, growth, impact, connection, joy, belong in your masterpiece? Your definition of success is yours to craft.

Write down your definition of success. Let it be a living document that grows as you do, one that serves as a reminder of what truly matters.

Success is not a static end-goal but a dynamic process of living authentically, pursuing what brings you alive, and celebrating the steps along the way.

Your path to success is as unique as your fingerprint, and it's yours to shape with every choice you make. Let your heart's compass guide you to the success that resonates with your truest self.

Delving Deep with the Five Whys

In the quest to define success, we can utilize a powerful tool known as The Five Whys—an approach developed at Toyota by Taiichi Ohno to identify the root cause of problems.[24] But its application goes far beyond manufacturing. It's a technique that helps uncover our true motivations by peeling back layers of surface-level reasoning.

I was reminded of this concept during a mentorship session with students at Northeastern University. One of the students was frustrated with interview questions that seemed to have nothing to do with the job.

"What would you do if you won a million dollars?" she asked. "Why do interviewers even ask that? It feels so irrelevant!"

Instead of answering directly, I turned the question back to her. "Well, what would you do if you won a million dollars?"

"I'd travel," she said.

"Why?" I pressed.

"Because I want to experience different cultures."

"Why does that matter to you?"

"Because understanding different cultures helps me grow as a person."

"Why is personal growth important to you?"

"Because I want to be open-minded, adaptable, and connect with people from all walks of life."

By the time we reached the fifth "Why," she had an aha! moment. It was a revelation, not just to her but to the group: These seemingly disarming interview questions are not about eliciting a correct response but about understanding the candidate's thought processes, values, and what truly motivates them.

This method is just as valuable when applied to your definition of success. When contemplating success, ask yourself, Why is this important to me? Then ask again, and again, until the essence of your motivation is laid bare.

→ YOUR TURN: Use the Five Whys

Apply the Five Whys to your own success. Write down your definition of success. Then, answer, and continue answering,

Why is this important to you?
Why is this important to you?
Why is this important to you?
Why is this important to you?
Why is this important to you?

This technique reveals the core driver behind your pursuit of success, helping ensure that your goals align with your true values.

Simon Sinek said it best: "When we know why we do what we do, everything falls into place."[25] Your why is the compass that directs your steps to authentic success.

This exercise ensures that your pursuit of success is meaningful and aligned with your deepest values, not just a goal inherited from societal expectations.

When you uncover the deeper reason behind your goals, it becomes clear that success isn't just about what you accomplish, it's about who you become in the process. That shift in focus, from external outcomes to internal alignment, leads us to the powerful question: Who do you want to be?

Being Versus Doing: Who Do You Want to Be?

In his book *Originals*, Adam Grant explains how the words we use shape both our identity and behavior. He suggests that defining ourselves with nouns instead of verbs makes ethical behavior feel more natural and deeply ingrained.[26]

For example, saying "Don't be a cheater" instead of "Don't cheat" connects the action to identity, making it more personal. This subtle shift can influence decisions and strengthen integrity because it frames the behavior as a reflection of who we are, rather than just a temporary action.

Grant shares examples to show how this works. When children hear, "You are helpful," rather than, "That was helpful," they're more likely to keep helping because they see kindness as part of who they are.[27]

Similarly, calling someone a "mentor" rather than saying "You give good advice" reinforces mentorship as part of their identity. When people see themselves as mentors, they are more likely to take on the responsibility of guiding others, actively listen, and provide thoughtful support, not just in isolated moments, but as an ongoing part of who they are.

This approach can significantly influence behavior and choices because it encourages people to act in ways that align with their self-image.

By shifting from doing to being, just like Frances Hesselbein's advice that "Leadership is a matter of how to be, not how to do," we start thinking beyond isolated actions and focus on our character, and who we want to be. Instead of making choices to achieve a specific result, we begin choosing actions that align with our values and reflect the person we want to become.

Your Mission Statement: Who Do You Want to Be?

Success is not just about what we achieve, it's about who we become.

Garry Ridge is very clear about the kind of person he wants to be. He keeps his personal mission statement visible everywhere, on his computer, as a screensaver on his phone, to constantly remind himself of the kind of person he wants to be.

His statement reads:

> I want to be grateful. I want to be caring. I want to be empathetic. I want to be reasonable. I want to be a listener. I want to be fact-based. I want to have a balanced opinion. I want to be curious. I want to be a learner, and I want to throw sunshine, not a shadow.[28]

This is more than a set of aspirations, it's a guiding framework for his decisions, interactions, and leadership.

Miki's Mission Statement

Over the years, I've spent time reflecting on the kind of person I want to be, refining this statement as I continue to grow. Taking inspiration from Adam Grant's advice, I've framed it as an "I am" statement, a reflection of the person I aspire to become.

> I am a resilient woman, mother, and wife, a nurturing presence, an advocate, and a catalyst for growth. I am a positive force in the world. I live a healthy and active life, embracing adventure. I am the cornerstone of nurture in my family, putting my family first and providing steadfast support and care. Professionally and personally, I am devoted to unlocking human potential, guiding others and myself to realize their fullest selves.

This statement reminds me daily of my purpose, who I strive to be, the values I hold dear, and the impact I hope to create in the world.

Write It Down: Creating Your Personal Mission Statement

Research has shown that writing down your goals significantly increases the likelihood of achieving them. In a study by Dr. Gail Matthews at the Dominican University of California, participants who wrote down their goals were 42 percent more likely to achieve them compared to those who just thought about their goals.[29] But beyond goal achievement, the real power of writing down a mission statement lies in creating clarity, accountability, and intentionality. Putting your purpose into words anchors it in reality, and gives you a foundation to return to when distractions or doubts arise.

→ YOUR TURN: Write Your Mission Statement

Consider:

- Who are you at your best, most authentic self?
- What is your life's mission?
- What holds paramount importance to you, and how does this integrate into your daily existence?
- List the qualities that define who you want to be. Consider using nouns.
- Frame each as an I am statement.
- Make this statement visible, write it in your journal, save it on your phone, or post it somewhere you'll see daily.
- Ask yourself: How will your values and priorities be represented in your mission statement?

Your personal mission statement serves as a compass, guiding your decisions, helping you realign when you feel lost, and reinforcing the identity you wish to embody, one rooted in the character you aspire to build.

When embodying this persona, observe the sensations, the emotions that surface. This is not just self-perception; it's self-actualization.

Summary

Clarify: Key Takeaways

This chapter helped you define who you want to be as a leader and as a person by guiding you through five key areas of clarity and offering tools for greater self-awareness and intentionality:

- **Gain self-awareness:** Leadership starts with leading yourself. Understanding your values, strengths, priorities, and mission enables you to make intentional choices that align with who you want to be. If you don't lead yourself, others—external expectations, pressures, or cultural norms—will end up leading you.
- **The five key areas of "Clarity"—Define:**
  - *Values:* Your guiding principles that shape your decisions and actions.
  - *Strengths:* The unique qualities that set you apart and help you excel.
  - *Priorities:* What matters most at this stage of your life.
  - *Success:* Define success on your own terms, rather than societal expectations.
  - *Mission:* A guiding statement that reflects who you aspire to be and what drives you.
- **Living with intention:** Clarity simplifies decision-making, enhances confidence, and ensures that your actions reflect what truly matters to you.
- **Lead with authenticity:** The more aligned you feel across roles, the more you build authenticity, reduce stress, and increase integrity.

  Ask yourself: Who do I want to be? What truly matters to me? How do my values and strengths shape my leadership?

Tying It All Together

At this stage, you have gained clarity on your values, priorities, strengths, and personal definition of success. You have explored who you want to be, not just what you want to achieve. This process has required deep introspection, a willingness to challenge assumptions, and the courage to define success on your own terms. That in itself is an achievement worth recognizing.

Before moving forward, take a moment to pause. Re-read your mission statement. Ask yourself:

- Does my daily life align with the person I want to be?
- Do my choices support my values?
- Am I defining success in a way that feels authentic to me?

Recognizing what truly matters and gaining this level of self-awareness is no small feat. It is easy to rush past the progress made and immediately focus on what's next, but taking time to acknowledge and celebrate the clarity you have gained reinforces your commitment to this journey.

Celebrate the fact that you have taken the time to explore, challenge old definitions, and create a framework for a life that aligns with your values. Recognize the work you have done to gain clarity on your values, strengths, and priorities, insights that have guided you in defining success on your own terms and crafting a mission statement that truly reflects who you are and who you aspire to be.

What's Next: Moving from Clarity to Action

Now that you have done the deep work of understanding who you are and what matters to you most, the next step is operationalizing, translating these insights into daily habits, behaviors, and decisions that bring your vision to life.

In the next chapter, we will explore:

- How to align your daily actions with your long-term goals
- Strategies for sustaining momentum and staying accountable
- How to assess whether your current life supports your values and strengths

Clarity is powerful, but action is what transforms it into meaningful change. You have built a strong foundation. Now, it's time to put it into motion.

2
OPERATIONALIZE

A goal without a plan is just a wish.

Antoine de Saint-Exupéry, author, *The Little Prince*

The Shift from Clarity to Action

Achieving big goals takes planning and action. The saying, "A goal without a plan is just a wish, or a dream" reminds us that while dreams inspire us, they remain out of reach unless we take specific steps to make them happen. Those steps start not with giant leaps, but with small choices repeated consistently—your habits.

You have laid out your dream. You've clarified what you truly care about. Now it's time to bring that clarity to life. In this chapter, we'll focus on closing the gap between what you care about and how you actually live, how you spend your time, energy, and attention. This is where intention meets action, where your days begin to reflect your deepest values.

As designer Ayse Birsel puts it: "You are the user of your own life... if you can know yourself better and imagine your future based on your values, your chances of having a life that looks like you and feels like you are much higher."[30]

This chapter is about designing that kind of life, not just in theory, but in how you live each day, how you spend your minutes, your energy, and your focus.

We'll start by looking at your current habits, identifying which ones support your goals and which ones may be getting in the way. From there, we'll map out small, intentional shifts that build momentum and help align your actions with what truly matters.

But be careful not to try to change everything at once. Doing too much too fast can lead to burnout or disappointment. Real, lasting change comes from small, consistent steps. Start with adjustments that feel manageable and sustainable. Some changes may come easily; others will take patience, practice, and persistence.

That's why it's important to prioritize what matters to you most and begin integrating new behaviors gradually. Small changes build confidence. Confidence supports consistency. And consistent habits lead to transformation.

The goal isn't just to make a plan, but to embed your intentions into the rhythm of your daily life.

This is where you shift from default habits to deliberate design, from autopilot to intentional alignment. That process often begins with taking a closer look at how you're currently living and leading, your routines, assumptions, inherited expectations, and asking what no longer serves you.

As Ayse Birsel shared with me, this act of intentional change mirrors her design method: "There's always a point where I go from what I know to what I can imagine ... Deconstruction helps break your preconceptions. Reconstruction lets you build something new, guided by your values."[31]

You are, in essence, deconstructing how you currently use your time, energy, and attention—so you can consciously reconstruct a life and leadership style that reflects the life you truly want to lead. This isn't just about forming new habits; it's about designing your days to feel like *you*. And when your days reflect your values, you gain the energy and courage to move forward with clarity.

You need a bold vision of who you want to become, a clear sense of the big picture—and the daily rhythm, the grounded execution, the consistent steps that bring the vision to life. When your goals become part of your routine, you bring focus and direction to your efforts. Progress happens when action replaces ideas, when steps, no matter how small, move you forward.

In the next chapter, "Reflect," you'll explore how your thoughts, patterns, and internal narratives can either support or sabotage your goals. Growth isn't just about doing more; it's about understanding yourself at a deeper level. It's about thinking differently, so your actions stay aligned with what truly matters.

Aligning Actions with Values and Priorities

What Your Time and Choices Say About You

How do you spend your time, money, and energy? Every day, people and projects compete for your attention, often pulling you toward their priorities. When this happens, it can feel like you're not in control of your own life.

In *How Will You Measure Your Life?* author Clayton Christensen explores how many high-achieving Harvard Business School graduates struggled with balancing career success and personal fulfillment. They poured their energy into professional accomplishments, drawn in by the immediate rewards of promotions, raises, and achievements. Their intentions were good; they wanted to provide for their families. But long-term priorities, like nurturing relationships and raising children, didn't seem as urgent.

Years later, many found themselves divorced, disconnected from loved ones, and unhappy. Their careers had flourished, but their personal lives had suffered.[32]

It's easy to believe we'll get to what matters later, after the next big project, once things settle down, or when the timing is better. But in reality, the way we allocate our time and energy today determines where we end up. If we don't intentionally align our resources with our values, we may find ourselves far from where we truly want to be.

If a stranger looked at your schedule, your detailed credit card bills, your screen time report, what would they assume your priorities are? Would they align with what you say matters most to you?

I Don't Have Time

People often tell me they don't have time.

"I don't have time to read."
"I don't have time to explain this to my team."
"I don't have time to exercise."
"I don't have time to…"

But the truth is, we all have the same twenty-four hours. The difference lies in how we choose to use them. If something isn't getting your time, it's likely not a priority, at least not in practice. If you're unsure where your time is going, track it for a week. Use a notebook, an app, or an Excel sheet to log your activities. Then, review:

- Where is most of your time going?
- How much of it aligns with what you truly value?
- What activities bring fulfillment, and which ones drain your energy?
- What patterns emerge?

Now, decide: What do you want to make time for? What needs to shift?

→ YOUR TURN: Align Your Time

- Look at your schedule or your time-tracking exercise. What does it reveal about your true priorities?
- Are you spending time in ways that reflect what you truly care about?
- What changes can you make? What will you eliminate, delegate, or shift?

Time isn't something you find, it's something you allocate. Choose wisely.

Defining the Behaviors that Align with Your Values

Let's explore some examples of both personal and professional values and identify the specific behaviors that bring them to life. When values are reflected in daily actions, they become a guiding force in decision-making and interactions with others.

Integrity
- **How to operationalize it in daily life:** Follow through on commitments, even when it's inconvenient. Speak honestly, even when the truth is uncomfortable.
- **What it looks like:** You admit mistakes openly, correct them, and hold yourself accountable.
- **The impact:** People trust you. They know they can count on you to act with honesty and consistency.

Respect
- **How to operationalize it in daily life:** Give people your full attention when they speak. Acknowledge different perspectives without judgment. Show consideration for everyone around you.
- **What it looks like:** You listen more than you speak, avoid interrupting, and consider different viewpoints.
- **The impact:** Others feel valued and heard, and your relationships strengthen as a result.

Accountability
- **How to operationalize it in daily life:** Set clear expectations and follow through. Own both successes and failures.
- **What it looks like:** You meet deadlines, update stakeholders proactively, and admit when you fall short.
- **The impact:** Colleagues and friends know they can trust your word and rely on your commitment.

Innovation
- **How to operationalize it in daily life:** Challenge existing ways of doing things. Experiment with new approaches.

- **What it looks like:** You brainstorm, eager to find smarter ways to work, propose fresh ideas, and take calculated risks.
- **The impact:** You're always involved in the next big project. You are known for driving progress and embracing change rather than resisting it.

Empathy
- **How to operationalize it in daily life:** Pause before reacting. Consider the emotions behind someone's words or actions. Understand what others are going through.
- **What it looks like:** You acknowledge people's struggles, ask thoughtful questions, and adapt your approach based on their needs.
- **The impact:** People trust you as a compassionate listener who truly understands their perspective.

Commitment to Quality
- **How to operationalize it in daily life:** Pay attention to detail and refuse to cut corners, even under pressure.
- **What it looks like:** You double-check your work, request feedback for improvement, and strive for excellence in every task.
- **The impact:** Your work stands out as reliable and consistently high quality.

Leadership
- **How to operationalize it in daily life:** Lead by example. Support and develop others rather than simply directing them.
- **What it looks like:** You inspire and empower your team, provide encouragement, and help others grow into leadership roles.
- **The impact:** People look up to you. They seek your guidance and trust your ability to lead with clarity and integrity.

Family Comes First
- **How to operationalize it in daily life:** Set boundaries to protect family time. Show up fully present, without distractions.

- **What it looks like:** You prioritize important family events, put away your phone during shared moments, and engage meaningfully with loved ones.
- **The impact:** Your relationships deepen, and those closest to you feel your unwavering support.

Generosity
- **How to operationalize it in daily life:** Share your time, knowledge, and resources without expecting something in return. Offer help when others are struggling, even when it's inconvenient.
- **What it looks like:** You offer your support without being prompted, whether that means mentoring a colleague, sharing useful resources, or stepping in when someone is overwhelmed. You freely give credit, celebrate others' wins, and take time to uplift those around you.
- **The impact:** Your generosity builds trust and goodwill. People feel supported, valued, and more willing to collaborate. It creates a culture where help is offered freely, not just when asked, and where success is shared, not hoarded.

These are examples of what embodying these values in your everyday actions would look like. In doing so, you not only enrich your own life but also set a shining example for those around you. Remember, it's the small, consistent steps that make the big difference.

→ YOUR TURN: Turn Values into Actions

Go back to your list of values. How can you define them behaviorally? What specific actions will demonstrate your values? How will someone observing you know that you are living by your values?

For each value, write down at least one specific action that will help you embody it. Small, consistent actions create alignment between your values and your daily choices.

Think of specific actions you will take. No shoulds or coulds, rather, actual actions you *will* take.

Examples:

- **Integrity:** Follow through on all commitments, no matter how small.
- **Empathy:** Pause before responding in conversations and ask yourself, What might this person be feeling?
- **Accountability:** End each workday by reviewing what you accomplished and what you need to follow up on.

Aligning your values with your actions isn't just a theoretical exercise, it's about making deliberate choices every day. How will you become the person you want to be? What will you commit to doing?

Miki Working on Alignment

Looking at my values and behaviors, I identified a clear gap. I was not as active and fit as I wanted to be. As I turned fifty, I made a decision, I needed to prioritize getting fit. I wanted to live a more active life and be able to fully participate in the activities my family loved. This was not my natural way of living and being. I grew up with a father who weighed 350 pounds and exercise was not part of the mentality in my house. My husband is a natural athlete, a marathon runner who leads a very active life. My son runs ultra-marathons, and is an avid hiker and backcountry skier. My daughter danced for over fifteen years. Getting fitter meant that I could spend more time with them, aligning with my values of spending quality time with my family and living a healthy lifestyle.

To operationalize this goal, I set myself a goal, a very high goal: climbing Mount Kilimanjaro, the highest peak in Africa. I knew that this goal would keep me motivated and get me out exercising on a regular basis. I started going on long walks three times a week. I made sure to hit the hills in our town. I walked three to six miles on weekdays, ten miles on the weekends. I walked in the rain, which I would never have done otherwise. I made walking a priority and made time for it in my schedule. I delegated the route planning of the climb to my son, who was thrilled to join me on this adventure and was well-equipped to complete this task.

For those wondering about my goal's outcome, we'll come back to this escapade a little later on.

At the same time, I wanted to live my values of service and impact more fully. Being a catalyst for growth, both for myself and others, is at the core of who I am. I had always valued supporting others, but I realized I needed to be more intentional about making it a consistent part of my life. To operationalize this goal, I began offering pro bono coaching, mentoring women in career transitions, and guiding young professionals as they navigated their careers. These actions weren't just about giving back; they were a reflection of my deeper purpose, unlocking human potential and helping others realize their fullest selves.

Through these experiences, I wasn't just supporting others; I was shaping the person I wanted to become. Whether it was my commitment to living a healthy, adventurous life or my dedication to guiding and nurturing others, making intentional choices allowed me to actively live my values, not just aspire to them.

Let's get specific. What will your commitment to action, to aligning your actions with your values and priorities, with who you want to be, look like?

All behaviors are a value statement. What will your behaviors say about your values, about who you are? What behaviors will demonstrate your values and priorities?

If family comes first, what will that mean? What will demonstrate that? I have talked with many executives who said this, but their actions spoke differently.

→ YOUR TURN: Assess Your Alignment

Where are you now? How well do your daily actions reflect the person you want to be and the values you want to embrace?

Look at the values and priorities you identified and the mission statement you crafted. Then take a step back and assess how your behaviors align with them. Consider your routines, decisions, and interactions. Where do you see congruence? Where are the gaps?

Beyond self-reflection, consider seeking feedback from those around you, colleagues, family, and friends. Their perspectives can help highlight blind spots and patterns you may not notice on your own (more on that in the "Evaluate" chapter).

Reflect on the feedback and self-observations to identify patterns where behaviors may not yet fully align with your values.

Self-Assessment

For each of your core values and the behaviors you want to embody, rate your alignment on a scale of 1–10 (with 10 being full alignment and 1 being far from it). Now, take action:

- If you scored 7 or above, what is working? How can you reinforce and build on those behaviors?
- If you scored below a 7, what is one specific behavior you can adjust this week to move closer to alignment?
- What small shifts can you make to better embody your values?
- What behaviors need to change? What priorities need to shift?
- Where can you take immediate action, and what will require a longer-term approach?

Alignment isn't a one-time evaluation, it's an ongoing process of reflection and adjustment. Regularly revisit this exercise to ensure your actions continue to reflect the values that matter most to you.

Living Your Values Through Action
Start, Stop, Do Less, Do More

When you think about the actions you will take to better align your values with your actions, it helps to consider these specific adjustments:

- **Start** → Introduce new behaviors that support your goals and values.
- **Stop** → Eliminate actions that contradict your priorities and values.
- **Do Less Of** → Reduce behaviors that don't fully align but may still have some purpose.

- **Do More Of** → Strengthen existing positive habits that are working well.

Start

Shelley, like many of you, was in back-to-back meetings all day. She was thankful if she had time to run to the bathroom in between. She did not have time to exercise, or eat a healthy lunch. She had gained weight and wanted to lead a healthier lifestyle. She felt that if she didn't make a change, she wouldn't be around long enough for her kids.

With these priorities in mind, she started blocking time on her calendar for morning walks, gym sessions, and lunch breaks. She shared these priorities with her team, sometimes turning meetings into walk-and-talks to integrate movement into her day.

Along the way, Shelley recognized that healthy eating required preparation, and adjusted her schedule to grocery shop on weekends and began meal prepping the night before. Over time, she discovered that these small shifts made a big difference in her energy and well-being.

Similarly, Jane was an executive so focused on the operational side of her group that she rarely engaged with her employees on a personal level. Yet she valued her employees and cared for them and wanted to build personal connections with them. She started prioritizing regular one-on-one meetings, not just to discuss business but to show genuine interest in her employees' career aspirations and personal lives.

Stop

David, the executive I mentioned earlier who decided that he wanted to spend more quality time with his family, told his team that he would not be available between 6:00–8:00 p.m. every evening. That was family time. Yes, there were some emergencies, and he was not home every night, but he now spent most nights, present, with his family. And David was used to being on his phone. It wasn't that people were constantly bothering him, it was his go-to habit. He placed his phone in his home office for these couple of hours, to resist the habit of reaching out to it regularly. He stopped being constantly connected to his phone and work, so that he could be with his family.

What will you stop doing? Are there actions you need to stop because they clearly do not demonstrate your values, or because they are counterproductive and get in the way of living those values and showing up as your best?

George, a CEO, often found himself checking his email, glancing at his phone, or tapping his watch, even while others were speaking to him. This happened both at work and at home. Over time, people around him grew frustrated. Not only did they feel he wasn't fully present, but he also missed important details in conversations.

Through the 360° interviews I conducted as part of our coaching, George began to see the impact of his behavior. He prided himself on being efficient, but one of the core values he had identified was respect. And now, he realized that what he viewed as efficiency was actually undermining that value. He wasn't truly listening. He wasn't really present. And without meaning to, he was treating people disrespectfully.

George decided it was time to make a change. To reduce the temptation to check his screen, he began having conversations and meetings on the couches in his office instead of at his desk. He left his phone behind and set his watch to 'do not disturb.' If someone walked in while he was focused on something else, he paused to decide: could the task wait, or should the person come back later?

By stopping his multitasking habit, George began to show up differently, with presence, intention, and respect. It was a small behavioral shift, but it made a big difference. People felt heard. Frustration decreased. And George felt more aligned with the leader he wanted to be.

Do Less Of

This strategy focuses on minimizing behaviors that hinder success. This approach is about identifying and reducing actions that are counterproductive, or have minimal impact on your goals, enabling a more streamlined and effective workflow.

From my personal example of aspiring to live a healthy and active life, I noticed that late nights were sabotaging my commitment to exercise. Staying up too late meant I was too tired to work out in the morning, or I'd wake up late and skip my workout altogether. It is ok if I have a late night every now and then. But by doing less of my late-night habits, where I was mostly binge-watching TV, I improved my ability to stay consistent with my health goals.

Franc, a senior leader and a perfectionist, often spent excessive time overseeing every step of his team's work and fine-tuning details that had minimal impact on the overall success of projects. This micromanaging behavior was causing delays and frustration among his team. We worked on doing less of the oversight and control, and instead focused on empowering his team to take ownership of their responsibilities. The shift improved project timelines and significantly boosted team morale.

The balance of doing more of what works well and doing less of what doesn't is a dynamic and effective strategy for personal and organizational growth. It helps individuals and teams refine their actions and behaviors towards optimal performance and satisfaction.

Do More Of

This strategy helps reinforce successful behaviors by identifying actions that are already working well and finding ways to amplify them. This isn't just about doing more, it's about strategically scaling what is already effective to achieve greater impact.

This concept is rooted in Positive Psychology, which highlights the power of leveraging strengths and successes rather than focusing solely on fixing weaknesses. Neuroscientists like Earl K. Miller at MIT have shown that when the brain experiences success, it reinforces neural pathways that make future success more likely. In short, success builds upon success.

By identifying what is already working, whether it's a leadership strength, a management skill, or a productivity approach, and expanding those efforts, we create more opportunities for sustained growth and improvement.

To continue building my Executive Coaching business post-COVID, I needed to do more networking. Before the pandemic, in-person events were one of the most effective ways for me to meet potential clients and build relationships. But coming out of COVID, I found myself networking much less in face-to-face settings.

Long COVID had made me hesitant to attend events, and I had grown more comfortable in a virtual world. But I also realized that if I wanted to continue expanding my business, I needed to push myself out of my comfort zone and return to in-person networking.

I made a deliberate effort to attend more events, reconnect with my professional community, and seek out opportunities to engage face-to-face. It wasn't always easy, but with each event, I felt my confidence return, built new connections, and ultimately strengthened my business.

This is a great example of doing more of what had worked for me before, even though I had to overcome internal hesitation to make it happen.

Joe, an executive in a startup, wanted to spend more time thinking strategically. He had a natural ability to see the big picture and connect smaller issues to broader organizational goals. Yet he found himself constantly pulled into day-to-day operational details, leaving little time for high-level thinking.

Joe realized that his biggest contribution would come from dedicating more time to strategy rather than being caught up in execution. But to make this shift, he needed to create space for deep thinking.

He made a few deliberate changes:

- Delegated operational tasks to his team to free up time.
- Blocked off early mornings for strategic thinking, his most focused time of day.
- Set aside time each week for big-picture discussions with his mentors and peers.

By doing more of what played to his strengths, Joe was able to provide greater leadership and long-term direction for his company.

Marc, an executive in a software company, had always been skilled at fostering strong relationships within his organization. His ability to build and maintain close, trusted relationships internally, with his team, peers and senior leadership, had contributed to his career success.

However, he realized that his professional world was largely confined within his company's walls. While his internal relationships were strong, he lacked a broader industry network that could provide fresh perspectives, new opportunities, and potential collaborations.

Recognizing this gap, Marc committed to expanding his networking efforts beyond his company. He set a goal of attending at least one industry conference per quarter, scheduled coffee meetings with professionals outside his immediate circle, and joined a leadership roundtable to engage in discussions with executives from different organizations. Over time, he started forming valuable relationships with industry leaders, gained insights from different perspectives, and even uncovered business opportunities for his company.

By doing more of what he was already good at—relationship-building, but applying it in a broader context—Marc strengthened his leadership presence in the industry and positioned himself as a key player beyond his organization.

Learning From What Already Works

To identify areas where you can do more of what works, take a moment to assess what is already contributing to your success. Instead of focusing solely on gaps or weaknesses, shift your perspective to what you're already doing well.

If you rated yourself a 5/10 on your alignment assessment for a value; for example, integrity, ask yourself:

- Why is it a 5 and not a 4?
- What behaviors are already working that I can expand?
- What am I already doing well?
- How can I do more of it?
- What has led to my past successes, and how can I replicate that?
- Where are you already living your values? Utilizing your strengths?

Instead of focusing only on gaps, this reframing helps you see what you are doing right, rather than just what you are doing wrong. It highlights where you're already making progress, and how you can build on it.

When Jake took over as the head of a burgeoning software development team, he brought with him a highly analytical and critical eye. Fresh perspectives often illuminate overlooked issues, but his approach initially focused exclusively on the negative, on what was not working. During meetings, his critiques overshadowed commendations; he highlighted inefficiencies without acknowledging the team's strengths. This constant emphasis on faults without recognition of successes bred resentment rather than inspiration, distancing him from his new team.

The turning point came when, through coaching, Jake realized he needed to adjust his lens towards the positive aspects of his team's work. He intentionally started to look for what was working. He began to notice and praise the team's adept handling of complex projects and their innovative solutions to technical problems. Together they explored how they could build on these strengths, and leverage existing capabilities to solve bigger challenges, refine their processes and drive greater success. Over time, Jake's relationship with the team improved and the team atmosphere shifted. The team responded not just with increased morale but also with an invigorated commitment to their work.

Reflective Questions:

- What is your team doing well?
- What can you learn from their successes?
- How do you encourage them to build on these strengths?
- How can you increase impact by focusing on what's already working? What would it look like to amplify these strengths across the team?

→ YOUR TURN: Choose Your Stop/Start/More/Less

Reflect on how your current behaviors align with your values, your mission, and the kind of leader you want to be. Use the prompts below to assess and recalibrate your habits, and evaluate which behaviors you need to stop, start, do more of, or do less of to create stronger alignment.

Stop
- What behaviors, habits, or patterns are getting in your way?
- Are there actions that are misaligned with your values or counterproductive to your goals?
- What do you need to let go of in order to show up as your best?

Start
- What new behaviors would support your growth, impact, or well-being?
- Is there something you've been putting off that aligns with your aspirations or values?
- What is one small action you can start taking this week?

Do More Of
- What's working?
- Which habits already reflect your values and are helping you move forward?
- How can you double down and make those behaviors more consistent, increase your effectiveness, and expand your impact?

Do Less Of
- What habits or behaviors tend to consume your time or energy without adding real value? Where might you be overextending or overcontrolling?
- Are there habits or reactions that drain your energy or effectiveness?
- What could you scale back on to create more space for the behaviors that are more effective, meaningful, or aligned with your values?

Saying No

Our time is limited. There are only twenty-four hours in the day, so when you decide you want to do something, you often need to decide what it is that you won't do; what you will eliminate.

What will you say no to?

There's saying no to yourself, that's self-discipline. If you want to spend more time reading, do you need to say no to watching Netflix, Hulu, or Amazon Prime?

If you want more focused time for deep work, what meetings might you opt out of?

When you're clear about your priorities and your *why*, it becomes much easier to say no, whether that's to your own distractions or to the demands of others.

Whether you're saying no to yourself or to someone else, the goal is the same: to protect what matters to you most. Saying no isn't about deprivation or rejection, it's about honoring your time, energy, and values.

I often have conversations with clients around setting clearer boundaries and saying "No" when needed. For some, it's a recent focus. For others, it's an ongoing challenge.

But just like saying no to ourselves, saying no to others is essential for living intentionally. It's about protecting space for what you've deemed most important, your goals, your health, your family, your values.

Here are a few tips for saying "No" more often:

1. **Remember it's okay to put yourself first.** You're entitled to your time, energy, and resources. Saying "Yes" to everything can lead to resentment, burnout, and neglecting your own needs.
2. **Ask yourself: When I say yes to this, what am I saying no to?** Your time is limited. Every yes comes with a trade-off, something else you may have to delay or sacrifice.
3. **Don't react, respond intentionally.** Pause before giving an answer. Consider how the request fits with your priorities, current commitments, and your team's needs. If a clear "No" feels difficult, can you offer a thoughtful alternative, like helping with part of a project, or tackling it at a later time?
4. **Expect some surprise.** People may not be used to you saying no. Letting them know you're working on setting boundaries can help ease the transition, and even inspire their support.
5. **Watch for manipulative behavior.** Not everyone will respect your new boundaries. If someone tries to guilt or pressure you, name the behavior for what it is. That clarity can help you stay firm and centered in your decision.

If you're not used to saying no, it may feel awkward or uncomfortable at first. That's okay. It's a skill, one that takes practice. But developing this skill is essential for staying focused, maintaining your energy, and honoring your true priorities.

Saying no protects your time. It helps you prioritize the activities and relationships that align with your values. It prevents overcommitment, fights burnout, and allows you to show up more fully in the areas that truly need your attention.

Dorie Clark's advice for saying no offers a refreshing perspective that can help us set boundaries without unnecessary guilt. She reminds us that not everyone assigning you a request is giving it the same weight you are.[33] While you might only ask for help when it truly matters, others may be operating from a *can't hurt to ask* mindset, sending the same request to dozens of people.

Understanding that difference is freeing. Saying no to someone's wide-net request often has far less emotional weight than we imagine.

Dorie also shares a practical delay strategy that helps weed out non-serious requests. Instead of an outright no, you can respond with, "I'd be happy to consider this, but I'm currently overwhelmed. Please follow up with me in a week (or another specific time)."[34] By introducing this delay, you naturally filter out those who aren't committed enough to follow through, saving yourself time and energy. It's a simple yet powerful boundary that ensures you say yes only to the requests that truly matter.

In his book *Essentialism: The Disciplined Pursuit of Less*, author Greg McKeown talks about how learning to deliver a graceful no is one of the most important skills to master, it allows you to focus your time, energy, and commitments on the things that really matter.[35]

McKeown's book outlines four ways to say no:

The Polite No
- Express appreciation for the opportunity.
- Clearly and politely decline the request.
- Provide a brief and straightforward reason for your refusal.
- Suggest that you appreciate the offer but cannot commit due to other priorities.
  Example: *"Thank you for thinking of me. Unfortunately, I am currently working on other projects and won't be able to take on additional tasks at this time."*

The Grateful No
- Express gratitude for being considered or offered an opportunity.
- Clearly decline the request.
- Offer a sincere and appreciative response to convey that you value the relationship or the opportunity.
  Example: *"I'm truly grateful for the opportunity, and I've enjoyed working with you. However, I must decline at this time due to other commitments."*

The Firm No
- Clearly state your decision without excessive explanation.
- Avoid over-apologizing or providing too many details.
- Use a firm and confident tone to communicate your decision.
  Example: *"I appreciate your offer, but I'm unable to take on additional responsibilities right now."*

The No with a Rain Check
- Express gratitude for the offer or opportunity.
- Communicate that you are currently unable to commit but would be open to considering it in the future.
- Provide a specific timeframe or condition under which you might reconsider.
  Example: *"Thank you for thinking of me. I'm unable to take on additional commitments at the moment, but I would be open to discussing this again in six months."*[36]

Saying no is a skill that can be developed over time. The above four approaches can help you decline requests assertively, yet gracefully, without burning bridges. By using these techniques, you can maintain positive relationships while staying focused on your essential priorities. If saying no is challenging for you, practice with a friend or in front of a mirror. Get more comfortable with saying no. It is also helpful to consider if there are specific people who tend not to respect your boundaries; if so, think about what you are (and what you are not), ready to do for them. Prepare yourself for conversations with them, and how you would like to handle their demands.

Sandy, a director at a successful organization I coached, struggled with saying no. She loved helping her peers and whenever anyone asked for her help, she said yes. Naturally, everyone in the organization loved her. She was a wealth of knowledge and always happy to help. But Sandy was so busy helping everyone else that sometimes she didn't have enough time to get her own work done. It got to a point where she wasn't quite meeting her goals. Sandy's priorities needed to shift so that she could first meet her own commitments. Being collaborative and helpful was a core value for Sandy. She had to learn to be collaborative and helpful AND meet her goals. She needed to find a balance between helping others, being a collaborative team player, and saying no strategically. Sandy explained to her peers that she needed to make this shift. She practiced saying no. She learned to offer more limited support as well as redirect people to others who could assist. The result? In the next quarter, Sandy exceeded her goals!

→ YOUR TURN: Practice Saying No

Do you need to work on saying no more often?

What do you need to start saying no to, to be able to live by your values and your priorities?

Building Habits and Routines That Stick

"You don't rise to the level of your goals. You fall to the level of your habits."

Atomic Habits, James Clear

How Habits Work

Habits play a significant role in our lives, influencing our behavior, actions, and overall well-being. Creating new habits helps us grow, one step at a time. They can move us out of our comfort zone and create lasting change. Understanding how habits work can provide insights into how we can intentionally shape our routines and behaviors. Here's a simplified breakdown:

Cue/Trigger

- A cue or trigger is the initial signal that prompts your brain to initiate a behavior. It can be an external event, an emotional state, a specific time of day, or any other stimulus.
  Examples:
    - Feeling stressed (cue) triggers the habit of biting your nails.
    - Having a looming deadline (cue) triggers the habit of procrastination.
    - I wake up in the morning (cue) triggers the habit of drinking coffee first thing in the morning. Yep, that's me!

Routine/Behavior

- The routine is the actual behavior or action that follows the cue. It is the habit itself, the behavior you automatically engage in response to the trigger.
  Examples:
    - Biting your nails is the routine that follows the cue of feeling stressed.
    - Procrastinating by delaying work on the project is the routine that follows the cue of having a looming deadline.
    - Brewing and thoroughly enjoying my cup of double espresso is the routine that follows the cue of waking up.

Reward/Outcome

- The reward is the positive outcome or feeling that follows the completion of the habit. It reinforces the habit loop by providing a sense of satisfaction, pleasure, or relief.
  Examples:
    - Biting your nails may provide a temporary sense of relief or distraction, serving as the reward for the habit.
    - Procrastination may provide temporary relief from the stress associated with the task, serving as the reward for the habit.
    - Drinking my coffee in the morning provides me with a sense of comfort, increased alertness, and a pleasurable taste, serving as the reward for the habit.

Repetition and Reinforcement

- Habits become ingrained through repetition. The more consistently the habit loop is completed, the more automatic and ingrained the behavior becomes. Repetition strengthens the neural pathways associated with the habit.
  Examples:
  - If you consistently bite your nails in response to stress and experience the temporary relief, the habit becomes more entrenched over time.
  - If you consistently procrastinate in response to looming deadlines and experience temporary relief, the habit of procrastination becomes more entrenched over time.
  - Consistently drinking coffee in the morning upon waking up (if you can believe it, I have been drinking coffee every morning since I was six years old; I don't know what my parents were thinking!) and experiencing the positive outcomes, the habit of morning coffee consumption becomes more entrenched over time.

Habit Loop

- The cue-routine-reward sequence forms a habit loop, a neurological pattern that becomes increasingly automatic with repetition. This loop is orchestrated by the basal ganglia, a part of the brain associated with habit formation.
  Examples:
  - Every time you feel stressed (cue), you automatically bite your nails (routine), and the temporary relief you experience reinforces the habit loop (reward).
  - Every time you have a looming deadline (cue), you automatically procrastinate (routine), and the temporary relief you experience reinforces the habit loop (reward).
  - I have all kinds of portable espresso makers that I can take with me anywhere, so that I can ensure that every time I wake up (cue), I automatically drink coffee (routine), and the comfort, alertness, and pleasurable taste I experience reinforce the habit loop (reward).

Cognitive Loop

- Over time, habits may become more automatic, requiring less conscious effort. However, individuals can also engage in a cognitive loop, where they become aware of the cue, consciously choose a different routine, and still receive a reward. This process involves intentional habit modification.
  Examples:
  - Instead of biting your nails when stressed, you may consciously choose to take deep breaths or go for a short walk, still achieving a sense of relief without the negative consequences of nail-biting.
  - Instead of procrastinating when faced with a looming deadline, you may consciously choose to break down the tasks into smaller, manageable steps and start working on them. This alternative routine still achieves a sense of relief without the negative consequences of procrastination.
  - If, for some reason, I ever decide to reduce my caffeine intake, I may consciously choose to replace the routine of drinking coffee with a routine of drinking herbal tea in the morning. This alternative routine still provides a sense of comfort and a positive start to the day.
  - Understanding the components of the habit loop allows you to intentionally modify or create habits by identifying cues, adjusting routines, and ensuring rewarding outcomes. This awareness is the foundation for habit formation and transformation.

How Long Does It Take to Form a Habit?

In one well-known study undertaken by the psychologist Dr. Phillippa Lally, the average time it took to form a habit was sixty-six days, but the range varied widely depending on the behavior and the person. There's no exact formula, but research shows that forming a new habit typically takes between twenty-one and sixty-six days, sometimes longer for more complex behaviors.[37]

The key to forming a habit is consistency, not perfection. You don't need to be flawless, just persistent. Missing a day doesn't reset your progress, but giving up altogether does. And here's something crucial: Focus on building one habit at a time.

Trying to overhaul everything at once often leads to frustration or burnout. But when you commit to just one meaningful habit and repeat it consistently, you're far more likely to see lasting change, and stay motivated to keep going.

Sharon's Leadership Journey Through the Habit Loop

Meet Sharon, a high-powered executive known for her sharp focus on outcomes. While her drive delivered strong results, it also came at the cost of team morale. She was often perceived as dismissive and overly critical, and many high-potential employees felt discouraged or undervalued working with her.

During our coaching sessions, Sharon reflected on her core values: Achievement, Excellence, Respectfulness, and Teamwork. While she excelled at achievement and excellence, she realized she was falling short on respect and collaboration, two values she genuinely wanted to uphold.

To realign her behavior with her values, Sharon created a new habit loop:

- **Cue/Trigger:** Sharon chose the start of each meeting as her cue. As soon as a meeting began, she built in a moment of intentional pause to remind herself, *"Respect and teamwork matter just as much as results."* This mental reset helped her shift from purely task-focused to relationally aware.
- **Routine/Behavior:** Guided by this new awareness, Sharon began practicing active listening, acknowledged others' contributions openly, and encouraged discussion and collaboration. She also made a conscious effort to give constructive, rather than critical, feedback.
- **Reward/Outcome:** Her team responded positively. They felt heard, respected, and more motivated to contribute. Gradually, the culture of her team shifted, engagement rose, communication improved, and they started achieving better outcomes together.

In time, this habit loop profoundly transformed Sharon's leadership style and the culture of her team. Each time she paused to reconnect with her values and chose a more respectful, team-focused approach, she strengthened the loop. The behavior became more natural, and the rewards—greater trust, engagement, and collaboration—reinforced her commitment. By aligning her leadership habits with her core values, Sharon not only became a more effective leader but also fostered stronger relationships and a more motivated, cohesive team.

→ YOUR TURN: Design Your Habits

Take a few moments to reflect on the habits shaping your daily life. Notice the patterns in your behavior, what you do, when you do it, and why.

- Which ones are helping you move closer to your goals?
- Which align with your values and priorities?
- Which might be holding you back?

Try breaking them down into their habit loops:

- What is the cue that triggers the habit?
- What is the routine or behavior you follow?
- What is the reward you get from it?

Now choose one habit loop you'd like to shift. Identify a new behavior you can try in response to the same cue, one that aligns more closely with your goals and values.

Habit Stacking

It is not easy to create new habits. Habit stacking is a productivity and behavior change technique popularized by James Clear in his book *Atomic Habits*.[38]

The idea is to leverage existing habits as cues or triggers for new habits, making it easier to establish and maintain positive behaviors. By stacking a new habit on top of an established one, you create a routine that feels seamless and requires minimal mental effort. For example, if you regularly check your calendar first thing in the morning, you could pair that with reviewing your personal mission statement. The existing habit becomes a cue for a more intentional start to your day. Here's how habit stacking works:

Identify an Existing Habit
Choose a habit that you already do consistently as a part of your daily routine. This can be something simple and automatic, such as brushing your teeth, making your bed, entering a meeting, or having a cup of coffee.

Select a New Habit
Decide on the new habit you want to incorporate into your routine. It should be small, manageable, and aligned with your overall goals. Examples include doing a short workout, practicing mindfulness, or identifying your top three priorities for the workday.

Pair the Habits
Associate the new habit with the existing one by stacking them together. For instance, if you decide to do a short workout, you might link it with your habit of making your bed. After making your bed, you proceed directly to your workout.

Create a Trigger
Use the completion of the existing habit as a trigger for the new habit. The completion of one habit serves as a signal to start the next one. Over time, the association becomes strong, and the new habit becomes integrated into your routine. Example: **After** *(current habit)*, **I will** *(new habit)*.

> After I pour my morning coffee, I will spend ten minutes journaling.
> As I start my team meetings, I will spend five minutes inquiring how they are each feeling.
> As I sit at my desk each morning and turn on my computer, I will write down the top three work priorities for the day.
> After I finish my lunch, I will take a five-minute walk outside.
> As I walk in the door and say hello to my family, I will put my phone away.

Be Specific

Clearly define the new habit and the associated trigger to make the process more concrete and actionable. This clarity helps in building a routine that becomes automatic.

Habit stacking is effective because it leverages the power of existing habits, reducing the friction associated with starting something new. Over time, as the habit stack becomes ingrained, you can consider adding more habits to further enhance your routine. The key is to start small, be consistent, and gradually build upon your habits.

Putting Habit Stacking into Action

As you've probably gathered, I love my coffee, black espresso. Let's just say I drink a few a day, and yes, it's my addiction. As I made my coffee, I noticed a small but telling ritual: I'd stand in front of the cabinet, pausing to choose my next mug. Some days I reached for my dark blue one, others for the bright orange, the flowery Marimekko mug, or the one my best friend gave me.

Over time, I started noticing patterns. On blue mug days, I often felt a little down. On days I chose the flowery one, I was typically more upbeat. Sometimes I picked the mug from my friend simply because I missed her. I began paying closer attention, noticing how my mood influenced my choices and how my choices could influence my mood.

So I started making small, intentional shifts. On a day that might've started as "blue," I reached for the flowered mug instead. I asked myself, "Why does today feel off?" That pause gave me a chance to check in with myself and make a conscious decision about how I wanted the rest of the day to unfold, rather than letting the rain or someone's comment shape it for me.

In short, I took a habit I already did multiple times a day, making coffee, and stacked a moment of self-awareness onto it. It became a small but powerful emotional check-in. I put the habit stacking concept into action: I linked a new behavior (self-reflection) to an existing habit (coffee-making). By connecting the new behavior to something already automatic, I increased the chances it would stick.

At the office, I found another opportunity to stack a small but impactful habit. As I sat down with my coffee each morning, I used that moment to quickly pause and reflect on my top priorities for the day. It became a natural cue for a mini check-in: Was I focused on what mattered most? Was I making progress on the tasks that would move the needle? That morning coffee became more than a routine, it became a tool to stay aligned and intentional.

One of my clients, Ken, a senior manager, wanted to become more consistent in giving his team real-time feedback. With packed days, it often fell off his radar. Together, we identified a simple habit to stack: after each one-on-one or team meeting, he would jot down one piece of positive feedback or a growth opportunity for someone. He tied this to the natural transition of ending a meeting, whether clicking "Leave" online or standing up after an in-person session. That small pairing made feedback more consistent, less daunting, and eventually second nature.

Creating moments of self-awareness wasn't the only habit I stacked onto my coffee routine. Back in early November 2020, I was trying to establish an exercise routine, with the added goal of reducing stress around the elections. I committed to doing just three minutes of yoga a day. It felt doable, and I liked the idea of integrating yoga into my daily rhythm to build a new habit.

That month, I practiced yoga on twenty-three out of thirty days. Yes, there was still room for improvement, but when I compared that to October and September, when I practiced only four and five times respectively, it was real progress.

Three minutes a day was easy to commit to, and interestingly, I often ended up practicing for twenty-eight minutes on average. (Thank you, Apple Watch, for the tracking!)

Each day, I reflected on what influenced whether I practiced or not. I started noticing patterns. On weekends, without a structured schedule, time sometimes slipped away and, oops, I forgot. That's when I turned to habit stacking again. I paired yoga with my coffee: morning coffee, then yoga.

I also practiced self-forgiveness. Instead of beating myself up for missing a day, I focused on what I could do differently moving forward.

Remember the goal. The goal is simply to do more of what you set out to do. And I was. I felt more relaxed, stronger, more centered, and more aligned.

Transferring Habits Across Domains

In December 2023, as I reflected on the past year and looked ahead to the challenges of 2024, one priority stood out, again: maintaining physical fitness. Although I had made great strides in recent years, two years of grappling with long Covid had left me frequently fatigued, and I was still struggling to balance rest with movement.

On days when I felt especially tired or the weather turned gloomy, it was all too easy to give in to the comfort of Netflix or a quiet nap, letting my fitness goals slide.

As I considered how to stay consistent with daily exercise, I found inspiration in an unlikely place: my game apps. The visual rewards, the daily streaks, the dopamine hits, they worked. I played every day without fail.

Over coffee, I shared this realization with a friend. She suggested I try the Peloton app. And it was a game-changer. Drawn in by the streak feature, I soon found myself exercising daily. I built a twenty-six-week streak, six months of showing up, every single day.

Then, oops. Just two days after I wrote about this win, I had a big argument with my husband. (Yes, that still happens after thirty plus years of marriage!) I was upset, distracted, and completely forgot to do my Peloton workout. The next day, I opened the app and saw I was back to day one. I felt crushed. My first reaction was to focus on the loss.

Then I paused. I reminded myself of the bigger picture: the goal is to move more and feel stronger. One missed day doesn't erase my progress.

It's now been nearly eleven months, and in that entire time, I've only missed three days. That's progress.

This experience reminded me of a valuable insight I often share with my clients: When something works in one part of your life, it can often be adapted to strengthen another.

I often use the approach of transferring habits across domains in my coaching practice, helping clients transfer effective behaviors from one area of life to another.

Take Janice, for example. She struggled with speaking too quickly during team meetings, which often left her audience overwhelmed and created a false sense of urgency. Interestingly, when presenting to the board, she naturally slowed her pace and communicated clearly and calmly. Together, we analyzed what helped her shift gears in that setting, her mindset, preparation, and the tone she intentionally set.

By identifying those cues and replicating them in her daily meetings, Janice gradually learned to speak more deliberately and effectively with her team as well.

→ YOUR TURN: Stack Your Habits

What existing habits could you use as anchors for stacking new behaviors?

What can you learn from how you succeed in one area of life that might help you in another? As I did, for example, drawing from the motivational power of game apps to support my fitness, or as Janice did, applying her boardroom presence to her everyday team meetings. What habits or mindsets could you cross-apply to help you move closer to your goals?

As you reflect on how habits shape your daily actions, whether through small behavior shifts or by transferring what works in one area of life to another, it's helpful to zoom out and look at the bigger picture: how you show up when you're at your best. This is where your strengths come in. Your strengths are the throughline, often driving the habits that stick, the behaviors that cross domains, and the impact you have on others. Let's explore how these strengths come to life in your leadership and daily actions, and how you can harness them more intentionally.

Leveraging Your Strengths

The strengths you identified in the previous chapter don't just exist on paper, they show up in how you move through the world. Think about what other people may observe when you are using your strengths. What do they look like when you're in action, both in your leadership role and in your daily life and work engagements? Here's how you might see these strengths come to life:

- **Strategic Thinking:** Imagine you're in planning meetings, tossing around ideas that not only solve the issue at hand but also consider the long-term effects. This type of thinking involves proposing creative solutions to complex challenges, thinking three steps ahead.

- **Effective Communication:** This is all about clarity and presence. Whether you're presenting a new strategy or engaged in a one-on-one, you're listening actively and expressing your thoughts clearly, making complex ideas accessible to everyone.
- **Empathy:** It shows when you truly understand and acknowledge the feelings of your team members. In challenging times, it's about adapting your leadership style to the needs of your people, showing real compassion.
- **Decisiveness:** Here, you're the person who digests information swiftly, makes informed choices promptly, and takes responsibility for the outcomes of your decisions.
- **Adaptability:** This strength is crucial when the unexpected happens. You pivot strategies in response to changing market conditions, stay composed in crises, and always learn from these experiences to better handle future challenges.
- **Collaboration:** A collaborative leader seeks thoughts from the team, appreciates diverse viewpoints, and strives to build consensus, ensuring that everyone feels part of the journey.
- **Resilience:** This is about maintaining your performance level under pressure, bouncing back from setbacks, and learning from every failure without losing your drive.

Harnessing Your Strengths for Success

When you are fully aware of your strengths, it is easier to access them and utilize them when facing challenges.

Defining your strengths in behavioral terms not only helps you recognize them in real scenarios, it makes them real, tangible, and something you can continuously enhance to become an even more effective leader. Understanding how your strengths align with your goals can help you use them more intentionally and significantly boost your success, personally and professionally.

Take strategic thinking, for example. If your goal is to lead a major transformation, you'd use this strength to create a clear, compelling vision. You'd build a plan with milestones and identify the resources you'll need.

You'd bring others along by securing buy-in from key stakeholders. You'd anticipate roadblocks and think ahead with proactive solutions. You'd set clear metrics to track progress and adapt the plan as needed.

Similarly, if empathy is your strong suit and your goal is to strengthen family bonds, you'd let it shape how you relate with your family members. You'd listen actively and try to see things from their perspective. You'd offer emotional support during tough times. You'd spend meaningful time doing activities they enjoy. And you'd express appreciation often. These small actions build deeper, more connected relationships.

A clear understanding of your strengths, and how they play out in real life, gives you a powerful advantage. It helps you make smarter decisions, focus your energy where it matters most, and lead with purpose. When you use your strengths deliberately, you're not just reacting, you're building momentum toward your goals. That intentional alignment is what drives consistent, meaningful success.

→ YOUR TURN: Leverage Your Strengths

Take a moment to revisit your top strengths.

- How do they show up in your daily life, at work, at home, in how you lead, listen, or make decisions?
- In what situations do you feel most energized and effective?
- Where could you lean into them more intentionally to move closer to your goals?

Now consider: Are you creating the conditions that allow your strengths to thrive?

Sometimes we overlook a critical piece of the puzzle: our environment. Even the most powerful strengths need the right conditions to flourish. That's where we're headed next, exploring how you can shape your surroundings to support and sustain the habits, mindset, and behaviors to help you reach your goals.

Setting up Your Environment for Success

Setting up your environment for success is a fundamental step in aligning your daily life with your long-term aspirations. When your surroundings support your goals, the path to achieving them becomes clearer and less cluttered. This can mean organizing your physical space to eliminate distractions, or it can involve surrounding yourself with people and resources that inspire and motivate you. Just as a gardener prepares the soil before planting, so must we cultivate our personal and professional environments to foster growth and productivity. By intentionally shaping the spaces where we live and work to reflect our objectives, we enable a smoother journey toward realizing our dreams. Whether it's decluttering your workspace to enhance focus, setting up reminders of your goals, or curating a network that challenges and supports you, small shifts can make a big difference.

George, who was working on being more present, shifted his environment to support that intention. He started taking conversations away from his desk to avoid distractions and placed his phone at a distance during meetings so he could focus fully on the person in front of him.

Shelley, who was working on eating healthier, stocked her kitchen with fresh, nutritious ingredients and made sure tempting snacks were out of sight. She placed healthy options on the counter, so that during short breaks between meetings, she'd reach for the apple she could see instead of the chocolate hidden in the cupboard.

These changes may seem small, but they helped George and Shelley reduce friction and stay aligned with the people they wanted to be. Often, it's these manageable, practical tweaks that set us up for success.

And sometimes, the shift needs to be bigger.

For me, the environment I grew up in didn't support my growth; rather, it actively suppressed it. My father was dominant and deeply chauvinistic. My thoughts and opinions were dismissed. Despite being a strong student, I was told I wouldn't amount to much, that I wouldn't finish a degree, while my brother was praised and told he'd become a doctor or a lawyer. The message was clear: Expectations for me were low.

Instead of shrinking, I pushed back. I fought to be seen, to be heard, to assert my worth. But I also knew I couldn't truly grow in that space.

So, after high school, I made a pivotal decision: I moved to Israel. That move wasn't just about belonging or adventure and opportunity, it was about survival. It was a deliberate choice to put myself in an environment where I could think for myself, be taken seriously, and grow into who I wanted to be. It was the first time I chose a space that supported my potential instead of stifling it.

That experience taught me something profound: our environment shapes our sense of possibility. And when we're intentional about the spaces we create, physically, socially, emotionally, we set the stage for meaningful growth.

→ YOUR TURN: Design Your Environment

What changes, big or small, could you make to your environment to better support your growth and goals?

- What aspects of your current environment already support your progress?
- What's getting in the way? Clutter, distractions, or people who drain your energy?
- What small adjustments could reduce friction and help you make the helpful choice the easy choice?
- Are there bigger shifts you've been avoiding, ones that might unlock the next level of your growth?

Your environment shapes your habits, your energy, and your mindset. Take a moment to reflect: What would it look like to create a space, internal or external, that truly supports the person you're becoming?

From Environment to Accountability

While designing a supportive environment makes it easier to stay on track, it's not enough on its own. We all have moments of fatigue, distraction, or self-doubt—times when good intentions fade. That's where accountability comes in. Whether it's a check-in with someone you trust, a regular review of your progress, or an external system that keeps you honest, accountability turns your goals into shared commitments. It adds structure, motivation, and momentum to your efforts.

Accountability

Accountability is crucial for living a meaningful and purposeful life, ensuring that your actions align and are consistent with your values, fostering a sense of integrity and authenticity. Being accountable helps you stay focused on your goals and increases the likelihood of achieving them. It helps you take responsibility for your actions, learn from mistakes, and adapt to challenges contributing to personal growth and development.

Being accountable for your actions builds trust, both with yourself and others, demonstrating reliability and commitment.

Living in alignment with your values and being accountable for your choices minimizes the chances of regret and dissatisfaction.

Modeling accountability can inspire and positively influence those around you, creating a culture of responsibility and integrity.

Remember my story about the Peloton app's daily check-ins encouraging me to exercise daily? That is a form of accountability.

Accountability provides you with a regular time for self-reflection, a time to assess your actions and decisions against your values. It increases awareness of what you are doing, and what you are avoiding, making it easier to identify habits that support or derail your goals. It helps you stay on track and make necessary adjustments.

Accountability partners can provide powerful support as you work toward meaningful goals. In the Forefront program, a highly selective leadership initiative powered by Marshall Goldsmith and the 100 Coaches, we were paired with an accountability group that met weekly, led by the brilliant Rhett Power.

What made these sessions so impactful wasn't just setting goals, it was knowing that someone would be there each week to check in, ask how things were going, and challenge us to follow through. That consistent structure created a rhythm of action and reflection. Rhett helped us sharpen our focus, yes, but it was the shared commitment and mutual accountability that kept us moving forward.

Our group became a trusted space where we could speak honestly about challenges, celebrate progress, and hold each other to high standards. The simple act of saying something out loud, and knowing you'd report back, created momentum. It's often easy to break promises to ourselves. It's much harder when someone else is on the journey with you.

In our interview, Rhett shared that today's world is full of distractions, so many bright, shiny objects pulling our attention in different directions.[39] For him, living with severe ADHD, accountability has been a game-changer. It helps him stay focused on what matters most and maintain daily habits that move him toward his goals. It keeps him from chasing unproductive tasks or falling down rabbit holes.

Rhett's advice:

> One of the easiest things you can do is find an accountability partner. I can't say that enough. Write down your goals. Then find someone you can talk to every week, or even more often. The key is to choose someone who won't go easy on you. Someone who tells the truth.
>
> We all have that one brutally honest friend. That's the person you need. Not the one who says, 'Yeah, Rhett, that's great. No worries.' Don't choose someone who lets you off the hook. Pick the person who'll call you out if you didn't do what you said you would.[40]

Consider having an accountability partner or group, with whom you can share your goals and progress. This person/group can offer feedback, support, and hold you responsible for your actions. Who could serve as your accountability partner(s)?

Accountability has been a cornerstone of my coaching practice and has significantly helped my coachees achieve and sustain improvements in their behavior and leadership skills. By introducing a variety of accountability mechanisms, my coachees are reminded of their commitments and are encouraged to stay on track with their personal and professional goals.

Often in my coaching, my coachees are held accountable not just by me, but by their colleagues and stakeholders as well. They regularly check in with them about their progress towards achieving their development goals. This creates a powerful dynamic where the coachee is motivated to demonstrate change because they know others are invested in their progress and are observing them. The external perspective that accountability partners provide can also be invaluable in offering insights that the coachees might not see themselves. The regular check-ins and updates create a sense of responsibility and urgency that internal motivation alone may not provide.

Daily Questions

Every day, no matter where in the world he may happen to be, Marshall Goldsmith receives a call from someone who asks him a set of questions. This person, his accountability partner, asks Marshall about the effort he has made that day towards achieving specific goals. Why does he do this? He has found this process to be incredibly practical and efficient for him and his many successful clients. "I find that it does a wonderful job of keeping what is most important to me 'in my head,'" says Marshall. So every day he challenges himself by answering a set of questions that represent his values and the behaviors that he knows are important, but are often easy to neglect.[41]

Marshall pays this person to call him every day. And she just listens to his answers. The accountability is that simple.

I like using the Daily Questions App. I am prompted daily to answer on a scale of 1–10 about my effort in achieving certain behaviors.

Focusing on the effort is a critical aspect here. While we can control our effort, sometimes we cannot control the results. For this reason, each of Marshall's questions begins with "Did I do my best to..."

As Marshall says, "The good thing about beginning these questions with 'Did I do my best to...' is that it is almost impossible to blame someone else for my failure. No one can be responsible for 'Did I do my best to...' but me!"

Marshall begins with six active questions that have been proven (in his research involving over 2,500 people) to lead to higher satisfaction with life.[42]

Did I do my best to...

1. Set clear goals?
2. Make progress toward goal achievement?
3. Be happy?

4. Find meaning?
5. Build positive relationships?
6. Be fully engaged?

Marshall also added the following questions:

- How many minutes did you spend writing? This helps him stay consistent, as it is sometimes hard for him to sit by himself and write.
- How many sit-ups did you do? A reminder to focus on his health.
- Did you say or do something nice for your wife? Your son? Your daughter? His relationship questions accept that he is not a perfect husband or dad, and this process helps him get better.[43]

The questions are intended to reflect individual values, so they will be different for each person. So, for example, in addition to Marshall's six questions, I also ask myself:

- Did I do my best to treat my husband with love, respect and patience? After a day of coaching and being fully present and patient with my clients, I sometimes felt that I would not be as patient and present with my husband. I wanted to change that.
- Working on greater self-compassion, and taming my inner critic, I ask myself, Did I do my best to not criticize myself?
- To increase my focus I ask myself, Did I do my best to do my highest priority tasks first?
- Focusing on my health: Did I do my best to exercise today?

These questions are designed to encourage active engagement with one's goals and responsibilities, fostering a sense of personal accountability and continuous improvement. They can be tailored to fit individual needs and focus areas, whether that's improving personal relationships, advancing career objectives, enhancing health and well-being, or any other personal or professional aspirations.

My client George, the CEO who wanted to be more present, be a better listener and treat people with respect, added the question, Did I do my best to treat my employees with respect? And, Did I do my best to be fully present in meetings?

Shelley, who wanted to eat healthier: Did I do my best to eat healthy today?

David, the executive who was trying to spend more quality time with his wife and young family added, Did I do my best to spend quality time with my family?

Sharon, the high-powered executive who was dismissive of others' ideas added, Did I do my best to listen to others' ideas? And, Did I do my best to build a collaborative work environment?

Why does this process work so well?

It forces us to reflect and confront how we actually live our values, day by day. It helps us form new habits and track real progress. If your daily score is consistently low, it's a sign to pause and ask, Is this something that truly matters to me? If the answer is yes, think again about what might help you gain traction. If a score is consistently high, it may be a habit that's already well-established, and perhaps no longer needs to be on the list.

Importantly, this practice also reminds us that every day is a restart. No matter what happened yesterday, you get another chance to show up, to try again, to live your values with intention. That daily reset helps build not just discipline, but self-compassion too.

Try it out. Imagine a person was going to call you every day and listen to you answer questions about your life. Write out the questions that you should ask yourself daily. Even the process of writing the questions will help you better understand your own values and how you live or don't live by them on a daily basis. You can try using the Daily Questions app (search Marshall Goldsmith Daily Questions in the app store) or have someone you can text or who will listen to your answers every day, or partner with someone where you will each ask the other daily questions.

→ YOUR TURN: Ask Your Daily Questions

What questions would you want to ask yourself, every day? Write them down. Remember, it's about your *effort*, not perfection. Start each question with: *Did I do my best to...*

Whether you use the Daily Questions app or an accountability partner, start by writing your list of questions as a powerful step toward greater clarity and accountability.

From Accountability to Gratitude
Accountability helps us keep stock of what we're doing, and what we're not doing. But without balance, it can lead us to focus too much on what still needs fixing. That's where gratitude comes in. It shifts our attention to what is working, what we've accomplished, what is positive, and who has helped us along the way. With gratitude, we create a fuller, more accurate picture, one that keeps us grounded in both progress and possibility.

Staying Motivated on the Journey
Gratitude–Practicing Optimism
When you're stressed or your mind is clouded by negative thoughts, it's easy to lose sight of what's going well, both the big and the small. Practicing optimism helps counter that. It invites us to consciously look for the good, and writing those things down helps bring them into focus.

Start with Yourself
People often use a gratitude journal to note what they're thankful for. Writing down what you appreciate helps you slow down, reflect, and bring attention to the positive moments in your life. According to Robert Emmons, a professor at the University of California, Davis, and leading expert in gratitude research, "Writing helps to organize thoughts, facilitate integration, and helps you accept your own experiences and put them in context... It allows you to see the meaning of events going on around you and create meaning in your own life."[44]

One simple but powerful practice is to write down three good things that happen each day. These could be moments, people, or even small pleasures. Go for depth over breadth, be specific. Rather than writing "coffee," describe the aroma, the quiet moment before your day began, or the warmth of your favorite mug. Rather than just "Julie," reflect on how she cheered you up during a hard moment.

If you're stuck, try imagining life without something you take for granted, your car, your job, a close friend. This shift in perspective can help unlock gratitude for things that otherwise fade into the background.

This practice not only uplifts your mood in the moment but can reveal progress over time. Looking back through your journal can remind you of how far you've come, what's improved, what's stayed steady, and what continues to bring you joy.

Practicing Optimism With "The Glad Game"

When you find yourself struggling to identify something to be grateful for, try Pollyanna's approach: look for something to be *glad about*. Inspired by Eleanor H. Porter's classic novel, *Pollyanna*, this deceptively simple practice helps shift your mindset, even when things feel overwhelming.

Pollyanna would find something to be glad about in every situation, no matter how disappointing. When she received crutches instead of a doll from a charity, she was glad she didn't need to use them. It's an invitation to look for the silver lining, to train your brain to focus on what is still possible, still good.

While people have often poked fun at Pollyanna for being overly cheerful or naive, she actually offers a valuable lesson: Choosing optimism isn't about denying reality—it's about expanding it. It's not about pretending things are perfect, but about finding a thread of light in the dark.

A good friend of mine, who read the book as a child, introduced me to this game. She used it as a resilience tool throughout her life. Inspired by her, I started playing the game with my family, and even introduced it to clients. It's surprisingly powerful.

I had a chance to put it into practice myself in the winter of 2023. We found out that a pipe had burst at our lake cabin in Maine. Water had been pouring from the upstairs bathroom for days, flooding the downstairs. It was a mess. We immediately went into action, called the plumber, the insurance, a restoration company. But what surprised me most was my reaction.

I was calm. Positive, even. I remember thinking, What's done is done. What can I control now?

Just a few years ago, this would have unraveled me. But instead, I found myself playing "The Glad Game" in real life.

- I was glad no one was hurt.
- I was glad we had insurance.
- I was glad it wasn't our main home.
- I even found myself imagining how beautiful the cabin might look after the repairs.

This mindset helped me not just cope, but truly stay grounded.

Gratitude and Leadership

Gratitude isn't just a personal practice, it's also a powerful leadership tool. In *Leading with Gratitude*, authors Chester Elton and Adrian Gostick describe how appreciation, when expressed consistently by leaders, improves morale, reduces stress, strengthens trust, and leads to better business outcomes.[45]

Chester shared a memorable example during our interview. On the International Space Station, a team of astronauts practiced daily acts of kindness, cleaning, preparing meals, or covering for each other. The result? Zero interpersonal conflict and record-setting productivity.[46]

He also shared a personal ritual that makes gratitude tangible. He carries small stones inscribed with the word *gratitude* in his pocket and gives them out to people who've made a positive impact. As he explained, "The stone symbolizes that we're all different, a little flawed, but capable of creating ripples of positivity, like a stone in a pond."[47]

These small acts create moments of connection. A handwritten note. A sincere thank you. A moment of acknowledgment in a meeting. They don't take much, but their impact is lasting.

And here's something else that's important: Showing gratitude isn't just good for the recipient, it's good for the giver too. Research shows that expressing appreciation and doing kind things for others can significantly boost your own well-being and happiness. Gratitude is a gift we give that gives back.

As a leader, gratitude can:

- Reinforce your values.
- Build a culture of trust.
- Increase engagement and motivation.
- Improve team cohesion and performance.

When you use gratitude intentionally, it becomes part of your leadership identity, clarifying what matters, operationalizing appreciation, and reflecting your commitment to leading with authenticity and heart.

→ YOUR TURN: Practice Gratitude

Gratitude isn't just a mindset, it's a practice. It's not just about feeling thankful, it's about showing it, living it, and building it into your daily rhythms.

- How will you practice gratitude in your personal life?
- How will you demonstrate it in your leadership?

Whether it's three good things in a journal, a game of finding what to be glad about, or a simple thank-you note, you get to decide how gratitude shows up in your life. But when you do, it will ripple outward, in ways you may not expect.

When we take time to notice what we're glad about or grateful for, even in difficult circumstances, it naturally leads to something else: a moment of celebration.

Celebrating Progress

Celebrating your successes, no matter how small, is a powerful part of growth. Each celebration releases dopamine in your brain, reinforcing the link between effort and reward. That little boost of motivation helps you keep going, especially on the hard days.

It's not just about giving yourself a pat on the back; it's about acknowledging the progress you've made, which can significantly boost your morale and encourage you to continue pushing forward. Even the smallest step deserves recognition.

Celebration doesn't need to be elaborate. It can be a smile, a mental "I did it," a note in your journal, a text to a friend, or a moment of quiet pride. What matters is that you pause to notice and appreciate what you've done.

As a leader, celebrating wins, your own and your team's, is equally important. When teams take time to celebrate, it builds connection, boosts morale, and reinforces a culture of effort and progress. People feel more engaged and more likely to give their best when their contributions are seen and appreciated.

And just like gratitude, celebration trains your mind to see what's working, not just what still needs fixing. It's a habit worth building.

Steve, a senior leader at a fast-growing startup, had been working on giving more timely recognition to his team. In our coaching, we talked about the importance of celebrating progress, not just outcomes, as a way to build morale and reinforce positive behavior.

Steve often got so caught up in project momentum that he'd forget to acknowledge individual contributions until much later, if at all. He decided to try something simple: pausing at the end of each milestone to recognize one team member's effort in real time. The first time he did it, just a brief, specific thank you during a team huddle, he noticed the energy shift. People sat up straighter, smiled. A few even thanked him afterward.

Instead of brushing it off as "Just doing my job," Steve took a moment to recognize his own growth. That small act of celebration helped him see the impact of showing appreciation, and motivated him to make it a regular part of his leadership.

Celebration is not the end of the journey, it's a vital checkpoint. But as we grow, we inevitably hit bumps in the road. Progress isn't linear. After the high of accomplishment often comes a dip, a period of frustration, confusion, or doubt. That's why understanding *The Learning Dip* is so important. It helps us anticipate the hard moments and stay committed when things feel uncertain.

Navigating the Learning Dip

Learning something new, be it a skill, behavior, or mindset, takes time. It's hard. At times, it doesn't seem like it's working and we feel incompetent. That's often when people give up. We have all experienced the frustration of learning something new many times.

Think back to when you first learned how to type. There was likely a sense of excitement—finally learning to use a computer like a pro! Then came the challenge. You had to concentrate hard just to find the right letters. You looked down often, typed slowly, and made lots of mistakes. But over time, you built muscle memory. You stopped thinking about where each key was. Your fingers just knew. It became second nature.

If you've ever tried to learn a new language, you might recall how in the beginning, there was a thrill, imagining yourself traveling, connecting, speaking fluently. But then reality kicked in and the difficulty of stringing together even basic sentences was overwhelming. Still, with practice and repetition, your understanding grew. So did your confidence. Eventually, some words and phrases began to come naturally.

What about the last time you learned to use a new software program, a new app? The excitement, the frustration in getting the hang of all the nuances, and then the joy when you can fully use it!

Often, when we start learning something new, we're excited. We are curious to learn a new skill. Once the excitement wears off, frustration can kick in.

It takes us some time to really master the new skill. It is important to understand that the frustration, the hardship, really is a stage in the learning process. In his book *The Dip*, Seth Godin calls this the Learning Dip.[48] If we are aware that it is part of the process, and that if we stick with it success will come, our likelihood of succeeding is much higher.

Think of it this way, you have to be bad at something before you are good at it. It takes time to become good at something.

The changes you are working on here are not easy, they require effort, intention, and patience. There will be ups and downs. So the next time you feel frustrated, discouraged, or tempted to say, "This is not for me," remind yourself that this is part of the process.

When you're deep in the learning dip, it's easy to fixate on how far you still have to go. That's when it helps to look back and acknowledge the progress you've already made. It's also an opportunity to pause and reconnect with the bigger picture. What is your why? Why are you doing this? Who do you want to become?

In the moment, in the thick of frustration, ask yourself: Who do I want to be right now? This question brings you back to the present. It reminds you that you have a choice to act in alignment with your values, right now, when it is especially hard.

In the learning dip, while trying to change your behavior, it may feel like you are back to your old self, that you are not making progress. Don't lose heart. You're not off track. You're in the work of becoming. Keep going.

Am I Being the Person I Want to Be Right Now?

Garry Ridge keeps a sign on his desk that reads: Who do I want to be right now? It's a simple but powerful reminder to stay conscious of his behavior and the impact he has on others. In every interaction, Garry uses this question to realign with the kind of leader, and person, he aspires to be.

He explains why he needs this daily prompt:

> The world pulls you off track, and that's when you need these reminders most. As human beings, we're just these basic beings bumbling down the pathway of life. And in the bushes are thieves, thieves of anger, envy, greed, short-term thinking. While we're in the bushes, we might feel good for a moment, but that's not where we want to be. So the number one thing is staying aware of who you want to be, and keep reminding yourself, because we will screw up. I guarantee it. I've done it thousands of times.[49]

It's easy to be your best self when things are going smoothly. But when stress kicks in or you're outside your comfort zone, staying aligned with your values takes real intention.

Garry shares, "I could leave a conversation knowing I wasn't the person I wanted to be, and then head into the next interaction. But I don't want to carry that version of me forward. I want to show up better for the next person."

To stay grounded, Garry keeps his question front and center, on his computer, notebook, even his phone screensaver. He also keeps a list of the specific behaviors that represent his best self. When he feels off course, he revisits the list and reminds himself, Center yourself. This is the best you. Please be that you.[50]

It's intentional. It's human. And yes, you'll still mess up. But having this question, and the self-awareness it prompts, helps you recover faster, show up better, and stay connected to who you truly want to be.

Garry Ridge isn't the only leader to use this powerful question as a tool for alignment. In fact, Carol Kauffman first popularized this question.51 Carol shared a pivotal story of how this concept can transform a leader's presence, especially under stress.

Carol described working with a CEO who had back-to-back meetings at the peak of COVID, a time when leadership was tested in every way imaginable. By the time she reached her sixteenth meeting of the day, the CEO felt exhausted, unmotivated, and ready to disengage. But in that moment, she paused and asked herself: Who do I want to be right now?[52]

This simple pause was transformative. It shifted her mindset and reminded her that while this meeting felt unimportant to her, it might be the most critical meeting of the day for the people attending it. By realigning her actions with her values, she showed up as the leader she aspired to be, leaving a lasting impact on her team.[53]

Carol's story and Garry Ridge's practice illustrate a powerful truth: We are not defined by our previous moments, but by the choices we make in this one. Who do I want to be right now? allows us to reset, center ourselves, and act in alignment with our values, no matter how stressful or unfamiliar the situation may be.

This practice is in line with the principles of mindful leadership and self-awareness. It's a tool that helps leaders pause and reflect on their choices. It ensures that they are not acting on autopilot but are instead making deliberate decisions that reflect their best selves and serve their organization and team members effectively. It's about being present in the moment and making choices that are congruent with one's leadership goals and personal values.

Who do I want to be right now? is a powerful form of self-inquiry that serves as a real-time check on our behavior and intentions. It reminds us that we are responsible for our actions at every moment. It's a question that cuts to the heart of accountability and self-reflection because it forces us to consider our actions in the context of our larger life goals and the kind of person we aspire to be. It encourages us to live intentionally and to align our behavior with our values and goals. By repeatedly asking this question, we create a habit of self-monitoring that can lead to more mindful and purposeful behavior.

It's a tool for staying focused on our personal development and for making adjustments as needed. When we are mindful of who we want to be, we are more likely to make choices that support that vision, leading to personal growth and improved performance in various aspects of life. Ultimately, this question is about continual self-awareness and the recognition that we have the power to shape our identity and our future through the choices we make right now.

Summary

Operationalize: Key Takeaways

This chapter helped you translate your values and intentions into meaningful action. It offered practical strategies to align your time, energy, and focus with what matters most:

- **Move from clarity to action.** Identify what matters to you most and embed it in daily life. Define your values as observable behaviors and take small, intentional steps to create lasting change.
- **Prioritize your resources.** Time, energy, and focus must be intentionally allocated, not left to chance. Protect them by saying no to low value demands; clear priorities prevent overwhelm and drive progress.
- **Start | Stop | Do More | Do Less.** Use this four-way lens to identify which behaviors demonstrate your values and align with your goals and which ones undermine them.
- **Leverage your strengths.** Notice where you are already effective, then amplify it. Success compounds.
- **Build sustainable habits.** Use habit stacking and small behavioral shifts to create sustainable success.
- **Stay accountable.** Strengthen follow-through with accountability tools, daily reflection questions, and trusted partners.
- **Practice gratitude.** Shifting attention to what's working lifts energy, builds resilience, and reinforces progress.

- **Expect the learning dip.** Frustration is part of the learning curve. When it hits, don't give up.
- **Celebrate progress.** Acknowledge small wins to build momentum and reinforce motivation.

Ask yourself: Are my daily actions aligned with what I value most? What adjustments will help me stay on track?

Tying It All Together

This chapter, "Operationalize," bridges the gap between your aspirations and their actualization. Previously, we uncovered the core values and priorities essential to your growth, and now, we've translated these ideals into tangible actions. By defining specific behaviors that support your highest priorities and values—and letting go of those that don't—you craft a solid framework that propels you towards tangible outcomes and enduring success. It's about converting your dreams into structured plans that mold your future, providing clear direction to navigate the path from aspiration to reality.

As we wrap up this chapter, I encourage you to take a moment and reflect on the exercises we've engaged in. These exercises aren't just tasks; they're stepping stones to aligning your daily actions with the broader vision of who you aspire to be. By applying these principles, you're not just dreaming of the future, you're actively shaping it. Remember, this process is about progress, not perfection. Celebrate the steps you've taken, no matter how small, and continue building on this foundation.

How will you mark this milestone? Maybe you'll take a well-deserved break, enjoy a gym session, catch up over coffee with a friend, or unwind with an episode of your favorite show on Netflix. These moments of recognition aren't just rewards; they are crucial in building and maintaining the momentum you need for long-term success.

By taking the time to celebrate how far you've come, you acknowledge the effort and commitment it has taken to reach this point. This acknowledgment is crucial, it not only boosts your morale but also invigorates your resolve to maintain this journey of growth and excellence. So, choose a celebration that resonates with your journey, one that reminds you of why you started and inspires you to press forward with even greater zeal.

What's Next: Preparing to Reflect

As we transition from operationalizing our values into the next phase, we turn the page to the "Reflect" chapter, and continue our journey inward. Moving from action to introspection, we gain insight into the mental patterns and stories that shape our decisions, reactions, and behaviors.

Personal growth is rarely a straight line. It's a cycle of trying, learning, and adjusting. As you reflect, you may uncover new realizations, ones that send you back to refine your actions or re-clarify your goals. That's a sign of progress.

So let's step into this next phase with curiosity and openness. Reflection helps us pause, learn, and reset with greater intention. It's where we deepen our self-awareness, so we can keep moving forward, not just with effort, but with clarity and purpose.

3
REFLECT

Follow effective action with quiet reflection. From the quiet reflection, will come even more effective action.

Peter Drucker

IN THIS SECTION, we dig deeper to understand the inner workings of our minds and the ways we often become our own obstacles. By exploring how our brain naturally functions and the profound impact our beliefs have on our thoughts, feelings, and actions, we embark on a journey of self-awareness and transformation.

This exploration through the reflective chapter will provide insights into the often-automatic operations of our minds. By dissecting how we think and react, we can start to see patterns, some of which may be holding us back. This awareness is the first step towards mental agility and resilience, allowing us to consciously choose responses that align with our goals and values, rather than being swept away by habitual reactions.

Together, we'll uncover the triggers that catalyze less-than-ideal behaviors and explore strategies for transforming these patterns. By the end of this section, you'll have a clearer understanding of how to harness your mental processes to support growth and reduce self-imposed barriers. This insight will help you move toward greater personal and professional fulfillment, and leading yourself more effectively.

This chapter contains a wealth of insights, and it's natural to feel overwhelmed at times. Some sections might immediately resonate with you and spark moments of clarity, while others may invite you to revisit them at a later time, and that's perfectly fine. If limiting beliefs have been holding you back, focus on reshaping them. If you tend to be your own harshest critic, work on transforming your inner dialogue into one of self-compassion and encouragement. Choose the element that speaks most strongly to you, reflect deeply, and apply the strategies outlined to create meaningful, lasting change.

The Power of Daily Reflection

The practice of daily reflection, central to Stoic philosophy, goes beyond preparation or review. It cultivates a deeper sense of self-awareness, resilience, and clarity. Marcus Aurelius, the Roman Emperor and Stoic philosopher, used this practice each day to look back on the challenges he had faced and anticipate those that might lie ahead. His reflections, captured in his *Meditations*,[54] reveal a commitment to personal growth and leading with wisdom and virtue.

For Marcus Aurelius, this daily habit wasn't just philosophical, it was practical. It helped him stay grounded amidst the pressures of leadership, evaluate his actions, and prepare to face future difficulties with calm and intention.

Likewise, we can use reflection to better understand ourselves, our thoughts, emotions, and behaviors. In the busyness of daily life, it may feel like a luxury, but it's a necessity for meaningful growth. It allows us to pause, look inward, and assess what's working and what needs to shift.

Reflection is a chance to slow down, adopt a mindset of curiosity, and consider multiple perspectives. It's how we learn from experience, recognize patterns, and make conscious, value-aligned choices, rather than reacting automatically to life's demands.

Most importantly, reflection puts you back in the driver's seat. It's how you take control of your story, take responsibility for your choices, and focus on what you can influence, rather than being swept along by external circumstances.

Slowing Down to Speed Up

Have you ever watched NASCAR drivers skillfully navigate the racetrack, accelerating to speeds that boggle the mind? It's thrilling! But even in the midst of all that speed, these drivers must occasionally pull over for a pit stop. It's an essential pause to ensure the car can keep performing at its best, a strategic pause where decisions made in seconds can determine victory or defeat. Without these stops, the relentless pace would soon take its toll on both car and driver.

This idea of a pit stop isn't confined to the racetrack; it applies to us, too. We may not be taking hairpin turns at two hundred miles per hour, but many of us are racing through life. We're juggling countless tasks, constantly pushing ourselves to go faster and do more. Just as in racing, where pit stops are essential for peak performance, in life, we too need these moments. A strategic pause isn't merely about stopping; it's about creating the space to choose our response wisely.

Take a moment to think about those times at work when you've hastily replied to an upsetting email. Maybe you hit send and immediately felt that twinge of regret as your words, now irreversible, flew through cyberspace. Or think about those days when frustration got the best of you, leading you to snap at a colleague, or perhaps say something a bit too sharp to your partner at home. Maybe there were times when your child was trying to tell you about their day, but your mind was miles away, tangled up in the stresses of work.

These moments happen to the best of us. We react in the heat of the moment, driven by our immediate emotions, only to spend days, or even weeks, mending the rifts created by a few hastily spoken words or an ill-considered email or text. The truth is, the effort required to repair these relationships and restore trust is often much greater than what it would have taken us to pause, take a breath, and respond with consideration.

Imagine how different those scenarios could be if you had given yourself just a few seconds to breathe, to reflect on the potential impact of your words before letting them fly. That brief pause could be the buffer that saves you from unnecessary heartache and preserves the harmony of your relationships, both at work and home.

"Between stimulus and response lies a space. In that space lie our freedom and power to choose a response. In our response lies our growth and our happiness."

Viktor Frankl

Viktor Frankl, a psychiatrist and Holocaust survivor, beautifully captures the transformative power of a pause.[55] Even in the face of unthinkable suffering, he found meaning, and discovered that while we can't always control what happens to us, we can choose how we respond. That choice, he believed, is where our growth and freedom lie.

This idea, the space between stimulus and response, has become a cornerstone of both psychological insight and leadership wisdom. Stephen R. Covey brought it to the mainstream in *The 7 Habits of Highly Effective People*, writing: "The space between what happens to us and our response, our freedom to choose that response and the impact it can have upon our lives, beautifully illustrate that we can become a product of our decisions, not our conditions... If we ignore this space, this freedom, this responsibility, the essence of our life and our legacy could be frustrated."[56]

Carol Kauffman emphasizes the importance of a pause as a tool for real-time self-leadership and intentional action. A small pause, just a moment to stop and reflect, can have a profound impact on how we show up, especially under pressure.

The story of the CEO, who paused between exhausting back-to-back meetings to ask herself, Who do I want to be right now? is a powerful example of this. That brief moment allowed her to reset, shift her mindset, and realign her actions with her values. Instead of carrying stress and fatigue into the next meeting, she showed up as her best self, fully present and aware of the impact she wanted to have on her team.

The Physiological Impacts of a Pause

While we often think of pausing as a mindful or emotional practice, it's also deeply physiological. A deliberate pause, especially one that includes deep, conscious breathing, can activate the parasympathetic nervous system. This is the body's natural calming system, responsible for slowing the heart rate, deepening the breath, and reducing levels of stress hormones like cortisol.

This physical shift helps move us out of fight-or-flight reactivity and into a state where we can engage more thoughtfully. It primes our brain for clearer thinking, emotional regulation, and connection. A pause isn't just a mental break, it's a whole-body recalibration that enables us to respond with greater wisdom and intention.

A deep breath, a moment to relax your shoulders, or simply feeling your feet on the ground can help calm your nervous system, anchoring you in the present and preparing you to respond with greater clarity and intention.

In this way, the pause becomes more than a moment. It becomes a gateway to self-awareness and intentionality, ensuring that our next action contributes to our growth, integrity, and goals. The pause empowers us to lead ourselves and others with clarity and purpose.

System 1 and System 2 Thinking

The power of a pause isn't just emotional or physiological. It's also cognitive. Pausing gives us access to a different mode of thinking. Daniel Kahneman, a Nobel Prize-winning psychologist, introduced the concept of System 1 and System 2 Thinking in his book *Thinking, Fast and Slow*. These systems represent two modes of thinking that all of us use to process information and make decisions.[57]

The science behind creating a pause involves understanding our automatic, habitual reactions (System 1 thinking), and developing the ability to engage our more reflective, deliberate mode of thinking (System 2).

System 1 operates quickly and automatically, requiring minimal effort and conscious control. It is responsible for rapid, instinctive, and emotional reactions to stimuli.

This system is efficient for routine tasks, recognizing faces, driving on familiar routes, and making simple judgments.

System 2 is the slower, more deliberate mode of thinking that involves conscious reasoning and analysis. It requires effort, attention, and mental resources to engage in complex problem-solving and critical thinking. System 2 is involved in tasks that demand concentration, logical reasoning, and the evaluation of evidence.[58]

In every task that we learn, we start in System 2. The first time you started driving, you had to think about everything, when to turn the wheel, use the indicators, press the brakes, or hit the accelerator. But as an experienced driver, it becomes automatic. We've all had that moment of arriving at a familiar destination and thinking, How did I get here? Our minds wander, and the actions happen on autopilot.

Sometimes it can be frustrating when you are operating in System 1, quickly and automatically, and someone else is still in System 2. Take, for example, my husband's and my attempt at hiking together. Coincidentally, we were listening to Kahneman's *Thinking, Fast and Slow* on our way from Boston to hike in New Hampshire on a beautiful fall day.

I am a slow hiker. As we hiked up and down the rocky trail, my husband was often ahead of me, walking at a much faster pace. He struggled to walk slower. I couldn't hike any faster. This hiking-together idea was not working out so well. My husband is like a mountain goat, easily maneuvering tree roots and boulders, happily and effortlessly steering his way up and down the mountain. I, on the other hand, am not. I didn't hike as a child and don't have that natural ability. Hiking requires more effort from me. On the uneven terrain, I watch every step, where I place my foot, what I hold on to, how I climb every rock. A steep incline seems tough to me and unremarkable to him.

It dawned on me: I hike in System 2, and he hikes in System 1. Yes, this wasn't a deep revelation, but it helped us understand how each of us was experiencing the same path differently. In some ways, it gave me comfort in explaining my slowness and the differences between us.

This tension between fast and slow thinking often plays out in the workplace. Picture a team working on a big presentation. One person quickly jumps to conclusions, drawing from instinct and experience, operating in System 1. Another takes time to think through implications, checking data and exploring multiple options, clearly in System 2. The first team member may feel frustrated: "Why is this taking so long?" while the second may feel dismissed: "Why aren't we thinking this through?"

Both modes have value, but when we aren't aware of the disconnect, it can create friction within the team. Recognizing which system you're in, and which one others might be using, can shift the dynamic from frustration to curiosity and understanding.

System 1 is quicker. Yet the quick, automatic thinking can also lead to biases and errors due to its reliance on heuristics (mental shortcuts). System 2, on the other hand, is more accurate but consumes more cognitive resources, and our brain, at times lazy and attempting to be efficient, may often default to the quicker and less effortful System 1 thinking. We react, rather than thoughtfully respond.

While System 1 can lead to biased or impulsive decisions, it's also important to recognize that not all intuition is flawed. In his book *Blink*, Malcolm Gladwell explores the power of intuition, describing it not as a mysterious or magical force, but as the distillation of our experiences, learning, and pattern recognition. Our intuition, he suggests, is often our brain's way of drawing on a deep reservoir of knowledge in an instant.[59]

Gladwell's perspective offers a helpful reminder: System 1 can serve us well when it's grounded in expertise and experience. The goal isn't to eliminate quick thinking, but to discern when to trust it and when to pause. We can't deliberate every decision, nor should we. The key is developing the self-awareness to know when a situation calls for more thoughtful analysis and when our instincts may be enough.

We rely heavily on the intuitive and error-prone System 1 thinking. According to Kahneman, we use it about 95 percent of the time.[60] When we pause, we can create a shift, we can slow down and allow the more deliberate, reflective, thoughtful System 2 thinking to take charge. By creating a pause, we give ourselves the chance to respond thoughtfully rather than reacting impulsively.

In my own career, I learned just how important it is to shift intentionally from System 1 to System 2 thinking. Over the years, I interviewed thousands of candidates. I began to notice a pattern: within just a few minutes, I was already forming strong opinions, shaped by first impressions, body language, or even how someone shook my hand. I was no longer neutrally evaluating; I was searching for data that confirmed my initial instinct. That's System 1 at work.

To counteract this, I developed the habit of pausing mid-interview and asking myself, What assumptions am I making? What biases could be coloring my view? This deliberate shift into System 2 helped me assess candidates more fairly and make better hiring decisions.

The same skill became invaluable in high-stakes meetings, whether negotiating partnerships or managing sales discussions. In those moments, I'd pause to reevaluate how the conversation was going. What was the other person really trying to communicate? Was I truly listening, or just filtering things through my own lens? By shifting into System 2, I could step back, reconsider my assumptions, and sometimes redirect the conversation more effectively. It helped me better read the room, stay aligned with our goals, and make more intentional choices in the moment.

System 2 helps us move beyond instinct into thoughtful, intentional action. Whether you're interviewing a candidate, navigating a conversation, or making everyday decisions, slowing down allows you to widen your perspective.

Pausing isn't just about shifting into System 2, it's about creating space to evaluate which system is most appropriate. Sometimes, slowing down helps you recognize that thoughtful analysis is needed. Other times, it reveals that you're overthinking and need to trust your instincts and move forward. The goal isn't to live in System 2, which would be exhausting, but to develop the awareness to shift between systems with intention and agility.

By pausing, you create the space to evaluate more carefully, question assumptions, and choose a response that reflects your intentions, not just your impulses.

Here's an example: Alex was a director known for delivering projects on time and taking great pride in his achievements. But while he consistently met deadlines, his team members didn't always enjoy working for him. They often felt he wasn't open to their suggestions and dismissed ideas without real consideration.

Alex was focused on the immediate task and the pressure of delivery. He would rush through decisions, relying heavily on System 1 thinking, his fast, automatic, and intuitive mode of thought.

Under pressure, Alex's System 1 responses would lead him to quickly shut down suggestions. His automatic response was rooted in a desire to maintain the current course, avoid disruptions, and meet the deadline. But in doing so, he compromised his team's engagement and the project's long-term quality.

Through our coaching, Alex realized his approach wasn't working. He made a conscious effort to pause and engage System 2 thinking. When a team member offered a suggestion, he took a breath and shifted to curiosity. Instead of reacting, he asked questions: "What are the key assumptions behind this? How does this align with our goals? What potential risks or opportunities does this uncover?"

This shift allowed Alex to evaluate ideas more thoughtfully and created a more inclusive environment. His team felt heard and valued. Together, they uncovered flaws in the plan and discovered new opportunities. Over time, switching between System 1 and System 2 thinking became a core leadership skill for Alex, helping him balance speed and quality in decision-making.

The act of pausing, taking a moment to consciously engage System 2, is critical. It creates a deliberate break in the decision-making process. It allows you to step back from automatic reactions, reflect, engage your critical thinking capabilities, and make more thoughtful choices.

→ YOUR TURN: Pause to Shift Your Thinking

Where in your day-to-day life, at work or at home, do you find yourself reacting quickly, without pausing to reflect?

- Think about recurring challenges or misunderstandings. Could slowing down and engaging System 2 lead to a better outcome?
- In those moments, what would it look like to pause and shift into more deliberate, System 2 thinking?
- Are there times when you find yourself overthinking or getting stuck in analysis paralysis? What would it look like to trust your instincts and lean into System 1?
- Are there specific situations, meetings, or certain conversations, where an intentional shift from automatic to deliberate thinking would make a difference?

Try to pinpoint a few patterns. Identifying where you typically default to System 1, or overuse System 2. The pause is the first step to creating space for more intentional, grounded action.

Positive Intelligence

In his book *Positive Intelligence: Why Only 20% of Teams and Individuals Achieve Their True Potential and How You Can Achieve Yours*, Shirzad Chamine presents an approach that aligns well with Daniel Kahneman's concept of System 1 and System 2 thinking. Chamine's concept of Positive Intelligence measures our mental fitness, how often our mind acts as our ally, enhancing our ability to flourish and reach our full potential, as opposed to when it becomes our saboteur, hampering our progress.[61]

Chamine explains that saboteurs are internalized voices developed early in life as survival mechanisms, strategies we adopted to cope with perceived threats or to gain approval. Over time, these strategies become ingrained, forming our automatic responses to stress, conflict, or uncertainty.[62] In this way, they operate much like System 1, fast, reactive, and subconscious.

Some of the most common saboteurs include the Judge (harsh self-criticism or constant evaluation of others), the Hyper-Achiever (driven by external validation), the Controller (needing to take charge to feel safe), and the Avoider (dodging conflict or discomfort). While they may have once served a protective role, these mental habits often become limiting patterns that hold us back in adulthood, undermining both our effectiveness and our well-being.[63]

> **Curious About Your Saboteurs?**
> If you'd like to identify which saboteurs are most active in your life, Shirzad Chamine offers a free online assessment that maps your top saboteurs and how they influence your thoughts, behaviors, and performance. Just Google: Shirzad Chamine Saboteur Assessment, or see the link in the notes section.[64]

Much like the pit stop in racing, Chamine encourages us to take brief, intentional mental pauses, what he calls 'PQ reps' (Positive Intelligence repetitions), to strengthen our 'sage' brain. These moments are designed to interrupt our reactive, saboteur-driven responses and shift us toward wiser, more centered choices.[65]

In practical terms, this means taking a deliberate mental break to disengage from the negative, automatic patterns of System 1 and engage the more thoughtful, sage-driven responses of System 2. These mental pit stops allow us to choose responses that align with our best selves, ultimately enhancing our ability to navigate challenges with wisdom and composure. This practice not only boosts our mental fitness but also impacts all areas of our lives, from personal relationships to professional endeavors, by fostering resilience and proactive growth.

PQ reps are practical exercises that help strengthen the 'sage' part of your brain, shifting away from the negative influence of 'saboteurs.' These exercises are brief yet powerful and can be done almost anytime, anywhere. Here are some examples to consider incorporating into your daily routine:

1. **Focused breathing:** Take slow, deep breaths for a minute or two. Concentrate solely on the sensation of the air moving in and out of your lungs. This can help quiet the mind and bring your focus back to the present, reducing the influence of saboteurs like anxiety or stress.
2. **Sensory awareness:** Engage deeply with your surroundings using your senses. For a few moments, focus on what you can see, hear, touch, or smell. This practice helps pull you away from ruminative thoughts and towards a state of mindful awareness, enhancing your sage's presence.
3. **Body scanning:** From your toes to your head, slowly scan your body in your mind's eye, noting any sensations or feelings. This not only helps in grounding yourself in the moment but also interrupts negative thought patterns, fostering a calm and collected mindset.
4. **Silent counting:** Count slowly to ten in your mind, focusing fully on each number. This simple cognitive exercise can act as a circuit breaker for stressful or negative thoughts, resetting your mental state.

These PQ reps are designed to be quick and effective, requiring only a minute or two. They serve as mental pit stops that recalibrate your thoughts. By regularly practicing these reps, you strengthen your mental fitness, enhancing your ability to choose more sage-driven responses in daily life.[66]

Many of my clients have found tremendous value in incorporating the Positive Intelligence approach into their routines. It's not just about catching those pesky saboteurs in the act, it's about nurturing and strengthening their inner sage. We explore together to find PQ reps that seamlessly integrate into their daily lives, turning moments of stress into opportunities for growth.

Some of my clients find the subtle but powerful technique of gently rubbing their fingers together under the table helpful during tense meetings. For others, grounding themselves by feeling their feet firmly planted on the floor is another easy-to-implement technique when at work. These simple physical connections act as a quick mental reset, pulling them away from the edge of anxiety or frustration.

Others have embraced the practice of taking deep, calming breaths, not just before a potentially heated meeting begins but also right in the thick of it. This pause is crucial; it allows them to compose themselves before reacting to an upsetting remark or reading an inflammatory email. These small practices are lifelines that bring them back to a state of calm and control, enabling them to respond from a place of sage wisdom rather than knee-jerk emotion. Mastering my own saboteurs through these techniques, like taking a moment to breathe deeply, has greatly improved my relationships, especially at home. I remember times when my teenage daughter was pushing every boundary imaginable. Those moments when I chose to pause before reacting made all the difference, preserving peace in our household. At work, these same skills have helped me navigate challenging conversations. Whether it's delivering difficult feedback as an HR leader or mediating conflicts between colleagues, pausing before reacting has allowed me to approach situations thoughtfully and with emotional intelligence. It's a practice that not only enhances relationships but also leads to better outcomes across the board.

These small practices are not just coping mechanisms; they are transformative tools that foster neuroplasticity, the brain's ability to form new connections and reorganize itself based on experience. Each time you pause before reacting, you're not only choosing a more thoughtful response, you're strengthening the neural pathways that support emotional regulation and clear thinking. These moments of choice transform everyday challenges into opportunities for growth, gradually reshaping both your brain and behavior toward a more positive and productive state.

→ YOUR TURN: Practice PQ Reps

Are there moments when you feel overtaken by your saboteurs, those inner voices that criticize, catastrophize, or push you toward perfectionism?

Try the PQ reps listed above. Which ones feel easiest for you to implement? Maybe it's a deep breath, gently rubbing your fingers together, or grounding your feet on the floor. Choose one.

Set a one-minute timer, and practice it now. Notice how this small act of mindfulness can help quiet your saboteurs and shift you into a calmer, more centered state.

You've created a pause. Now what? This moment of space is powerful, but it's what you do with it that shapes your impact. The following two frameworks, the 4 Ps and the Five Cs, can guide your next steps with intention. They help you shift from reactive System 1 thinking, where your saboteurs take charge, to deliberate System 2 thinking, where your wiser sage self leads. Use them to move from automatic reactions to thoughtful, values-aligned action.

The 4 Ps Heuristic

One practical way to use the space you've created is the 4 Ps heuristic: **Pause, Process, Plan, Proceed.**[67] This framework offers a simple but powerful structure to shift from reactivity to intentionality. When a challenging situation arises, it helps you stop and interrupt your automatic response, reflect on what's happening, make a thoughtful plan, and move forward with clarity and purpose.

Samantha, the Head of HR at a fast-growing tech company, had just finished her morning coffee when a message pinged in her inbox. The subject line caught her attention immediately: Formal Complaint Against Team Leader. Her stomach tightened as she opened the email to find a detailed account from an employee who felt demoralized by their manager's overly critical feedback. The complaint also hinted at broader team morale issues under the leader's watch.

Samantha felt a wave of defensiveness rise. This team leader, Mark, was someone she had personally recruited and always regarded as a high performer. Her initial instinct was to dismiss the complaint as an overreaction and mentally side with Mark. But before responding, she remembered the 4 Ps heuristic we discussed in our coaching: Pause, Process, Plan, Proceed.

- **Pause:** Samantha closed her email and took a moment to gather her thoughts. She reminded herself not to jump to conclusions or let her personal bias dictate her response. A few deep breaths helped her reset emotionally and create mental space for a more measured approach.
- **Process:** Later that morning, Samantha revisited the complaint with fresh eyes. She reviewed the company's feedback policy, reflected on her knowledge of both the employee and Mark, and began gathering additional context. She considered how both individuals might be experiencing the situation differently: Mark likely saw himself as a no-nonsense leader pushing for excellence, while the employee might perceive his style as overly harsh. Samantha also recognized the need to separate her personal respect for Mark from her role as an impartial HR leader.
- **Plan:** After reflecting, Samantha drafted a plan. She decided to hold one-on-one conversations with both Mark and the employee to understand their perspectives. For Mark, she would frame the meeting as an opportunity to explore his leadership style and its impact on his team. For the employee, she would provide a safe space to share concerns without fear of retaliation. She also planned to review the team's feedback surveys to get a broader sense of morale and ensure her response addressed potential systemic issues.
- **Proceed:** Samantha set her plan into motion. Her meeting with the employee revealed specific examples of Mark's tone and approach that felt overly critical, leaving the team feeling undervalued. When Samantha met with Mark, she discovered that his intentions were positive, but his feedback delivery lacked tact and empathy. By weaving together insights from both conversations, Samantha worked collaboratively with Mark to create a leadership development plan focused on improving his communication style and emotional

intelligence. She also ensured the employee felt heard and took proactive steps to monitor team morale going forward.

What could have escalated into a tense conflict or a breakdown in trust became an opportunity for growth. Samantha's ability to pause and engage in thoughtful reflection before acting allowed her to handle the situation with empathy and professionalism. Mark appreciated the constructive feedback and was motivated to improve, while the employee felt validated and supported. The broader team benefited from a leader who was more attuned to their needs, and Samantha strengthened her reputation as a fair and thoughtful leader.

→ YOUR TURN: Use The 4 Ps

- Identify a challenging conversation coming up this week.
- How might you apply Pause → Process → Plan → Proceed?

Samantha's story shows us the power of intentionally using the space between stimulus and response. But when emotions run high or time is short, how do we practically access that space and lead from it?

The Five Cs: A Framework for the Power of Pause

Carol Kauffman offers a simple yet powerful framework to help leaders navigate moments of pause with intentionality. She calls it the Five Cs: **Calm, Clear, Curious, Compassionate,** and **Courageous.**[68] The Five Cs framework helps us make the most of the pause between stimulus and response. We become more aware of how we are showing up and where we might need to adjust on these Five Cs:

1. **Calm:** Are you centered and in control, or are you reactive and scattered?
2. **Clear:** Do you have clarity of thought, or are you overwhelmed and confused?

3. **Curious:** Are you open to learning and understanding, or are you judgmental and closed off?
4. **Compassionate:** Are you showing kindness and empathy, or are you dismissive and detached?
5. **Courageous:** Are you brave enough to take action or speak up, or are you hesitating out of fear?

These five qualities allow us to center ourselves, assess our state of mind, and recalibrate in the pause. By tuning in to them, we can intentionally decide how to show up as our best selves, particularly when stress, uncertainty, or conflict threatens to derail us.

In our interview, Carol shared a story that beautifully illustrates the transformative power of the Five Cs. She had been coaching the CEO of a multi-billion-dollar private equity company. Before a critical executive committee meeting, this CEO was feeling unsettled and on edge, pressures were mounting, and tensions were high.

Carol introduced him to the Five Cs and asked him to pause and reflect on his state of mind:

1. **Calm:** "On a scale of 1 to 10, how calm are you right now?" The CEO answered confidently, *"Ten. I'm always calm."*
2. **Clear:** "How clear is your thinking?" *"Ten. I know exactly what I need to do."*
3. **Curious:** "How open and curious are you feeling about this meeting?" *"Ten. I'm always looking to learn and gather insights."*
4. **Courageous:** Carol didn't even need to ask. For a leader of this magnitude, courage was a given.

But then came the final question:

5. **Compassionate:** "How compassionate are you feeling right now?"

The CEO paused. He realized that this was his blind spot. "Honestly," he admitted, "I'm not great at that." Carol immediately reframed the question to highlight strengths: "When are you a 10 out of 10 on compassion?"

He glanced at a photograph of his son on the desk and replied, "I can be completely compassionate with him."

This reflection planted a seed that would soon bear fruit. Later that day, in the middle of the meeting, a member of the executive team, the CFO, shared deeply personal news. His father was dying, and he needed to take a leave of absence. Overcome with emotion, the CFO began to cry.

In that moment, the CEO had a choice: revert to old habits of stoic detachment or step into a more compassionate version of himself. He paused and reflected on the Five Cs. Instead of freezing, he stood up, walked over to the CFO, and placed a hand on his shoulder. "We've got you. We'll take care of this. You focus on your family. We'll be here for you."

The room, usually a bastion of stoicism and toughness, was stunned. The team witnessed a leader who was not only clear, calm, and courageous but also compassionate, showing up as his best self.

This one act of compassion shifted the CEO's leadership brand. It became a moment that people talked about for years, a moment when a leader chose to embody not just strength but also humanity.[69]

Putting the Five Cs into Practice

The beauty of the Five Cs is their practicality. They don't require hours of reflection, they can be applied in a matter of seconds. Here's how you can use the framework in your daily life:

1. **Pause before key moments:** Before a meeting, a conversation, or a presentation, take a deep breath and ask yourself: How am I doing on the Five Cs?
2. **Rate yourself:** Quickly rate yourself on a scale of 1 to 10 for each C. Where are you strong? Where are you falling short? Consider addressing anything under a five.
3. **Adjust intentionally:** If you notice you are not calm, take a moment to steady your breathing. If you're not feeling compassionate, remind yourself of a moment when you were, and choose to show up that way.

Pausing to reflect on the Five Cs doesn't just improve how you show up in a single moment; it also strengthens your self-awareness over time. Carol reminds us that leadership is not about perfection; it's about intentionality. When we pause and check in with the Five Cs, we shift from autopilot to intentionality. Whether it's a moment of compassion, clarity, or courage, the pause gives us the space to choose our best selves, right now. By building the habit of reflection, you create a powerful feedback loop that allows you to grow, adapt, and show up as the leader, and the person, you aspire to be.

→ YOUR TURN: Rate Yourself on the Five Cs

Take a moment to reflect on the Five Cs: Calm, Clear, Curious, Compassionate, and Courageous.

- Which of these comes most naturally to you?
- Which one tends to fade under stress or pressure?
- How might reminding yourself of that "weaker C" shift how you show up in difficult moments?
- Are there patterns where a particular C shows up strongly (e.g., courage in crisis) and others where it's harder to access (e.g., compassion during conflict)?

The power of a pause is the fundamental first step in creating the mental space necessary for self-awareness, emotional regulation, and thoughtful action. Much like a moment of rest between sets in training, pausing allows us to recalibrate, engage our more deliberate System 2 thinking, and avoid automatic, impulsive System 1 reactions. It is within this pause that we create a buffer between stimulus and response, enabling us to choose actions aligned with our goals and values.

Without this foundational step, the following tools and strategies for overcoming triggers, changing our negative thoughts, transforming habitual behaviors, and fostering personal growth would be far less effective. The pause becomes the gateway to thoughtful reflection, setting the stage for intentional and meaningful change.

→ YOUR TURN: Integrate the Pause

You've explored the many ways a pause can shift how you show up, from calming your body and quieting your saboteurs to choosing how to respond in the moments that matter. Whether it's creating space to shift from System 1 to System 2 thinking, resetting with a PQ rep, walking through the 4 Ps, or checking in with the Five Cs, each approach helps you use the pause with greater intention. Now, bring it together:

- When are you relying too heavily on System 1, the fast, intuitive mode, and where would shifting to System 2's slower, more deliberate approach serve you better?
- Are there recurring situations where you could benefit from slowing down, thinking critically, and choosing your response more thoughtfully?
- Where do you tend to operate on autopilot (System 1) in your daily life or leadership?
- Which techniques resonate most with you, PQ reps, the 4 Ps, or the Five Cs? Try them to see what works for you.
- What's one cue you could use to remind yourself to pause, like linking it to an existing habit (e.g., checking your calendar, opening your inbox, walking into a meeting)?

This chapter isn't about mastering everything at once—it's about starting small.

Start with just one: one pause, one shift, one small moment of choosing how you show up.

Over time, these intentional pauses become a powerful practice—one that helps you lead yourself with greater awareness, composure, and purpose.

Identify a moment, habit, or behavior that you want to approach differently. Then commit to pausing and reflecting in those situations. That single choice, repeated consistently, can transform your relationships, your leadership, and your ability to respond with intention and purpose.

The pause is powerful, but it's not always easy. Sometimes, what makes pausing so difficult are the underlying forces that hijack our attention, our emotions, and our actions before we even realize it. These are our triggers.

Triggers are the sparks that often ignite our automatic responses. They're the moments that shorten or steal the pause. To lead ourselves with intention, we need to recognize and understand them. Let's explore what triggers are, where they come from, and how we can respond with greater self-awareness and control.

Triggers

Triggers are stimuli that impact our thoughts, actions, or behaviors. They can be external, like a colleague's comment, a facial expression, or a sudden change in the environment, or internal, such as a memory, emotion, or fleeting thought. These triggers are deeply embedded in our neural pathways, often linked to past experiences, and can provoke reactions that seem disproportionate to the moment. Some triggers cause quick, emotional responses that hinder relationships or derail goals, while others influence long-term behavioral patterns, shaping how we move through the world.

For instance, I grew up in a chauvinistic household where comments demonstrating a lack of respect for women were commonplace. Even today, when I hear something reflecting similar disrespect, it triggers an immediate emotional response. My reactions aren't always proportional to the situation, but recognizing this has been the first step in managing my response rather than being ruled by it.

Martin, a project manager, experienced financial instability during his childhood. As an adult, discussions about budget cuts at work provoke a wave of anxiety, even when the situation is manageable. This sometimes leads him to overreact, either by becoming overly controlling or withdrawing from the conversation altogether, affecting his ability to lead effectively. Through coaching, Martin learned to recognize this pattern and now uses a brief pause, grounding himself with a breath or a reminder like, Present, not past, to separate the current reality from old fears. He also began preparing for budget meetings by clarifying facts beforehand and mentally rehearsing calm responses. These small steps helped him respond with steadiness rather than fear.

Jane, a seasoned executive, faced gender bias early in her career, frequently being passed over for promotions and seeing her ideas dismissed. Though her current role is more equitable, situations like being interrupted in meetings or having her suggestions overlooked still trigger frustration. Through reflection and deliberate practice, Jane learned to manage these reactions by identifying emotional cues, reframing situations, and responding assertively rather than impulsively.

How to Identify Your Triggers

Understanding and managing your triggers begins with self-awareness. Triggers vary widely. What rattles one person may not even register with another. Here are some ways to uncover yours:

- Notice your overreactions. If your emotional response feels outsized for the situation, it may be a trigger.
- Track recurring frustration. Are there certain people, situations, or topics that consistently provoke irritation, anxiety, or defensiveness?
- Reflect on past patterns. Think about times when you later wished you'd handled something differently. What set you off?
- Tune in to your body. Physical sensations like a racing heart, clenched jaw, or shallow breathing can be early signs of a triggered state.
- Ask for feedback. Sometimes others notice our reactions before we do. Trusted colleagues or loved ones can offer insights if you're open to hearing them.

By recognizing our triggers, we can prepare for them, adjust our environment, and reduce their power. This process of identification and reflection allows us to transform impulsive reactions into thoughtful, aligned responses.

Managing Responses to Triggers

Once we've identified our triggers, the next step is learning how to respond to them with intention. When triggered, our bodies often revert to conditioned responses like anger, withdrawal, defensiveness, or anxiety. While these reactions may have once served a protective purpose, they often no longer reflect who we are, or how we want to show up.

Managing our responses isn't about suppressing emotion. It's about noticing the moment we've been triggered, pausing long enough to disrupt the automatic response, and choosing a more constructive path.

Simple techniques can help:

- Grounding in the body through deep breathing, feeling your feet on the floor, or gently rubbing your fingers together.
- Stepping away, even briefly, when you feel emotionally hijacked.
- Reframing the situation by asking, "What else could be true here?" or "What kind of impact do I want my response to have?"
- Name it to tame it, labeling your emotion ("I'm feeling anxious") can lessen its hold. More on reframing and naming your emotions later in this chapter.

Over time, this practice builds emotional regulation and flexibility, allowing us to stay connected to our values, even when emotions run high.

Martin, for example, began using a short breath exercise and a mental reminder, this isn't then, this is now, to calm his nervous system during tense budget conversations. By separating present facts from past fears, he shifted from control to collaboration. His ability to stay centered improved not only his leadership but also his team's trust in him.

Building Resilience Over Time

The goal is not to erase emotional responses but to reduce their intensity and expand your choice in the moment. With repeated practice, the space between trigger and response becomes more accessible. As Marshall Goldsmith notes in his book *Triggers*, awareness is the gateway to change. By anticipating situations that push your buttons, you can prepare and engage more skillfully. This is how reactive moments become opportunities for growth.

→ YOUR TURN: Map Your Triggers

Take a moment to reflect on your own triggers and how they shape your decisions and interactions.

- What patterns do you notice—certain people, phrases, or settings that spark a strong reaction?
- What emotions do they stir?
- Are your reactions serving your well-being and goals?
- What helps you interrupt the cycle? A deep breath, a mental reset, or physical grounding?
- What new strategy could you experiment with the next time you feel triggered?

By exploring these patterns, you can begin to make thoughtful, intentional choices. You don't have to get it perfect. Just start by catching one trigger. Notice it. Pause. Choose. This is the work of self-leadership, and it begins one moment at a time.

From Triggers to Meaning-Making

Understanding our triggers is a vital step in managing how we respond, but the story doesn't stop there. Our reactions don't come from the trigger alone; they're shaped by the meaning we attach to what's happening. And that meaning is often based on the stories we tell ourselves, sometimes consciously, often not. While triggers can expose these stories more vividly, storytelling is how our brains operate all the time. We are constantly interpreting, labeling, and connecting dots to make sense of our world.

In the next section, we'll explore how this natural storytelling process works, how our minds construct meaning, why it's so powerful, and how it can help or hinder our ability to lead ourselves and others with clarity and intention.

The Stories We Tell Ourselves

Every Wednesday, we would get a call from the Montefiore Home where my mom was living, telling us that she was very upset and was screaming at the workers. Mom was in her early seventies and had Alzheimer's. She would wake up Wednesday morning, open the closet in her room, and to her dismay, discover her clothes were missing. She had to make sense of what happened to them. The only explanation she could come up with was that her clothes were stolen. Her mind took the fact that her clothes weren't in the closet and constructed a story around it, that someone had taken them. My mom, who, prior to living with Alzheimer's, was the kindest, most conflict-averse, non-aggressive person, would now be screaming at the employees, accusing them of stealing. Wednesday was laundry day. Every Wednesday was laundry day. And every Wednesday, mom told herself the same story, got upset, and we would be called in.

Mom, with Alzheimer's, no longer had the ability to create a new story in her mind, learn from what happened the previous week, and find an alternative explanation to the missing clothes. We all create stories as a cognitive tool to understand the world; the mind naturally does this as a way of processing and understanding information. This inclination towards storytelling is deeply ingrained in our cognitive processes and has evolutionary roots. Our brains are adept at recognizing patterns in the information we encounter. Creating a narrative helps organize and make sense of these patterns, turning disparate pieces of information into a cohesive and understandable whole. These stories are more memorable than isolated facts. When information is presented in a narrative form, it becomes easier for our brains to encode, store, and retrieve. Stories provide a framework for understanding cause-and-effect relationships. By attributing meaning and significance to events, we can make sense of the world around us. This sense-making function helps reduce the uncertainty and complexity of our experiences.

This is how it works. We look at the available data. Select information to focus on. Make assumptions based on the data and our past experiences. Draw conclusions. Take action.

In the story of the missing clothes, each action my mom took was driven by the narrative her mind constructed from limited, interpreted data. Each

Wednesday, when she discovered her clothes missing from the cupboard, an unsettling and confusing occurrence, her Alzheimer's-impaired mind relied on past experiences and cognitive patterns to make sense of it. Unable to recall that it was laundry day and her clothes were simply being washed, she concluded they were stolen, a story which felt coherent in the moment. Her reaction was to accuse the staff, an action fueled by her distress and the urgent need to address the perceived wrong. This cyclical pattern, where data selection, assumption, conclusion, and action intertwine, illustrates the profound influence of the stories we construct based on perceptions and behaviors.

The stories we tell ourselves don't just arise in moments of emotional intensity; they are the default way our minds interpret the world. From daily misunderstandings to major decisions, we are constantly constructing meaning through mental shortcuts and past experiences. These internal narratives can help us make sense of ambiguity, but they can also lead us astray. That's where the Ladder of Inference comes in. It gives us a step-by-step look at how we unconsciously move from a simple observation to a firmly held belief or action, and, more importantly, how we can learn to pause and question that process.

The Ladder of Inference

This is a helpful model for understanding how our minds turn observations into conclusions and actions, sometimes so automatically we don't even notice. Popularized by organizational psychologist Chris Argyris and shared widely through Peter Senge's *The Fifth Discipline*, the model offers a way to slow down and unpack the rapid leaps our brains make when interpreting the world.[70]

At the base of the ladder is observable reality, raw data and facts. As we climb the ladder, rather than absorbing all this information, we filter it selectively, a process driven by our existing assumptions and beliefs. Our selection isn't random but is guided by what we've noticed and deemed important in the past, highlighting how our focus can narrow based on prior experiences.

Next, we interpret what this data means, adding personal significance and creating a narrative that aligns with our worldview. This interpretation

FIGURE 3: The Ladder of Inference, Chris Argyris's model of the steps we use to make sense of situations, and to act.

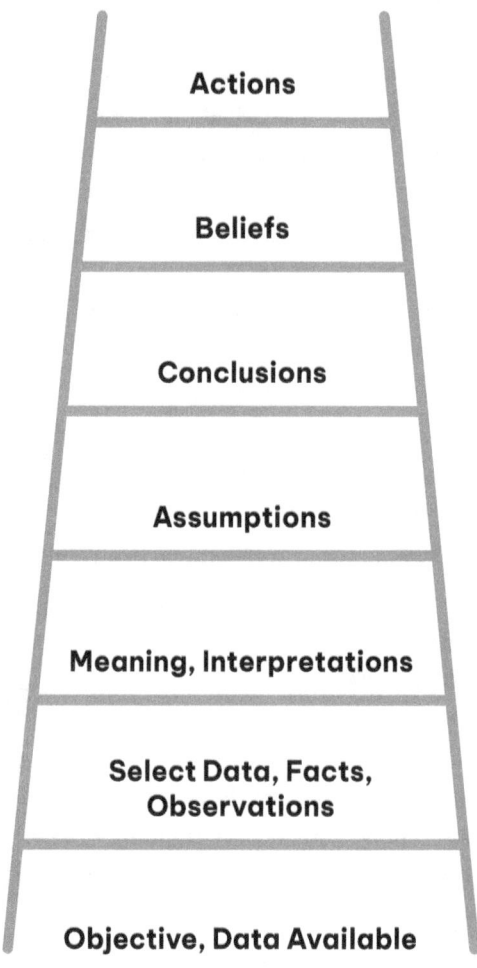

is a crucial step. It's where subjective meaning is formed, and where much of our cognitive bias cements itself. For example, if we believe a colleague is uncooperative, we might interpret their neutral actions as negative.

From these interpretations, we make assumptions. These assumptions can escalate quickly into conclusions, often without us realizing we're skipping steps or failing to question our initial data selection. These conclusions then inform our beliefs about the world, reinforcing our existing views or adjusting them slightly. Each step on the ladder builds upon the previous one, making it increasingly difficult to separate objective reality from our construed interpretation.

Finally, we act. Our actions are based on the beliefs formed through this inferential process, often without conscious awareness of how our ladder has shaped these actions. By the time we act, our behavior is informed less by objective reality and more by an internalized story shaped through each rung of the ladder. The process is fast, efficient, and often invisible to us.

Understanding this progression allows us to reflect more intentionally. By stepping back down the Ladder, questioning the data we focused on, the meaning we assigned, and the assumptions we formed, we can interrupt automatic responses. We can begin to see how our interpretations may not be the only way to view a situation. Recognizing this cognitive pathway reveals much about why we think and behave the way we do, offering a chance for self-reflection and a deeper understanding of the interplay between beliefs and behavior. This understanding is crucial not just for personal growth but also for improving communications and relationships in both personal and professional contexts.

As a manager, I often used the Ladder of Inference with teams when people held opposing views or struggled to understand each other's perspectives. Rather than debating conclusions, we would walk back down the ladder together. We'd start with the observable facts, then look at what each person had chosen to focus on, how they interpreted that data, and what assumptions followed. This process helped uncover the root of the misalignment and often revealed that people were operating from different stories, not necessarily different intentions. Once we had clarity on that, more constructive dialogue could follow.

When working with clients, we often use this process to explore new possibilities, challenging assumptions and interpretations at each step of the Ladder.

Pam, one of my coaching clients, was struggling with her relationship with her boss. Each email from her boss seemed to amplify her irritation, a reaction that peaked during one of our sessions when she read aloud an email that had particularly upset her. As an outsider, the content of the email appeared entirely benign to me, suggesting that Pam's reaction was less about the words on the screen and more about the spectacles through which she viewed them.

As we delved deeper, it became apparent that Pam was not just reacting to a simple email; she was navigating a labyrinth of personal assumptions and biases. These assumptions were not just filters but barriers, barriers that distorted her interpretation and magnified conflict where it might not have existed. Pam was assuming bad intent where there was none. Pam's interpretations were not just reflections of the words in the email but were heavily influenced by layers of past interactions and her emotional responses to them. This realization was a pivotal moment for Pam, as it opened a pathway to reevaluating her assumptions, aiming to clear the lens through which she viewed her interactions with her boss. As a result, she could approach her communications with her boss in a more neutral, less charged perspective.

People selectively choose what to pay attention to while ignoring other perceivable information. The famous Invisible Gorilla Experiment, where subjects were asked to watch a short video of two groups of people (wearing black and white T-shirts) passing a basketball around, demonstrates this point well. The subjects were told to count the passes made by one of the teams. In the video, a person walks through the scene wearing a full gorilla suit. After watching the video, the subjects are asked whether they noticed anything out of the ordinary taking place. In most groups, 50 percent of the subjects did not report seeing the gorilla.[71] When people concentrate, and look for one thing, they often do not see other things.

Our focus and assumptions have a great power in coloring our perceptions and relationships. By examining these internal filters, we not only improve communication and reduce conflict, but also gain deeper insight into our own thinking, insight that shapes our behavior, decisions, and ultimately, our character.

→ YOUR TURN: Reevaluate Decisions

Think of an action or decision that you would like to re-evaluate, a story you are telling yourself that you would like to see from a different perspective.

Let's start with the facts. Are you looking at *all* the facts? Only a subset of the data? Hearsay—what your colleague/neighbor told you? Where did you get your information? Sometimes you do not have access to all the facts, and then it's important to acknowledge that the decisions are based on partial information.

Now, what part of this information, the data, have you selected to focus on? The negative? The positive? Just a small part of it? Have you ever talked about a shared past experience with others, and noticed that each remembers it in their own way, focusing on different details? Look back at the facts. Could someone see them differently? What else can you consider?

What assumptions have you made based on past experiences and previous knowledge?

People may wrongly assume that a woman of a certain age is a mother; that the guy in the room is the manager; that you must have certain experience to qualify for a certain role; that others have verified the information they are presenting, etc. Ask yourself, have you verified your assumptions? Is this the only way to look at and interpret the data?

What conclusions are you drawing? What story are you telling yourself? Your conclusions lead to actions. Imagine other people you know. What conclusions would they reach? What story would they tell? Try and think of other possibilities.

Now that you have reassessed the data you're looking at and the assumptions you've made, are there other conclusions you could reach? Other actions you could take? What plans could you make? What new story could you tell?

When we step back down the Ladder of Inference, we begin to see how easily our assumptions and interpretations solidify into beliefs, beliefs that shape not just our actions, but our relationships, our self-perception, and our leadership. These beliefs don't stay on the Ladder, they follow us into every interaction, often operating beneath our awareness, influencing what we see, how we feel, and ultimately, who we become.

This brings us to a deeper truth: our thoughts, shaped by our beliefs, don't just inform our momentary actions, they shape our identity, our habits, and the course of our lives. As Lao Tzu, the ancient Chinese philosopher, and later thinkers like David Bayer remind us, what we think, we become.

What We Think, We Become

How Our Thoughts Become Our Reality

Our thoughts and beliefs shape the way we experience the world, sometimes without us even realizing it. Let's look at how this unfolds.

Lao Tzu said it best:

> Watch your *thoughts*, they become *words*.
> Watch your *words*, they become *actions*.
> Watch your *actions*, they become *habits*.
> Watch your *habits*, they become *character*.
> Watch your *character*, for it becomes your *destiny*.
> What we *think* we *become*.[72]

How Our Beliefs Impact Us

My client Sofia, a marketing executive, constantly found herself stuck in cycles of frustration and self-doubt. Every week, her team meetings seemed to drain her energy. She believed her team lacked initiative and were overly dependent on her for direction. The thought, Why can't they figure things out themselves? echoed in her mind before every meeting.

As a result, Sofia often entered the room feeling tense and braced for disappointment. Her tone became sharp, her feedback curt. Her belief shaped her actions. Over time, her team grew quieter in meetings, hesitant to share ideas, afraid of being dismissed. This only reinforced Sofia's belief that they weren't proactive, creating a self-fulfilling prophecy.

When we unpacked this in a coaching session, Sofia had a realization. Her belief that her team lacked initiative was coloring everything she saw. She acknowledged that this belief was deeply tied to her fear of failure and the pressure she felt to deliver results. She was micromanaging, not because her team lacked initiative, but because she was afraid of letting go.

Then, we flipped the belief. What if my team is capable, but they need more space and encouragement to take ownership? Sofia decided to test this new belief.

At the next meeting, she paused before speaking and opened with curiosity instead of critique: "What do you think is the best way forward?

Let's hear your ideas." She forced herself to hold back, giving her team time to respond. The team was hesitant at first, and then, to Sofia's surprise, ideas started flowing. Her team offered thoughtful suggestions and even pointed out areas for improvement she hadn't considered.

Over time, this shift in belief reshaped Sofia's behavior. Instead of assuming the worst, she started believing in her team's potential. Her tone softened, her trust grew, and her team began stepping up in ways they hadn't before. The meetings transformed from draining to collaborative, and Sofia realized how much her belief had been holding them all back.

Our beliefs are powerful. They frame how we interpret the world and how we respond to it. If we hold onto beliefs that limit us, whether about others or ourselves, we limit our potential and our relationships. But when we challenge those beliefs, we open doors to growth, connection, and success.

The Hidden Impact of Limiting Beliefs

In his book, *A Changed Mind: Go Beyond Self Awareness, Rewire Your Brain & Reengineer Your Reality*, author David Bayer outlines how our beliefs drive our feelings, actions, and results in his model, the 5 Primary Drivers.[73]

The 5 Primary Drivers state simply the following:

1. What we Believe determines what we Think.
2. What we Think determines our Feelings.
3. How we Feel determines our Actions.
4. Our Actions, over time, become our Habits.
5. Our Habits determine the quality and ultimate outcome of our life or, our Destiny.[74]

David Bayer adds the beliefs and feelings to Lao Tzu's formula. At a subconscious level, your beliefs dictate your thoughts at any given moment. You cannot think differently to what you believe. Depending on the quality of your thoughts, your brain releases chemicals that influence how you feel. Whatever you think, you feel. Your feelings motivate your actions and your actions produce your results.

If we pause and think about this for a moment, it makes perfect sense. If you believe that the earth is flat, you will only look for evidence that supports this proposition. Only when you are ready to question it, or let go of this belief, will you be open to seeing contradictory evidence. If you believe that you can't do math, you will likely not attempt to do any, and will only look for evidence supporting this belief. If you succeed in solving a Math problem, you will likely still see it through the same lens and attribute your success to chance, rather than your capabilities.

Limiting Beliefs

Most of your beliefs are formed early on in life and they reform and reshape throughout your life as you encounter new experiences. As a child, you observe and take in information without having the ability to evaluate it. Dr. Bruce Lipton, author of the bestselling book *The Biology of Belief*, talks about how from birth to around age seven, you operate primarily in brain wavelengths that are very close to a hypnotic state. When you are a kid, you are literally a sponge, soaking up every little thing around you in order to record *bad* and *good* behaviors and emotions. This means that everyone develops beliefs from early childhood, some of which are supportive, and some of which are limiting. For instance, children who are treated as though they are loved and valued will develop the belief that they are loved and wanted. On the contrary, children who are abused or neglected will tend to develop the belief that they are unworthy and unwanted.[75]

These conclusions you drew from different experiences in your life come from the brain's desire to protect you from future pain. If your parents fought a lot, you may have concluded that relationships are difficult. If you were often criticized, you may have concluded that you needed to be perfect to be loved. If you were bullied in school, you may have concluded that you weren't good enough. If one of your parents was unemployed, you may have concluded that it is hard to find a job. If a parent did not like their work, and complained about it often, you may have concluded that work is not fun. You get it.

None of these need be truths, yet you have created these equations in your mind that subconsciously still guide you today. For some, these beliefs are not only untrue but also greatly disempowering. Functioning from a belief, you look, consciously or unconsciously, for information that will validate it.

Often when you are stuck, a limiting belief is holding you back. A limiting belief is a thought or a state of mind that you think is the absolute truth and stops you from doing certain things. These beliefs don't always have to be about yourself, either. They could be about ourselves, how the world works, ideas, and how you interact with people.

It was Mother's Day and, like many others, I found myself reflecting on the significance of my mother. That same weekend also happened to be the eighth anniversary of my mom's passing. As I reminisced, I recognized that my mother's nature as a caring, warm, and loving person was accompanied by a tendency to be silly and playful. My mother also struggled with asserting herself when faced with disrespect. She let people walk all over her. I didn't like this particular characteristic and didn't want to be like her.

What I realized that weekend is that subconsciously, I associated silliness with vulnerability and a lack of self-advocacy. Consequently, I convinced myself that being serious was the only way to garner respect.

Our upbringing plays a significant role in shaping our beliefs and self-image. As I pondered my mom's memory, I found myself confronting this personal belief I had held onto for years. The equation I had created in my mind, connecting silliness with disrespect, had limited my ability to express myself fully.

As humans, our minds have a natural tendency to form associations and create patterns. These mental equations help us navigate the world and make sense of our experiences. This is how our brains work. However, these equations can sometimes be flawed, limiting our perception and potential.

Recognizing the limitations imposed by false equations is a step towards personal growth. In my introspection, I realized that silliness and respect are not mutually exclusive. Being playful and lighthearted doesn't diminish one's worth or invite disrespect. It is entirely possible to be both silly and respected simultaneously. Embracing this newfound understanding, I am curious to see what being silly will look like for me.

We all have equations that we have unwittingly accepted as truth. They may pertain to our appearance, abilities, or our relationships. By challenging these false equations, we can uncover new possibilities and embrace our authentic selves. It is liberating to recognize that we are not bound by the limiting beliefs we have held onto for so long.

Part of my coaching process involves working with my coachees to understand their limiting beliefs, assumptions, and negative self-talk. These mental barriers can significantly impact a leader's effectiveness and ability to achieve their goals.

By bringing these limiting beliefs to the surface, we can begin to challenge and reframe them. This often involves a process of identifying the beliefs that hold them back, understanding where they come from, and then actively working to replace them with more empowering and constructive thoughts.

Several of my coachees believed that they needed to have all the answers in order to be respected by their team. This belief can lead to overworking, stress, and a reluctance to delegate, which in turn can stifle the team's development and innovation. By recognizing this limiting belief, the coachees could start to let go of the need for control, learn to trust their team, and foster a more collaborative environment.

The impact of addressing these mental barriers is profound. It can lead to improved leadership effectiveness, better decision-making, and a more positive organizational culture. It also helps leaders to become more resilient and adaptable, crucial qualities in today's fast-paced business world.

Before we move on, take a moment. Do you also believe that to gain your team's respect you need to have all the answers? What other equations might be quietly shaping how you show up as a leader?

My client John, a gentleman in his late fifties, is an executive in a successful Pharma company. John's day, like most executives' nowadays, was in back-to-back meetings all day, every day. John, frustrated, trying to get some of his work done, would be multitasking, answering emails, and going through his long list of to-dos during the meetings. This did not go unnoticed by John's colleagues and employees, who complained that John was always in back-to-back meetings and that while he was physically there, he was not really present in most meetings. John thought that a lot of the meetings were a waste of time and there was no need for him to be there. When I asked John why was he involved in all of these meetings if he thought his presence was not necessary there, he replied, "Because I was invited."

His response surprised me. Here was a smart, successful professional whose default was to attend any meeting that he was invited to. John believed that it would be rude to decline meetings he was invited to, especially meeting requests from people at levels below him. In John's home, being respectful was the number one rule. As an older sibling, he was often told to treat his younger siblings with respect. Thus, it was very important to John to be respectful and avoid coming across as an arrogant executive. He would not behave in what he perceived to be a rude manner to anyone. This is what he had always done. It took time for John to understand how the equation he had in his mind—declining meetings = being rude and disrespectful—was hurting him and negatively impacting the people around him. John started exploring what declining meetings, graciously, could look like. He was surprised to see that it was well received, and that people appreciated him attending only those meetings where he was fully present and contributing.

We often have more than one limiting belief. Here is another one of mine. Marshall Goldsmith, my mentor, created the 100 Coaches Community, which brings together the world's premier leadership thinkers and provides them with the opportunity to learn from his practiced and proven methods. Being part of this coaching community is considered an honor. I very clearly remember my first time attending an MG100 event and I was thrilled to spend the weekend with Marshall and the top coaches and management thinkers. We gathered in Nashville, Tennessee at Belmont University. We learned from Marshall, from each other, and listened to some amazing country music—we were in Nashville after all! I was inspired. I had found my tribe. I connected with incredible people who I felt 'got me.' I was also anxious and self-conscious. I didn't feel completely me, with my regular contagious energy and confidence. My fellow Forefront members all talked about Imposter Syndrome, but it didn't feel quite like that.

This feeling didn't leave me, and I felt that I needed to get to the bottom of it. I was talking with my lovely, incredible mentor, Liz Kislik, also a member of the MG100, and we were trying to work out what was going on there for me. Liz knew my history, the environment I grew up in. She could help me 'peel the onion' and uncover my deep "I am not good enough" limiting belief. Now this limiting belief is really not that surprising, considering I grew up in a home where I was frequently told by my father that women are inferior to men, that I was not capable, that I would not finish a degree.

Since I had finished two degrees, cum laude, including a masters, and had been a successful executive, it seemed that this belief didn't hold me back in most situations, yet being part of the best of the best didn't feel right. There was too great a distance, a gap, between the *no good* and *one of the best*. I had to digest this. Digest that the impact of what I had heard at home growing up was still with me in my fifties. When I reflected back, I could see that in many aspects of my life I considered doing well, but the best was not really an option; that was for other people. I could suddenly see how this limiting belief had always impacted my thinking. I was always determined and believed that I could do anything I set my mind to. Obviously the anything had a glass ceiling. This was my opportunity to break it.

It was time to come up with a new belief, one that served me better. What worked for me is this: I can do anything I set my mind to. No glass ceiling. I *can* be the best. The next MG100 event I showed up differently. I was a confident, relaxed me.

> "What we can or cannot do, what we consider possible or impossible, is rarely a function of our true capability. It is more likely a function of our beliefs about who we are."
>
> Tony Robbins

→ YOUR TURN: Challenge Limiting Beliefs

We all carry beliefs that once served us, but may no longer be helping us thrive. Often, we don't even realize they're there, quietly shaping our choices, our relationships, and how we see ourselves.

Let's explore yours, gently and honestly.

1. **Notice the Voice**
   Start by tuning into your self-talk, especially when you feel uncertain, stuck, or self-critical. What are the phrases or thoughts that repeat themselves?

What do you hear yourself saying when you're frustrated, hesitant, or holding back?

2. **Name the Belief**

   What belief might be underneath that voice?

   What equation have you created in your mind that feels like an unspoken rule (e.g., If I don't say yes, I'm being selfish or If I ask for help, I look weak)?

   Try finishing this sentence:

   I believe that _____, I _____.

3. **Trace It Back**

   Where might that belief come from?

   Was it something you picked up in childhood? A moment that left a mark? A message you absorbed over time?

   Remember, these beliefs weren't born in malice. They often formed to protect you. The question now is: Are they still protecting you, or limiting you?

4. **What Has It Held You Back From?**

   In what areas of your life has this belief limited you?

   How has it shaped your actions, relationships, or self-image?

   Has it kept you from speaking up, trying something new, setting boundaries, or simply being yourself?

   Has it prevented you from feeling joy, connection, or confidence in certain spaces?

   This isn't about blaming, it's about gently uncovering what might be possible if this belief weren't in the driver's seat.

5. **Challenge It**

   Ask yourself:
   - Is this always true?
   - Can I find any moments in my life that disprove it?
   - What's another possible perspective?
   - Have I ever seen the opposite be true?
   - How might someone who loves me see this differently?

   Try this reframing:

   Even though I've believed _____, I'm open to the idea that _____.

6. **Choose a New Belief**

   What's a more empowering, truthful belief you'd like to try on instead?
   - I can be both kind and clear.
   - It's safe to take up space.
   - Not knowing everything doesn't mean I'm not capable.

   What belief would serve you better now? What belief reflects the person you're becoming, not the person you had to be in the past? You don't have to believe it 100 percent yet. Just try it on. See how it feels.

7. **Put It Into Practice**

   What's one small action you can take to begin reinforcing that new belief?

   Maybe it's speaking up in a meeting, saying no with kindness, or allowing yourself to be playful without judgment.

   Start where it feels possible.

Let this action be your first step toward rewriting the story, and living more fully as the person you already are, underneath that old belief.

From Beliefs to Self-Talk

Our limiting beliefs don't just sit quietly in the background, they find their voice in our daily self-talk. That inner dialogue, shaped by years of assumptions, experiences, and subconscious conclusions, becomes the steady hum that influences how we see ourselves and navigate the world. Sometimes it motivates us. Other times, it holds us back.

Self-Talk

The most conversations you will ever have are with yourself. This inner dialogue, the continuous stream of thoughts and narratives that echo through our minds, plays a profound role in shaping our reality. This self-talk, whether a silent whisper or a loud roar, directly influences our emotions, decisions, and overall mental health. When positive, it can propel us forward, bolstering confidence and resilience. Conversely, when it veers into negativity, it limits us, casting a shadow over our capabilities and prospects.

The perils of negative self-talk are potent and insidious. A person who habitually thinks, I'm not good enough, may unknowingly set a ceiling on their potential, avoiding challenges where they fear failure might confirm this identity. Someone who constantly tells themselves, I'm not good at handling pressure, may find themselves overwhelmed in high-stakes situations, reinforcing a cycle of stress and underperformance. These self-critical patterns often become self-fulfilling prophecies, where the fear of failure creates barriers to growth and success.

We are often our own harshest critics, saying things to ourselves that we would never dream of saying to others. This inner voice, unchecked, can amplify doubt and imposter syndrome, leaving us paralyzed when we most need courage. When your inner critic speaks up, pause and reframe by asking yourself, "What would my best friend say to me?" Your best friend wouldn't belittle you for making a mistake; they would remind you of your strengths, encourage you to try again, and put the situation in perspective. Imagining this kinder, supportive voice helps interrupt the spiral of self-judgment and replace it with compassion and clarity.

Another strategy for managing this relentless critic is to give it a name, something like Taco, Psycho, or Banjo. By personifying your inner critic, you create separation between your true self and the irrational negativity. When you catch yourself thinking, I can't do this, or, I always mess things up, you can pause and ask, "Is this something Taco would say?" This small shift transforms your critical inner monologue into an external dialogue, one you can engage with, challenge, and even dismiss.

Pair this with the powerful reframe, asking yourself what a trusted friend would say, and you start to consciously rewrite the narrative in your head. These simple tools may seem lighthearted, but they can be powerful in softening the sharp edge of self-judgment and inviting in more grace and possibility.

Positive self-talk isn't about ignoring challenges or pretending everything is fine; it's about fostering a balanced, empowering mindset that supports growth. By stepping back, reframing your thoughts, and engaging with your inner dialogue, you transform self-talk into a tool for resilience and success.

The goal isn't to silence your inner voice, but to teach it a new tone, one of truth, strength, and self-compassion.

→ YOUR TURN: Rewrite Your Internal Dialogues

- What does your self-talk say about your beliefs in your abilities?
- How does it shape your daily experiences?
- Are you an architect of your own confidence, or are you unwittingly undermining your potential?
- Could imagining your best friend's words, or naming your critical thoughts, help you gain perspective and foster a more compassionate self-narrative?

Engaging with these strategies is the first step toward turning your self-talk into a source of empowerment. By replacing your harshest critic with a kinder, wiser voice, you build resilience, clarity, and confidence, setting yourself up for success in every challenge you face.

This voice, our self-talk, the one we hear most often in our lives, where does it come from? Often, it begins with a thought. A quick, automatic, and usually unnoticed flicker of meaning.

- I'm not prepared.
- This won't go well.
- They probably think I'm not good enough.

These are negative thoughts, and they're usually the starting point of a loop. Our self-talk responds, either reinforcing the fear (Why do I always mess this up?) or gently interrupting it with a more compassionate voice (I've done hard things before; I can handle this too).

When left unchecked, negative thoughts can become the background music of our minds, quietly shaping how we show up, how we feel, and what we believe is possible.

Negative Thoughts

These thoughts are distracting, diminishing one's confidence, and often leading to lethargy and depression. It's natural to have negative thoughts; everyone has them. The question is how to deal with them. Do we let them take over and diminish our confidence and possibly debilitate us, or do we learn to overcome them?

Research suggests that a significant portion of our thoughts, often as much as 80 percent, tend to be negative. Even more striking is that around 95 percent of our thoughts are repetitive, meaning we tend to loop through the same worries, doubts, and judgments day after day.[76] This pattern isn't a personal flaw, it's how our brain evolved. We are wired to scan for threats, detect potential dangers, and anticipate worst-case scenarios. This negativity bias helped keep our ancestors alive, but today it often leads us to fixate on what's wrong, or what could go wrong. We're quick to notice negative cues (someone's frown) and quick to take it personally or assume negative intent (they must be upset with me). Our mind takes a single cue and builds an entire story around it.

A fleeting doubt becomes a familiar inner script. Over time, those scripts begin to shape how we feel, what we believe, and how we show up. We don't just think these thoughts, we start to believe them. We tend to accept our thoughts as truths—but the truth is, our minds often trick us.

How the Mind Tricks Us

View the two illustrations below: You see two lines: one with arrowheads at each end pointing outward, and the other with arrowheads pointing inward.

Examine Carefully: Look closely at both lines. Decide if one line appears longer than the other, or if they seem to be the same length.

Measure for Accuracy: Use a ruler or another measurement tool to measure the actual length of each line. This will help you verify your visual impression against the actual dimensions.

Reflect on Your Perception: Think about your initial perception and compare it with the actual measurements. Were you surprised by the results?

This is the Müller-Lyer illusion, a famous optical illusion that shows how our perception can be misleading, leading us to accept as true something that is not.[77] It consists of two lines of equal length; one with arrows pointing outwards, the other with arrows pointing inwards. Despite being the same

FIGURE 4: The Müller-Lyer illusion, where two lines of the same length appear to be different.

length, the line with arrows pointing inwards appears longer than the one with arrows pointing outwards.

This illusion demonstrates how our minds can trick us into accepting our perceptions as absolute truths. Just as the lines in the illusion are the same length—but our brains tell us they're different—our interpretations of reality are shaped by mental filters, biases, and preconceived notions that can distort our understanding.

The Ebbinghaus illusion (sometimes known as Titchener circles) is an optical illusion of relative size perception. Named for its discoverer, the German psychologist Hermann Ebbinghaus, the illusion was popularized in the English-speaking world by Edward B. Titchener in a 1901 textbook *Experimental Psychology: A Manual of Laboratory Practice*, hence its alternative name.[78]

Look closely at the images in Figure 5: You'll see two central circles, each surrounded by several other circles. Are the two central circles (the circles in the middle) the same size?

Notice the difference in perception: Despite the central circles being the same size, one may appear larger than the other due to the sizes of the surrounding circles. The circle surrounded by smaller circles tends to look larger, while the one surrounded by larger circles appears smaller.

These optical illusions can serve as a powerful metaphor for understanding the impact of negative thoughts. Just as these optical illusions trick our eyes into seeing lines of equal length, or circles of equal size, as different, negative thoughts can distort our perception of reality. They

FIGURE 5: The Ebbinghaus illusion, an optical illusion of visual size perception.

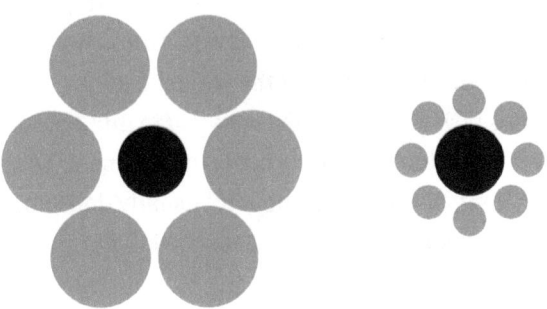

demonstrate that what we see isn't always the truth; our brains interpret visual cues in ways that can mislead us. Similarly, negative thoughts can alter our perception of situations, making challenges appear more daunting or insurmountable than they truly are.

Just as the illusions result from cognitive biases in visual perception, negative thoughts often stem from cognitive biases in our thinking patterns. For example, we might overgeneralize bad experiences or focus excessively on negative details, leading us to draw incorrect conclusions about ourselves or our circumstances. Our perceptions can deceive us, making us see things not as they are but as they appear through the lens of immediate context or emotional impact. These biases can make negative thoughts seem more significant than they are, altering our reaction to and recollection of events.

Usually, when we try to suppress our thoughts, it only makes us think about them more. A great example of this is known as the White Bear Problem, based on a 1987 study by Wegner, Schneider, Carter, and White. It refers to the psychological process in which we make deliberate attempts to suppress certain thoughts, only to end up making them more likely to surface.[79]

Let's do a little experiment: Read the next few lines slowly, pausing after each one. Take a moment to picture the image in your mind as vividly as you can.

Close your eyes. Imagine a white bear as vividly as you can.
Can you see its features?
Do you see its snow-white fur?

Are its nostrils flaring?

Is it lying on an iceberg or is it in a zoo?

Now don't think about the white bear. I want you to think about anything but the white bear. Try it for a few minutes. Most people can't help themselves, and continue to think of the white bear.

This illustrates how when we actively try *not* to think of something—like a white bear—we may actually be more likely to imagine it. Yes, this is why the advice we often hear, "Don't think about it" usually does not help. By trying not to think about it, suppressing thoughts, we keep going back to them.

Reframing: A Better Alternative to "Don't Think About It"

How we interpret challenges shapes how we experience them. Reframing is the powerful practice of shifting perspective, changing the way we interpret a thought, event, or situation so it feels more constructive and empowering.

Unlike simply telling yourself, Don't think about it (which usually backfires), reframing helps you change the story you're telling yourself. It's not about ignoring difficulties or putting a positive spin on everything. Rather, it's about adjusting your lens so you can see beyond the immediate setback and uncover new possibilities. A reframed thought can change not just how you feel, but what you believe is possible.

Take, for instance, the frustration of a flat tire. Imagine this: you're driving to an important meeting, feeling good about being on time, when suddenly you hear that unmistakable thump-thump-thump. You pull over, get out, and there it is, a completely flat tire. Your initial reaction might be frustration or even panic: This is a disaster. My entire day is ruined. You feel the clock ticking, the meeting slipping out of reach, and a flood of negative thoughts starts to overwhelm you.

But then you catch yourself. Instead of spiraling, you take a moment to reframe the situation. Yes, the tire is flat, and yes, it's an inconvenience. But does it have to ruin your day? You remind yourself that this is simply an hour-long detour, not the end of the world. You pull out your phone, call for roadside assistance, and while you wait, you take a few deep breaths. You realize this moment of stillness, forced though it may be, is a chance to regroup. You might even use the time to reschedule your meeting or catch up on emails.

And then a new thought arises: imagine not having a car at all. Suddenly, you feel a spark of gratitude for having reliable transportation most of the time. Instead of focusing on the annoyance of the moment, you appreciate the bigger picture, that you'll get the tire fixed, the meeting rescheduled, and your day will move forward.

This shift in viewpoint can transform an entire day from a series of frustrations to a narrative of overcoming and resilience. This practice of consciously shifting perspective is not just about making the best of a bad situation; it's about shifting your mindset and creating a mental space where you are in control of your reactions. You can choose how to respond and thereby empower yourself to continue your day with a renewed sense of purpose and positivity.

This mental shift, from spiraling to steadying, is the essence of reframing. Below are some tools to help you do it more deliberately, especially in moments of stress or disappointment.

Reframing Toolbox: How to Shift Your Perspective

- **Awareness:** Begin by tuning in. Pay attention to your thoughts. Become aware of your negative interpretations about a situation, especially in moments when you're feeling stressed, disappointed, or stuck. What are you telling yourself? What's the story running through your head? For example, imagine you didn't get the promotion you worked so hard for. Your negative thoughts might sound like, This is unfair! I'll never get ahead! or I'm just not good enough.
- **Challenge Your Negative Thoughts:** Question your assumptions and the beliefs underlying the negative thought. Determine whether there's actual evidence supporting your interpretation. Ask yourself: Is this thought based on facts, or fear? Is it always true? Have I seen exceptions?
- **Consider Alternatives:** Open up space for other interpretations. Explore alternative explanations or perspectives that might provide a more balanced or constructive view. Could someone else

have simply been a better fit for this particular role? Is it possible you're capable, but need to gain experience in a specific area?

- **Reframe:** Look for a more helpful or neutral reinterpretation of the situation. Create a narrative that supports growth, learning, or possibility. Instead of seeing the missed promotion as a failure, view it as feedback, and a chance to reassess your goals. Could this be an opportunity to gain new skills? To clarify what you want next? Perhaps it's a nudge to have a career conversation with your manager, or a sign that a better-suited opportunity is just ahead.
- **Language Shift:** Watch the words you use, even in your own head. Replace harsh or absolute terms with more accurate and compassionate language. Swap failure for a temporary setback or a learning moment. Change, I always mess up to, That didn't go how I hoped, but I can try again.
- **Perspective-Taking:** Step outside your own viewpoint. Put yourself in someone else's shoes or zoom out to gain a broader perspective. How would a trusted friend, coach, or mentor interpret this moment?
What would they remind you of? What might they see that you're too close to notice? If a friend were in your shoes, how would you respond to them?
- **Mindfulness and Acceptance:** Mindfulness techniques like deep breathing or grounding can help you stay present and interrupt spirals of negative thinking. Take a few moments to pause, breathe, and reset. This helps calm your nervous system and creates space for a new perspective.
- **Acceptance:** Some things are out of your control. Acknowledge what you can't change, and shift your focus to what you can influence. You can't undo the decision, but you can choose how you respond and what steps you take next.
- **Gratitude:** Even in hard moments, there's often something to be grateful for. Shifting your focus to what's going well, what's positive in your life, can help balance your perspective. What can you be grateful for? Your health? Your family? Your support

system? A lesson in the experience? Maybe it's the skills you've developed, the projects you've been trusted to lead, or simply the fact that you still have a job. Gratitude doesn't dismiss disappointment, it adds context and builds resilience.

- **Seek Support:** You don't have to reframe alone. Sharing your experience with someone you trust can bring clarity and encouragement. Talk with a mentor, coach, trusted colleague, or friend. They can offer insight, perspective, and help you realign your focus toward growth.

By applying these steps, a missed promotion, or any setback, can be transformed from a demoralizing disappointment into a stepping stone for future growth. Reframing doesn't deny the difficulty but rather opens the window to see the opportunity within the setback. Whether it's gaining insight, developing resilience, or finding a new direction, reframing gives you the agency to move forward with clarity and strength.

Reframing can happen after the moment, in retrospect, and in the moment, when your thoughts begin to spiral and anxiety starts to take over. The shift doesn't have to be dramatic; even a small reframe can stop a negative thought loop before it gathers momentum. Let's look at how one of my clients used this kind of real-time reframing to turn her anxiety into momentum.

Turn Your Anxiety into Success

Gabriela loved her work and was deeply committed to her organization. For some time, she had been developing an idea for a new initiative, something beyond her usual responsibilities, but close to her heart. As one of the few Hispanic women in the company, and the only one in a leadership role, she wanted to create a program to empower other Hispanic women in the workplace.

She poured her energy into the idea, building a detailed presentation and setting up a meeting with her boss to share it. But as the day approached, anxiety crept in. Her thoughts began to spiral: What if my boss doesn't get it? What if I fail? What if this idea I care so much about gets dismissed?

Looking for comfort, Gabriela called her mom, one of the few people she had confided in. Her mom, always encouraging, said, "Relax, it'll be fine."

Though well-meaning, the advice didn't soothe her. In fact, Gabriela felt more unsettled. She couldn't just *relax*. This mattered too much.

So what *does* work in moments like this? One surprisingly effective technique is to reframe anxiety as excitement. Instead of saying, I'm anxious, try saying, I'm excited.

Studies show that this small mental shift can have a big impact on your performance and confidence. In her article "Can Three Words Turn Anxiety Into Success?" from *The Atlantic*, Olga Khazan explains that both anxiety and excitement are aroused emotions.[80] In both cases, your heart races, cortisol spikes, and your body gears up for action. The difference isn't what your body is doing, it's the interpretation you associate to it.

That's why telling someone to calm down doesn't work. The leap from a high-arousal state (like anxiety) to a low-arousal one (like calm) is too far in the moment. But moving laterally, from anxiety to excitement, is more accessible. It's a shift in meaning, not energy.

Here's how it helps:

- Anxiety focuses your attention on potential threats, what might go wrong, and how you could fail.
- Excitement shifts your attention to possibilities, what might go right, and what you care about.

By telling yourself, I'm excited, you are able to get yourself out of the threatening mindset, and shift into an opportunity mindset, focusing on what could happen if you did well.

You can do this with other high-arousal emotions that are reactive, negative and depleting, such as irritation, frustration, anger and stress. You can shift to high-arousal renewing emotions like happiness, joy, passion and enthusiasm.

And this doesn't just apply to high-arousal emotions. You can use similar shifts with low-arousal emotions, too. If you're feeling low-arousal negative emotions, like sadness, shame, self-doubt, or resignation, it's helpful to gently guide yourself toward low-arousal positive states, such as calm, compassion, gratitude, or love.

Instead of telling yourself to "snap out of it" (which rarely works), ask:

- What can I feel grateful for right now?
- Can I give myself some kindness in this moment?
- What would calm look like right now, not as an escape, but as a choice?

Whether you're shifting from high-energy panic to excitement, or from quiet discouragement to peaceful steadiness, the goal is the same: to redirect your attention from threat to possibility, from depletion to renewal.

And that brings us to the heart of the next practice: Where are you placing your attention? Our attention shapes our reality. And learning to direct it intentionally is one of the most empowering things we can do.

Your Attention, Your Most Valuable Resource

Redirecting your attention, from fear to possibility, from depletion to renewal, isn't just a mindset shift. It's a practice. And at the heart of this practice is one of your most powerful tools: your attention.

We often think about time, how little we have of it, how to manage it better. But we rarely pause to consider our attention. What we choose to focus on shapes how we experience the world.

What are you choosing to focus on?

In the constant stream of thoughts and inputs that fill our days, attention is both precious and underappreciated. Moment by moment, we decide, consciously or not, where to place it:

- On our limitations or our capacities.
- On what's beyond our control or what's within it.
- On problems or possible solutions.
- On the tiniest flaw or the broader perspective.
- On fear or hope.

And that choice, what we give our attention to, shapes not only how we feel, but who we become.

Pause to take a deep breath. It isn't just about catching your breath; it's a deliberate act to bring your attention back to the present moment. That breath creates space, space to notice, to shift, and to choose. It moves you out of autopilot and into awareness. And in that awareness, you get to decide where to direct your mental energy.

Harnessing your attention becomes a pivotal exercise in rewriting the stories you tell yourself about who you are and what you're capable of achieving. Each pause, each breath, and each moment of awareness brings with it the chance to steer your focus away from the negative and towards affirming your potential and capabilities.

Is This Thought Useful?

This is Eric Barker's advice on how to direct your attention, which also resonated well with some of my clients. Eric Barker runs the blog *Barking Up the Wrong Tree*. He explains that though we can't control which thoughts pop up in our minds, we can control the thoughts we focus on.

"You're the thing that decides which thoughts are useful and should be taken seriously," he writes. "You're not your brain; you're the CEO of your brain. You can't control everything that goes on in 'Mind, Inc.' But you can decide which projects get funded with your attention and action."[81]

Seeing yourself as the CEO of your thoughts gives you control over what you spend time thinking about. The next time a negative thought pops into your brain, ask yourself, Is this thought useful? Is it worth spending my time on it?

As Eric Barker says, "If it is a reasonable worry, do something about it. If it's irrational or out of your control, recognize that."[82] Studies in neuroscience have shown that this small decision can reduce worry and anxiety.[83] The idea is not to ignore and suppress the thought but to evaluate it. Am I really hopeless at interviewing and never going to get a job? No. I had a bad interview today. I have to improve the way I answer a few questions...

Asking yourself if the thought is useful forces you to use a different perspective when looking at yourself. Become the CEO of your mind, consider if the thought is improving your company or if it needs to be dismissed.

Try this strategy. When you find your mind wandering to negative thoughts, ask yourself, Is this thought useful? If it isn't, drop it. If it is, do something about it.

→ YOUR TURN: Direct Your Attention

Your attention is one of your most valuable resources, so how are you choosing to use it? Are you pausing to notice which thoughts you're feeding, and asking yourself if they deserve your focus?

Try this:

- When a thought arises, especially one that feels heavy or repetitive, pause and ask: Is this thought useful? Is it helping me move forward, grow, or feel more grounded?
- If it is, what action might it be inviting you to take?
- If it's not, can you gently let it go, or shift your attention to something more helpful?

Think of yourself as the CEO of your own mind. Would you invest time and energy in this project? Or would you redirect those resources somewhere more productive?

In every moment of attention lies the power to shift your experience, from anxiety to curiosity, from self-doubt to possibility. You are not your thoughts, you get to choose which ones you follow. And just as you are not your thoughts, you are not your feelings, either.

You Are Not What You Feel

Language shapes our perception, influencing how we interact with our emotions and navigate challenges. Consider the difference between saying, "I am devastated" versus "I feel devastated." This subtle shift in phrasing can profoundly impact our psychological state.

When we say "I am devastated," we define ourselves by that emotion, as if devastation is a fixed, unchangeable part of who we are. It makes the feeling feel more permanent, reducing our perceived ability to move beyond it.

By contrast, saying "I feel devastated" acknowledges the emotion without letting it define you. It places the feeling outside your core identity, presenting it as a temporary state. This framing promotes emotional agility, the ability to observe and manage feelings as passing experiences, rather than as defining characteristics.

Compare:

- "I am insecure" vs. "I'm noticing some self-doubt in this moment" → Acknowledges the feeling without letting it define you.
- "I am overwhelmed" vs. "I feel overwhelmed right now" → Reinforces that emotions are temporary.
- "I am angry" vs. "I'm feeling anger rise in me" → Creates distance from the emotion, allowing space to respond.

These distinctions are powerful. They remind us that while we may experience intense emotions, those emotions are not who we are. They are emotional states, and no matter how intense, are just that: impermanent states. And when we recognize their transience, we gain the agency to navigate through them more effectively.

Linda, a senior director, found herself very upset after a strategy session where her proposal was critically challenged by her colleagues. Her tendency was to internalize the experience and tell herself, I am not cut out for this. This perspective began to affect her self-esteem and her interactions with her team. We worked on shifting her self-talk to, I feel upset and disappointed because my ideas were challenged. This allowed Linda to understand her emotions as a response to a specific event rather than a reflection of her competence.

Acknowledging her disappointment as a momentary reaction enabled Linda to then take proactive steps. She organized follow-up meetings with a few key skeptics to understand their concerns and to explain her vision more clearly. This not only helped in refining the proposal but also restored her relationships with her colleagues, demonstrating her openness to feedback and collaboration. By labeling her emotion as disappointment linked to a particular instance, rather than, I am a failure, Linda was able to engage more constructively.

This shift in language helped her see the moment more clearly and regulate her emotions, a small change with a big impact.

Another powerful way to regulate emotion? Naming what you're feeling. It's called affect labeling, and it's a surprisingly simple but effective practice.

Affect Labeling

This practice allows you to take control over your emotions by identifying and naming them as they arise. Research has shown that this simple act can significantly reduce physiological arousal and activity in the amygdala, the brain's fear center. In doing so, it helps calm the nervous system and allows for a more thoughtful, measured response.

It isn't about suppressing or pushing emotions aside. It's about acknowledging them clearly. Instead of saying, "I'm fine" when you're anything but, you pause and name what's real: "I feel anxious," "I'm disappointed," or "This hurts." Naming an emotion doesn't make it bigger, it helps loosen its grip.

Affect labeling also echoes ancient wisdom: that knowing and naming something gives you power over it. The more precisely we can name our emotions, the more empowered we are to choose how we respond. That clarity creates room to respond in ways that are aligned with our values and goals, rather than reacting on autopilot.

Let me tell you about Sophie. She was a leader at a fast-growing startup, deeply passionate about her work and fiercely committed to the company's success. But Sophie had a challenge: her emotions often got the better of her, especially in high-pressure situations. She was known for her sharpness in meetings, and while her intentions were always good, her reactions often left her team feeling deflated.

I was brought in to work with Sophie after her CEO noticed that, despite her brilliance, her leadership style was creating tension within the team. One story in particular stood out. During a big strategy meeting, a team member suggested an alternative approach to a project that Sophie was championing. The suggestion caught her off guard, and she felt her authority being questioned. Without a second thought, she interrupted them, her voice tinged with frustration, and dismissed the idea outright. The room went silent. The energy completely shifted, and what could have been an opportunity for collaboration became an uncomfortable stalemate. Later, Sophie admitted that she regretted how she handled it, but in the moment, her emotions had simply taken over.

When I started working with Sophie, it was clear she cared deeply about her team and wanted to improve. What she needed was a way to manage those intense emotional moments. I introduced her to the concept of affect labeling, naming her emotions as they arose. At first, Sophie was skeptical; it sounded almost too simple to be effective. But after I shared some of the research showing that naming an emotion can significantly reduce its intensity, she was open to giving it a try.

Not long after, she found herself in another heated meeting. Voices were rising, ideas were flying, and Sophie could feel that familiar wave of frustration bubbling up. Her heart started racing, her thoughts became scattered, and she could sense that if she didn't pause, she might fall into the same pattern. But this time, instead of snapping, she took a deep breath. In her mind, she said, "I feel angry and threatened." Just naming those emotions, angry and threatened, helped her gain a bit of distance from them. It was like flipping a switch; suddenly, she wasn't as overwhelmed by the feeling.

In that moment of clarity, Sophie made a conscious choice. Instead of firing back, she leaned into curiosity. She asked the person across the table, "Can you explain your idea a bit more? I want to make sure I fully understand it." The tension in the room softened. Her team, who had braced themselves for another clash, visibly relaxed. The discussion turned productive, and by the end of the meeting, they had refined the idea into something everyone felt good about.

Sophie later told me how surprised she was by the power of such a small shift. By simply naming what she was feeling, she was able to regain control and steer the conversation in a completely different direction. Over time, this practice started to reshape how she approached challenging moments, not just in meetings, but in her day-to-day interactions at work and at home. Her relationships improved, her team felt more heard and valued, and Sophie herself felt more in control of her emotions.

The thing about Sophie's story is that it's not unique. We've all had moments where our emotions take the wheel, and we say or do things we later regret. But a little bit of awareness can go a long way. By pausing, naming what we're feeling, and creating that small bit of distance, we open up the possibility to respond instead of react. It's not always easy, but it's a game-changer.

Emotions as Insight, Not Interference

By now, you've learned how naming your emotions can help loosen their grip. When you clearly acknowledge what you're feeling, you create enough distance to respond more intentionally. But labeling emotions doesn't just calm the nervous system—it also reveals something more. Emotions aren't just obstacles to manage. They're also useful data.

Think of your emotions as internal signals. They can tell you when a boundary has been crossed, when something you care about is at risk, or when something meaningful is unfolding. When you pause to notice what you're feeling and why, you gain valuable insight into what you deeply care about.

One of the simplest and most effective ways to help regulate your emotions is also the most overlooked: sleep. When we don't get enough of it, the part of our brain responsible for regulating emotion, the prefrontal cortex, loses its grip, while the amygdala, the emotional alarm system, becomes overactive. That's like turning your emotional volume up to full blast with no volume control.

I've experienced this firsthand. On days when I haven't slept enough, I'm more reactive. I interrupt more. I'm less thoughtful and more easily irritated. I don't show up as the leader or the person I want to be. That's why I've made sleep a priority. Going to bed earlier is one of the most reliable habits I've built to help me show up more grounded, present, and thoughtful.

Understanding your emotional landscape is essential for leading yourself. But it's also essential for leading others. Tuning into what the people around you are feeling, especially when they don't say it aloud, can help you better understand their behavior, build trust, and navigate difficult moments with greater skill.

Emotions are always part of the conversation, even if unspoken. Ignoring them is like flying a plane without checking your instruments. You don't have to be ruled by your feelings, but you do need to read them.

Treat your emotions as information. Notice them. Learn from them. Use them to make wiser, more emotionally intelligent decisions. This emotional awareness is the foundation of the next tool we'll explore. Because once you've noticed what you're feeling, the next step is to examine your thoughts and shift what's no longer serving you.

The Three Cs

This is a simple yet powerful framework from Cognitive Behavioral Therapy that builds on the tools we've already explored. It helps you take the next step: turning insight into action.

The Three Cs stand for **Catching, Checking**, and **Changing**.[84] When negative thoughts arise, you can follow these steps to help quiet those thoughts and shift toward a more constructive mindset. By catching your thoughts, checking their accuracy, and choosing a more empowering response, you create space for possibility, confidence, and growth.

Let's see how this would work for Andy and his negative thoughts around getting a promotion:

- **Catch It:** Andy is aspiring for a promotion. This has been on his mind for a while now. In fact, it keeps him up at night. It starts with a negative thought: I'll never get the promotion. Recognizing this negative thought is the first step in the Three Cs method. Andy catches the thought as it arises and acknowledges its impact on his career aspirations.
- **Check It:** Andy then proceeds to check the negative thought by asking a series of questions: Is this thought really even true? (Reflecting on past achievements, performance, and potential opportunities for growth.) Should I actually feel defeated every time I have this thought? (Questioning the emotional weight attached to the thought.) Is it worth dwelling on this negative thought? Does it help me reach my career goals? (Evaluating the usefulness of dwelling on negativity and its impact on future career success.) Through this checking process, Andy gains

insights into the validity of the negative thought and begins to understand potential distortions in his thinking.
- **Change It:** Having caught and checked the negative thought, Andy now focuses on changing his mindset. If the thought is deemed inaccurate or unhelpful, he will now reframe it into a more positive and constructive perspective. For instance, he might think, While the promotion is uncertain, I can actively seek feedback, develop new skills, and showcase my contributions to increase my chances.

The Three Cs method empowers Andy to actively engage with and reshape his negative thoughts about the promotion. This helps him foster a more positive and proactive outlook on his career growth and aspirations.

→ YOUR TURN: Name Your Feelings

How can naming your feelings and rephrasing your emotional experiences help you maintain perspective and a sense of control during emotional upheavals?

Next time a strong emotion hits, try pausing to name it. How does that shift your perspective? What changes when you remind yourself, This is a feeling I'm having, not who I am? How might this practice influence your ability to respond to emotional challenges with resilience rather than resignation?

The words we choose, especially the ones we say to ourselves, don't just describe our experience, they *shape* it. Whether we're naming an emotion to calm our nervous system or reframing a belief to unlock new possibilities, language is the tool we use to make change real. And sometimes, the subtlest shifts in wording can carry the biggest impact.

Which brings us to our next insight: Words Matter.

Words Matter

In his book *Atomic Habits*, James Clear emphasizes the importance of language with this example: Two people who have quit smoking are offered a cigarette. One responds, "I don't smoke," the other, "I am trying to quit." They've both quit smoking, but it's very clear who is more likely to succeed.[85]

On a lovely fall weekend, I ran a 5k fundraiser for cancer in my hometown of Lexington, MA. I am not a fast runner, but I enjoy the energy of the races and am happy to help raise money for a good cause.

I listen to music while I run. It is usually quite meditative and I don't even really hear the words, it is more the rhythm that matters and keeps me moving. I have a Spotify running playlist that I play on random shuffle.

The second-to-last song on my run happened to be "Working in the Coal Mine," with the chorus, "I'm so tired, how long can this go on."

Running this race, I heard the words for the first time. My first reaction was, Yes, I *am* tired, how much longer? As someone who only started running in the last few years, this would usually be true. But then I paused for a second and checked in with myself, thinking, I'm actually okay. I can push myself a little harder.

Then, in the last push to the end, this last song came up: "Harder to Breathe," with the chorus: "Is there anyone out there 'cause it's getting harder and harder to breathe." Again, I initially sympathized with the words, then checked in and thought, I'm okay.

I had a good laugh at the coincidence of those two songs both playing randomly at the end of my race. Nevertheless, the words did impact me. My immediate reaction was, I'm tired, it's hard to breathe. Not quite words of encouragement. What if I had listened to "I'm So Excited" or "I'm on Fire"?

Words matter, the words we tell ourselves, our self-talk, the words that others say to us, how we perceive ourselves and how we believe others perceive us.

This little background music coincidence also reminded me of the research included in Carol Dweck's book *Mindset, The Psychology of Success*. Dweck shares research on the power of words, and how they influence people's performance. In her research, she demonstrates that White men perform worse than Black men on athletic tasks when they are told that performance is based on natural ability. Asian women perform better on math tests when they are reminded of their Asian identity rather than of their female identity. Just a few words mentioned to the people before completing a task impacted their performance.[86]

In or Out of the Box

When I started running I kept telling myself, I am not a runner. Yes, I had never been a runner. And, yes, I am not like my husband and his running buddies. They run marathons, and run nearly every day, rain or shine. But I had been running regularly two-to-three times a week, three to six miles. Guess what? If I'm not a runner, it is much easier to not go running when it is cold outside, or I'm tired, or any other excuse. But when I *am* a runner, why would I not go running? So I decided that from then on, I am a runner. No excuses.

Whatever you are *not*, you are far less likely to embrace opportunities in that area.

Many people I coach tell me that they are not this or that. They are not great speakers because they have not talked at conferences like their CEO. They are not *real* people managers because they've only managed small teams. They are not innovators because they don't have patents to their name. They are not project managers, even though they have been managing projects. They are not techy, because they are not engineers, even though they're great with technology. And so on.

Naturally, there are situations where telling yourself that you are something, placing yourself in a box, is limiting and works against you. For example, thinking that if you are an HR professional, this means you are not—and can't be—a marketing professional.

Yet could you become a marketing professional if you so desired? I did. I didn't let HR define me. I ran a marketing department in my post-HR career.

→ YOUR TURN: Upgrade Your Self-Talk

What can you stop telling yourself that you are not and start telling yourself that you are? Listen to your self-talk. Where is it working for you? Where is it working against you?

Instead of engaging in negative self-talk, ask yourself:

Would I say the same thing to someone I care about? You can insert a specific person's name to make it more personal.

Where is the proof that this thought is true? This will help uncover any biases and limiting beliefs.

Asking, Is it really always or never? can help you put the issue into perspective and gain some objectivity.

What would ____ my best friend, partner, boss (insert what works for you) say?

Who told me that and why should I believe it? may help you create some separation between you and the voice, and discredit it.

Am I expecting myself to be perfect?

What can I learn from this? What's a positive? Try to see a possible opportunity here. You can also think, How can I reframe this?

What we tell ourselves shapes what we believe is possible. Whether it's labeling ourselves as not a runner or not a techy, these identities can limit our potential and close doors to growth. But just as harmful as boxing ourselves out is boxing ourselves in, believing we can't be more than one thing. These mental boxes are often built on fixed beliefs. To step beyond them, we need a different mindset, one that sees skills as buildable rather than predetermined.

Nurture a Growth Mindset

What shapes our capacity to grow and change often comes down to one powerful factor: our mindset. Changing our negative thoughts can help us build a positive, growth mindset. A can-do attitude.

The way we think about our abilities, whether we see them as fixed traits or skills we can develop, has a profound impact on how we approach challenges, setbacks, and success. When we reframe our thinking, we begin to build what's known as a growth mindset: the belief that skills and intelligence can be developed through effort, learning, and persistence.

This mindset isn't just positive thinking, it's rooted in research. Psychologist Carol Dweck, a Stanford University professor, introduced the concept of the growth mindset through her groundbreaking studies on motivation, achievement, and learning.

According to Dweck, people with a fixed mindset tend to believe that their intelligence or abilities are innate and unchangeable. As a result, they may avoid challenges, give up easily, or interpret failure as a personal flaw, a threat to their self-concept. If they receive a bad grade, lose a deal, or miss a promotion, they might think, I'm just not cut out for this. This perspective can create a results-only focus, which can be detrimental. It isn't constructive; it can lead to feelings of helplessness and a loss of confidence, stifling growth and improvement.

In contrast, those with a growth mindset believe that effort and learning lead to improvement. They see challenges as opportunities to grow, and setbacks as feedback, not a verdict on their worth or ability. The emphasis is on the process of learning rather than the end result. This perspective makes people more resilient and more likely to persist through difficulty.

Carol Dweck frequently highlights Michael Jordan as a quintessential example of the growth mindset. Jordan is renowned not just for his triumphs but also for his resilience in the face of setbacks. Jordan tried out for his varsity basketball team during his sophomore year of high school. The coach chose another sophomore for the varsity spot and placed Jordan on junior varsity instead. Later on in his career, Jordan had also missed crucial shots at critical game moments. Instead of letting these failures define or discourage him, he viewed them as catalysts for growth and improvement. Jordan's response to failure was not to assign blame externally or to retreat; rather, he intensified his practice efforts, focusing on perfecting the very skills that had faltered. This relentless commitment to practice and self-improvement underscores a core tenet of the growth mindset: viewing challenges and setbacks not as barriers, but as valuable opportunities for personal development. Jordan's mindset reveals that true success in any domain is rooted in the perseverance to continually evolve and learn from one's errors.[87]

Developing a growth mindset is about growing and learning from everything you do. It is understanding that failure is not the opposite of success, it's part of success.

If you want to improve, change, it is not about winning or losing, it is about enjoying the journey and not just reaching the destination.

Acknowledge that the path to success is a learning process and focus on what you can learn from the experience.

Ask yourself: What can I learn from this? What will I try next time?

It's important to note that our approach to growth and challenges isn't uniformly distributed across all facets of our life. It's possible to exhibit a growth mindset in one aspect of life while maintaining a fixed mindset in another. For instance, you might embrace challenges and the potential for development in your professional life, eagerly learning new skills or technologies that could advance your career. Yet, in personal hobbies or relationships, you might feel hesitant, sticking to familiar routines and avoiding new experiences that could lead to growth. This dichotomy reveals the nuanced nature of our mental landscapes, where confidence and openness to growth in certain domains don't automatically translate across all spheres of our existence.

Such variations might stem from previous successes or failures, perceived natural abilities, or even the value we assign to different aspects of our lives. For example, one may think, I can improve my public speaking with practice, (growth mindset), while simultaneously believing, I'm just not good at Excel (fixed mindset).

I had a fixed mindset when it came to my fitness. Exercise was never part of my life. At different points I tried different activities but never stuck with anything. I always felt that I was no good at it and never could be. But I reached a point where I wanted to make a change. At fifty, I wasn't getting any younger and I wanted to live healthier.

I had to develop a growth mindset. Make the shift to believe that my fitness capabilities are **not** predetermined. Effort and attitude will determine my ability. And that is when I decided that I am just not fit, yet, and I went big and took on the challenge of climbing Mount Kilimanjaro.

The Power of Yet

Carol Dweck's concept of the "power of yet" centers on the transformative potential of embracing a growth mindset. In her research, Dweck highlights how a small linguistic tweak, adding the word yet to the end of a sentence, can profoundly alter one's perspective on abilities and challenges. For instance, changing a statement from, "I can't do this" to, "I can't do this yet," implies that the ability or understanding is achievable with time and effort. It transforms fixed statements like, "I don't know this" into growth-oriented ones like "I don't know this yet," implying that learning and development are ongoing processes. This approach fosters a resilience in individuals, encouraging them to view challenges as opportunities for growth rather than insurmountable obstacles.[88]

The application of *yet* has shown significant positive impacts in educational settings, such as schools in Chicago that used "not yet" instead of failing grades, giving students the motivation to persevere rather than feeling defeated.

Dweck's work encourages us to recognize that our potential is not fixed and that our intelligence and abilities can develop with dedication and perseverance. This mindset not only supports personal achievement but also enhances the way we handle life's setbacks, reinforcing the belief that with effort, a path forward is always available.

Einstein once said, "It's not that I'm so smart, it's just that I stay with problems longer." His words capture a core tenet of Carol Dweck's growth mindset: that ability is developed through sustained effort, not innate talent. Einstein's success wasn't rooted in instant brilliance, but in persistence and the willingness to stay engaged with difficult problems and keep going when others might give up. Like Dweck's work, his approach reminds us that progress comes not from perfection, but from perseverance.

→ YOUR TURN: Shift to a Growth Mindset

In what areas do you find yourself open to growth and challenges, and where might you be holding onto fixed beliefs?

Listen to your self-talk. What are you telling yourself when faced with a challenge?

What does this say about your beliefs in your own potential to grow and evolve?

What should you be adding a "yet" to? I'm not good at it, yet.

How can recognizing these patterns help you foster more of a growth mindset in areas where you would like to create change?

Adopting a growth mindset doesn't just change how you learn or recover from setbacks, it changes how you lead, how you collaborate, and how others experience you. The beliefs you hold and the thoughts you nurture shape not only your behavior, but the energy you bring into every interaction.

Which brings us to the next key question: What energy are you bringing to interactions?

The Energy You Bring

Your thoughts and beliefs don't stay inside you, they radiate outward. The mindset you hold quietly influences your tone, your posture, your facial expressions. It becomes the energy you bring into a room. And that energy is contagious.

This phenomenon is called emotional contagion: the idea that we catch emotions from others, often without even realizing it. We're wired for connection, and our brains are constantly scanning for cues, a sigh, a smile, a furrowed brow, the pace of someone's voice. These subtle signals can spark emotional mirroring, where your body and mood begin to sync with the people around you.

You've probably felt it:

- The tension that spreads after one person enters a meeting looking frustrated or one's sharp sigh, a furrowed brow, or an eye roll.
- The relief and hope that follow when someone calmly says, "We've got this," or another's steady eye contact and reassuring tone.
- The way one person's laughter, or even just a warm smile, can lift the whole room.

Your energy shapes how others experience you, and how they feel about themselves. It can inspire openness or defensiveness, confidence or doubt, momentum or hesitation.

That doesn't mean forcing positivity. What it does mean is being intentional. Checking in with yourself. Owning your mood. Becoming aware of what energizes you and what depletes you. Knowing that your inner state, your mindset, your emotions don't just affect you, they affect everyone you interact with.

So ask yourself not just, What energy am I bringing? but also, What's fueling it?

Are you running on stress, on gratitude, on exhaustion, on inspiration?

Are there specific tasks, people, or meetings that energize you? And others that consistently drain you?

If you really want to understand your patterns, try an exercise many of my clients have found helpful. Over the course of a few days, track the impact different tasks, meetings, and conversations have on you. Which ones give you energy? Which ones deplete it? Which are neutral? You might be surprised by what you learn.

Then pause. Assess your current energy. Is this the energy you want to bring with you into your next interaction? Because how you show up matters. And you get to choose how you manage and direct the energy you carry.

Here's a small but vivid reminder from my own life: Not long ago, I found myself in a long line at the post office. It was one of those days where everything felt like it was moving just a bit too slowly. My parking meter was about to run out, and I was returning an item with a QR code that I assumed, based on past experiences, wouldn't need to be fully taped up.

While I was in line, frustrated that it was taking so long, I noticed that the two tellers were being extremely patient with the people they were serving. People who were asking a lot of questions and clearly needed extra help.

When I finally got to the front, the postal worker scanned my code and calmly said, "You need to tape this closed." I asked if I could use her tape. She told me no, that I would have to buy my own. And that's when I lost my cool. Not dramatically, but enough. I was rude. Frustrated. Short. I pushed back about having to buy a whole roll of tape for the two inches I needed.

She stayed professional, but I could feel the tension rise.

What happened next stuck with me. A woman who had been ahead of me in line returned to ask a quick question. The teller next to mine, witness to my interaction, snapped at her to get back in line. The warmth in the room was gone.

And I realized: that was me. I had shifted the mood. With one small, snippy interaction, I had unintentionally made things harder for everyone around me. The woman behind the counter was doing her job. She didn't make the rules. And she certainly didn't deserve my irritation.

This was a good reminder to watch the energy I bring and to be responsible for my impact. Even when it's just a quick errand on an ordinary day. Especially then. It's often in the small, ordinary interactions—errands, meetings, quick check-ins—where our leadership and energy speaks loudest. We always leave a ripple. The question is: what kind?

→ YOUR TURN: Manage Your Energy

What kind of energy do you tend to bring into a room? Are there specific tasks, people, or meetings that energize or deplete you? What would change if you paused to assess your energy—and chose how you wanted to show up?

The energy you bring into a room isn't fixed. It's not just a personality trait, it's something you can work on, refine, and improve. Just like any skill, it starts with awareness. And it grows through practice.

Which brings us to a powerful truth: improvement doesn't happen by accident. It happens by design, when you choose to work on something, one step at a time, every single day.

Work On Improving New Things Every Day

The idea of improving something new every day is grounded in the belief that mastery isn't innate, it's built through consistent effort and practice. This is reflected in the popular "10,000-hour rule," which suggests it takes roughly ten thousand hours of deliberate practice to master a skill. This rule, popularized by Malcolm Gladwell in his book Outliers, emphasizes the power of persistence and long-term commitment to skill development.[89]

Practice makes perfect is more than just an adage; it's a principle supported by a wealth of research in various domains, from music to sports to academic subjects. Each practice session builds upon the last, helping to refine skills, increase speed, improve accuracy, and deepen understanding.

What can you do? As you embark on the journey of self-improvement, here are key strategies to consider:

1. **Incremental learning:** Focus on setting small, manageable goals. By breaking skills into smaller components, you can concentrate on improving one facet at a time, making the process less overwhelming and more achievable.

2. **One goal at a time:** Avoid the common pitfall of spreading your efforts too thinly across multiple goals. Concentrate on one specific area of improvement at a time. This focused approach not only enhances your efficiency but also ensures deeper learning and mastery before moving on to the next challenge.
3. **Feedback loops:** Integrating feedback is crucial in the learning process. Constructive criticism helps you adjust techniques, correct errors, and refine strategies, thereby accelerating your progress and effectiveness (more on feedback in the "Evaluate" chapter).
4. **Consistency over intensity:** Regular, dedicated practice sessions are more beneficial than infrequent, intense bursts. Consistency fosters skill retention and gradual improvement, laying a stronger foundation for advanced learning.
5. **Mindset:** Embrace a growth mindset, as championed by Carol Dweck. View challenges as opportunities and mistakes as essential steps in your learning curve. This perspective encourages resilience and persistent effort in the face of setbacks.
6. **Real-world application:** Actively apply new skills and behaviors in real-life situations. Practical application not only cements these skills but also underscores their relevance and effectiveness, enhancing your learning experience.

By focusing on one step at a time, learning, practicing, and applying, we set ourselves up for meaningful growth. Small, steady improvements compound over time. But growth isn't just about modifying or adding new skills or pushing harder. Sometimes, the most powerful step forward is letting go—of habits, expectations, or beliefs that are quietly holding us back.

Letting go isn't the opposite of progress. It's part of it.

Letting Go

Fall in New England is beautiful. The red, orange, and yellow leaves mesmerize me. The trees look different every day as the sun shines upon them and their leaves fall. I stop and watch with awe.

Walking past them last fall, I thought about how nature has so beautifully mastered the art of letting go. When we let go, we create space for new things to happen. We are able to release negative emotions and move on with life. Letting go is important to our well-being. Yet, as humans, we don't have such seasonality and process ingrained into our lives. How lucky the trees are, I thought, we all need to learn from them and let go.

It reminded me of the classic Zen parable of the two monks and the woman, a story I've often heard Marshall Goldsmith tell: A senior and a junior monk reach a riverbank. As they prepare to cross the river, a young woman asks them for help crossing it. The senior monk, despite his vow not to touch women, carries her across the river and gently places her on the other side.

The young monk is shocked. He's appalled and speechless. How could the senior monk touch a woman?

They continue on their journey. An hour, two, three pass without a word between them.

As they return to the monastery, the young monk can no longer contain himself and says to the older monk: "We took a vow not to touch women. How could you carry her across the river?"

The older monk looked at the young monk compassionately and responded: "I carried her across the river, and set her down on the other side. Why are you still carrying her?"

What are you still carrying that you should be letting go? Past behaviors—your own, or those of others? Emotional pain? Hurts from the past?

It is a conscious decision to hold on to the past, to continue to ruminate over past actions or events, and continue to let them weigh us down. It can also be a conscious decision to let them go.

The curious among you might be wondering how my Kilimanjaro climb turned out. Well, it wasn't just a physical challenge, it became a real-time field test for nearly every tool in this chapter. Letting go. Reframing discomfort. Managing my mindset. Directing attention. Practicing positive self-talk. Embracing gratitude. The mountain demanded not just physical strength, but emotional flexibility, mental discipline, and the ability to focus on what mattered most, one small step at a time. I didn't just write about these ideas. I lived them.

Trekking Up Kilimanjaro

I got fitter, but really not physically fit enough for the demanding climb up Kilimanjaro. Our trek spanned eight days. By the end of day three I was already exhausted, my muscles were sore. But I was determined, I was *really* determined.

Each day we slowly climbed higher and higher up the mountain. The beautiful terrain changed, and with the elevation, the air got thinner and it became increasingly difficult to breathe.

On day four, the huge blisters on my feet gained me new respect from our guides.

On day six, we climbed to base camp at 4680 meters (5,239 feet). We had a rest in the afternoon and at 11:30 p.m. we started our climb to the summit at 5895 meters (19,341 feet). It was dark outside; we used our headlights to guide us on our path and also enjoyed the light from the full moon. It was cold, bitterly cold even by Boston standards. I was wearing six layers on top, and four on bottom (including two down jackets and snow pants). We were lucky, and it was not a windy day. (Can you see that I was looking for the positive?) As long as we kept moving it was ok.

As we were climbing, the path was steep and icy. I would look at it and think, How am I *ever* going to come down this?

I very quickly realized that if I wanted to get to the top, I couldn't think about the way down. Those thoughts were not useful. I had to focus on the summit only, on the big goal. Instead of thinking about the entire climb, I focused on making it to the next marker or rock ahead. By breaking the journey into smaller steps, the challenge felt less overwhelming, and I could celebrate each small milestone along the way. When my legs felt like they couldn't take another step, I closed my eyes for a moment and visualized myself standing at the top of the summit, feeling the sense of accomplishment and the view all around me. That vision gave me the energy to take just one more step

I used many of the tools I mentioned in this chapter to stay positive and keep going. Every time a thought about descending the mountain popped in, I would dismiss it and say to myself, You are going to make it to the summit. Countless times I asked myself, Is this thought useful?

and worked hard to dismiss the many that were not and were out of my control. I closely monitored my self-talk to keep it positive and productive. I constantly reminded myself of who I wanted to be. I leaned into my strength of determination. I focused on moving forward, and just shifting one foot in front of the other.

A third of the way up, in the middle of the night, I was already exhausted both mentally and physically. We stopped for a snack and hot tea, and it was hard to continue. Adrenaline, and maybe a little stubbornness, must have kept me going.

We reached the summit just before 8:00 a.m.

It was cold, and to avoid altitude sickness kicking in, we only spent a few minutes at the top taking in the view and snapping some photos. Stopping for a long rest is not an option. Once you stop, you get cold quickly and feel how tired you really are.

This is where an unexpected test began.

I had no energy left. Every step downhill felt like a mountain of its own. On the steep parts I paused to take some deep breaths, steady my steps and calm my mind. I held on to our guide for support. We arrived back at base camp at 1:30 p.m. We had been going for fourteen hours straight at this point.

But we weren't done. We still had to descend further to a lower-altitude camp. I lay down, utterly depleted, but sleep wouldn't come. So I sat up, took a few deep breaths, and let go of the struggle behind me. I told myself, *It's just three miles. You've come this far, you can do this.*

It wasn't easy. I leaned on my husband and son the entire way, sick and running on fumes. We reached camp at 6:30 p.m., after more than eighteen hours of hiking. I collapsed into our tent and didn't emerge until morning.

I was re-energized after my sleep. The guides were surprised at how upbeat I was, joking and laughing again and able to enjoy the remaining 13.5 km (8.3 miles). I chose to focus on how far I'd come, and on the warm shower that awaited me. In the hard parts I chanted to myself, and sometimes out loud, "Shower, shower, shower." That tiny word became my motivation, my mantra, and my reminder to stay positive.

For those considering a mountainous adventure of their own, a side note from my son, the Avalanche Forecaster: After reading this story, my son picked up the phone and said, "Ima, (mom in Hebrew) focusing solely on getting to the top without thinking about how you'll get down is actually dangerous. That's how people end up needing helicopter rescues." He was right. While focusing on the summit helped me push forward in the moment, it's important to say this is not a recommended strategy for mountain safety. You must always plan for the way down too. Thank you, Arden, for the important reminder.

Summary

Reflect: Key Takeaways

This chapter helped you explore the inner world of your thoughts, emotions, and patterns—so you can respond with intention instead of reacting on autopilot. Through reflection, you created space to grow:

- **Pause to respond rather than react:** Create space between stimulus and response, engaging System 2 thinking to make more intentional choices.
- **Recognize self-sabotaging behaviors:** Identify your triggers and patterns where you might hinder your own progress.
- **Examine internal narratives:** Notice negative self-talk, limiting beliefs, and the stories you tell yourself, and how they shape your perceptions and actions.
- **Name emotions to loosen their grip:** Use affect labeling ("I feel anxious") to calm the nervous system and regain choice.
- **Reframe your perspective:** Shift language and meaning ("I'm excited" vs. "I'm anxious") to turn threat into possibility and fuel action.
- **Mind the energy you bring:** Your mood is contagious; choose the tone you want others to feel by doing a quick energy check.
- **Deploy quick reflection tools:** Lean on mindfulness PQ reps, the 4 Ps (Pause → Process → Plan → Proceed), and the Five Cs (Calm, Clear, Curious, Compassionate, Courageous) when stakes are high.
- **Cultivate a growth mindset:** Learn from challenges, add "yet" to your limits, and let go of beliefs that no longer serve you.

- **Ask yourself:** How do my thoughts and emotions influence my actions? What insights can I gain on how I get in my own way?

Tying It All Together

This chapter, "Reflect," has guided you through the vital practice of pausing to examine your inner world, the beliefs, thoughts, and emotions that shape your experiences. We explored how reflection is a powerful tool for uncovering patterns, managing triggers, and fostering emotional agility. By integrating practices such as reframing, affect labeling, and mindfulness, you've developed strategies to navigate challenges with greater clarity and intentionality.

As you conclude this chapter, take a moment to reflect on what you have learned about yourself. What insights resonated most deeply with you? What strategies or tools have you chosen to apply in your life, and which ones didn't feel relevant right now? Remember, growth is a journey, and not everything will resonate immediately. Some concepts may take root later when the time is right, so don't hesitate to return to this chapter in the future. Growth is incremental, and you can't work on all your challenges at once. Prioritize what feels most pressing or impactful, and allow yourself the space to tackle others as they arise.

Celebrate your discoveries and the progress you've made so far. Each insight, no matter how small, is a stepping stone on your journey of self-improvement. Recognize the effort you've invested in pausing, reflecting, and aligning your actions with your values. These are milestones worth honoring, as they reinforce your commitment to becoming the person and leader you aspire to be.

And remember, reflection is an ongoing process. Each moment of self-awareness is an opportunity to recalibrate and grow. As you move forward, continue to ask yourself, Am I being the person I want to be right now? This question is your guidepost, helping you stay true to your highest self.

What's Next: Moving from Reflection to Evaluation

As we transition to the next chapter, "Evaluate," you'll build on the insights from your reflections to assess your progress, uncover blind spots, and gain valuable feedback from others. Take this next step to determine whether your behaviors and actions are coming across as you intend, ensuring that your growth aligns not only with your personal goals but also with how you are perceived by those around you. Let's continue this journey into evaluation, where your reflections are transformed into tangible, actionable insights for lasting impact.

4 EVALUATE

We judge ourselves by our intentions. Others judge us by our impact.

Author unknown

I WAS brought in to work with Ellen, a director at a fast-growing software company. Ellen, a smart, ambitious, and hardworking individual, had recently transitioned from an individual contributor role to a management role. From the confidential 360° interviews I conducted, it was clear that Ellen's team felt she didn't care about them. This came as a big surprise to Ellen. Ellen genuinely cared about her employees. How could they not see it? she wondered. "I am the first to reach out to them and offer help," she said.

Ellen's way of demonstrating care was to ask, "What can I take off your plate?" when they faced personal challenges. In her mind, this was the most practical and respectful way to help—by giving them time and space to sort things out. She avoided asking about personal matters, not because she didn't care, but because she didn't want to intrude. She believed the best way to show concern was to lighten their workload, to step in where she could be useful.

However, her team interpreted this differently. To them, it seemed like she only cared about the work getting done, not about them as people.

Ellen had good intentions, and she genuinely cared about her team. But her behavior was not interpreted as she intended.

In this part of the book, we focus on evaluating whether our actions are producing the impact we intend. Are we leading in a way that reflects who we want to be? Are our efforts having the effect we hoped for—on people, outcomes, and relationships? This stage invites us to self-evaluate and step outside of our own perspective and ask, "Is it working? And if not, why not?"

To effectively evaluate, we must take a twofold approach: gaining feedback and pausing to assess. Seeking feedback allows us to see ourselves through the eyes of others, revealing blind spots we might not be aware of. My executive coaching clients have the privilege of working with an external, unbiased professional who conducts confidential 360° interviews to gather honest, comprehensive feedback. 360° interviews usually include multiple sources: peers, managers, subordinates, and sometimes customers or even their spouses. If you have the opportunity to gain 360° confidential feedback, don't hesitate, embrace it. Later in this chapter, I'll offer practical ways to seek honest feedback on your own.

At the same time, feedback alone isn't enough. We also need to pause regularly to self-assess the impact of our behavior. When we can ask ourselves, What's working? What's not? What adjustments can I make? sometimes we discover a misalignment between our intentions and the outcomes. Other times, we realize we've drifted from our values, or that what worked before no longer works now. These insights are not signs of failure, they're powerful invitations to grow.

By combining external feedback with intentional self-assessment, we develop a more complete picture of our impact. We shift from assumption to awareness, from defensiveness to possibility. The ongoing process of evaluation moves us closer to alignment—between what we believe, what we do, and what others experience.

Mind the Gap

We all want to be seen for who we truly are, for our good intentions, our effort, our heart. But the hard truth is that people don't experience us through our intentions. They experience us through our impact.

This disconnect between what we mean and how we're received is what's often called the intention vs. impact gap.

You might intend to be helpful but come across as controlling.

You might intend to be concise but come across as abrupt.

You might intend to empower but come across as uninvolved.

None of this means your intentions are wrong or that your behavior is inherently bad. But it does mean that your actions might not be landing the way you expect, and that awareness is the first step toward real alignment.

When we realize there's a gap between how we intended to show up and how we were actually experienced, it can feel deeply uncomfortable. Our instinct is often to explain or defend, "That's not what I meant." While offering context can be helpful, it doesn't erase the experience of the other person.

The goal isn't to invalidate your intention. It's to understand the gap, and take responsibility for your impact. Because your impact is what shapes trust, relationships, and results. And when there's a mismatch, it's not a failure. It's a signal. A chance to pause, reflect, and realign.

To begin uncovering possible intention vs. impact gaps, ask yourself:

- Where might my actions be misunderstood, despite good intentions?
- Am I assuming others just know what I mean or what I'm trying to do?
- When I've received surprising feedback, did I dismiss it with "But that's not what I meant"?
- How am I actively checking to see if my impact matches my intention?

You can also ask others:

- What's one thing I do that might come across differently than I intend?
- How do you experience me when I'm stressed or under pressure?
- What's something I've done that surprised you, positively or otherwise?

Recognizing the intention vs. impact gap helps you show up with more clarity, curiosity, and emotional intelligence. You stop assuming your message landed well and start checking in. You take responsibility not just for what you said or did, but how it was experienced. And that's the beginning of real growth.

Identifying Blind Spots and Expanding Self-Awareness

Understanding the intention vs. impact gap invites us to ask: What might others be seeing that we're not? Where are the blind spots we haven't yet uncovered?

Evaluating our impact isn't just about knowing what's working and what's not. It's also about uncovering what we don't yet see. This means moving what is hidden into the open and expanding our self-awareness. That process can be transformative. It helps us understand how others experience us and whether our intentions match our impact.

This is where the Johari Window becomes a valuable tool. Developed by Joseph Luft and Harrington Ingham, it highlights how self-awareness grows through both feedback and self-disclosure.[90] The model divides self-awareness into four quadrants:

1. **Open area (Arena):** Known to you and known to others. This is the space where communication flows freely, fostering trust and collaboration.
2. **Blind area:** Not known to you but known to others. This is where feedback becomes essential to uncover what we cannot see about ourselves.
3. **Hidden area (Façade):** Known to you but not known to others. Reducing this area involves self-disclosure, sharing more about ourselves to build deeper connections.
4. **Unknown area:** Not known to you and not known to others. This represents untapped potential and discoveries that can emerge over time.

FIGURE 6: The Johari Window, a visual representation of what you know about yourself and what others know about you.

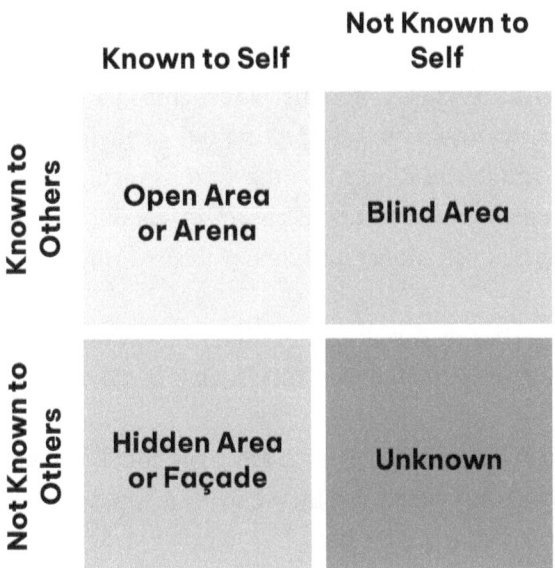

You want to expand the Open area, the part of you that is known to both yourself and others, because this is where trust, clarity, and collaboration thrive. The more others understand how you think, what you value, and how you work, the more effectively you can lead and connect. One way to grow this area is by reducing the Hidden area, which contains what you know about yourself but haven't shared with others. This might include your values, your concerns, as well as mistakes made. Sharing appropriately builds credibility and strengthens relationships.

In "Reflect," we focused on self-discovery and explored practices to uncover more of the Unknown area, the parts of ourselves we hadn't yet examined. Now, as we move into "Evaluate," we turn our attention to reducing the Blind area, what is known to others but not known to us, by seeking feedback from others. This process helps create alignment between how we see ourselves and how we are seen, enabling us to lead with greater impact and authenticity.

Admittedly, it requires courage to ask others how they experience us, but doing so can offer insights we simply can't access on our own.

As Chester Elton shared in our interview: "The greatest gift you can give someone is honest feedback delivered with care. When you ask for feedback, you invite others to hold up a mirror, helping you see what you can't see on your own."[91]

That mirror gives us clarity. It helps us recognize patterns we may not notice, reveals how others are interpreting our behavior, and shows us where a small change could lead to a big shift in results. When we pair this with reflection—those intentional pauses to ask ourselves what we're learning—we begin to see a more complete picture of who we are and how we lead.

Still, knowing that feedback matters doesn't always make it easy to receive. It can challenge how we see ourselves. It can feel personal. It can stir up emotion.

That's why in the next section, we'll focus on how to receive feedback well. We'll explore what makes it difficult, how to handle it skillfully, and how to stay open—even when it's hard.

The Art of Receiving Feedback

Receiving feedback is an art that requires openness, curiosity, and a willingness to grow. It's not just about listening; it's about engaging with the information provided as a vital resource for personal and professional development. When feedback comes your way, approach it with a growth mindset, seeing it as an opportunity to evolve rather than a judgment of your worth.

Why Receiving Feedback Is Hard

We long for people to accept us how we are. Receiving negative—hopefully constructive—feedback is hard; it sits at the intersection of our drive to learn and our desire to be accepted as we are.

Receiving feedback well is a layered process. You must engage skillfully in the conversation. You need to make thoughtful choices about how to use the information and what you're learning from it.

You must also manage your emotional triggers, and ultimately, be open enough to take in what's being shared and begin to see yourself in new ways.

How you show up in those moments, whether open or closed, curious or defensive, can make all the difference. That's where the idea of being above or below the line comes in.

Are You Above or Below the Line?

This concept is commonly used in organizational and personal development, especially when talking about accountability and mindset.

Being above the line means having an accountable mindset, being open, curious, committed to learning, and willing to take responsibility for your actions and their consequences. When you're above the line, you are receptive to feedback, eager to grow from mistakes, and focused on progress and possibility.

Being below the line, on the other hand, reflects a victim mindset. This includes being defensive, closed off to other perspectives, and more concerned with being right than with understanding, adapting, or finding solutions. People operating below the line tend to deflect responsibility, placing blame on circumstances or others rather than taking ownership of their actions and outcomes.

The idea of being above or below the line is closely related to the Johari Window and feedback. Operating above the line aligns with expanding the Open area of the Johari Window by seeking and incorporating feedback from others. Operating below the line often corresponds to remaining in the Blind or Hidden areas, resistant to feedback and personal growth.

Being above the line involves accountability, openness, and a growth mindset, while being below the line involves defensiveness, closed-mindedness, and a victim mindset. Recognizing and shifting from below the line to above the line behavior is crucial for your personal and professional development.

Above the Line

Mary, a Vice President of product management, considered herself a great listener. She was often called in to talk with difficult clients, hear their concerns about the product, and understand their needs. She was surprised when after a team meeting, her colleague, Gabe, approached her with some constructive feedback about her leadership style. He pointed out that Mary tended to dominate internal team discussions and sometimes overlooked input from quieter team members.

Mary paused to take it in. Instead of becoming defensive or dismissing Gabe's feedback, Mary listened attentively, thanked him for his honesty, and asked for specific examples to better understand his perspective. Mary could suddenly see that her internal behavior (toward her team), was different from her external behavior (toward their customers). She acknowledged that she might have been unintentionally overlooking valuable input and committed to making changes. Mary took Gabe's feedback as an opportunity for self-reflection and improvement, demonstrating her accountability and openness to learning.

Over the following weeks, Mary actively implemented strategies to encourage more participation from all team members, such as asking for input from quieter individuals and creating a more inclusive meeting environment. She started showing up for her team meetings the same way she did for her customer meetings. Her willingness to receive and act upon feedback not only strengthened her relationships with her team but also contributed to the overall success of their projects.

Below the Line

Jake, a sales manager, prided himself on being decisive and efficient. In meetings, he often interrupted others, dismissed ideas he disagreed with, and frequently cut discussions short to stay on track. While he believed he was keeping the team focused, others saw him as dismissive and impatient.

During his performance review, his manager, Lisa, provided him with feedback about his communication style, noting that it was affecting team morale. Several team members felt unheard or undervalued and were becoming increasingly disengaged.

Upon hearing this, Jake immediately pushed back. He insisted that his communication was clear and effective, and that his team members were simply overreacting. He pointed to external factors like workload and time pressure, arguing that he didn't have space for unnecessary discussion.

Despite Lisa's attempts to offer support and provide specific examples, Jake remained closed off. He viewed the feedback as a personal attack rather than a valuable perspective. He refused to acknowledge the impact of his actions, and ultimately, took no responsibility for the environment he was creating.

Lisa, frustrated and concerned, saw the toll his defensiveness was taking on the team. Productivity and morale continued to decline, and despite multiple efforts to help Jake course-correct, she eventually made the difficult decision to let him go.

Jake's inability to accept feedback not only hurt team morale, it stalled his own growth as a leader. Rather than exploring the effect of his behavior, he shut down the conversation and refused to engage.

When we are below the line, we fall into the common trap of defending our behaviors instead of examining their impact. We reject feedback, justify our actions, or look for someone else to blame.

Approach feedback when you are open, curious, committed to learning, and in an accountable mindset. When you are above the line, you're more likely to receive it with clarity and intention. Resist the urge to categorize feedback as good or bad, or to dismiss the giver.

When receiving negative feedback, we naturally tend to seek contradictory examples to the behavior mentioned. Fight this instinct and instead try to see where the feedback could be correct. Look for consistency rather than contradictory behavior.

I have often seen misunderstandings as both giver and receiver describe the impact of a behavior—they're describing the same behavior but interpreting it differently. In the case of Ellen, the software executive we discussed at the beginning of this chapter, those involved (Ellen and her team) were both describing the same thing; that is, Ellen's asking, "What can I take off your plate?" However, Ellen described it as a demonstration of care, while her team described it as, "She only cares about work."

Pause to identify the behavior described. If it is not clear, ask for examples. Is your passion perceived as overly emotional, or your straightforwardness as harshness? It's crucial to discern the impact of your behaviors separated from your intentions.

Take the time to consider if you have heard this feedback, or a version of it, in the past. Reflect on whether this feedback is a recurring theme. Even if you initially disagree, consider what elements might hold truth and what you might glean from this perspective.

Nobody is fond of receiving negative feedback. We don't want to hear that we are not perfect. It is natural for feedback to sometimes be overwhelming, particularly when it's unexpected. In these moments, pause to ask yourself four critical questions:

- What am I feeling?
- What's the story I'm telling myself?
- What's the actual feedback?
- And is my story distorting the feedback?

By answering these questions, you create space to process the feedback more thoughtfully. This simple act can shift you into a more open and balanced mindset, one that is better equipped to learn, grow, and respond with clarity.

Understanding your tendency to react to feedback is also key. Do you dismiss it, react defensively, or take time to absorb and respond? Being aware of these patterns can help you manage your responses more effectively.

But these reactions often aren't random, they're rooted in deeper emotional responses known as feedback triggers. These triggers can distort how we hear feedback and whether we're able to take it in constructively. Understanding them is essential if we want to respond to feedback with greater clarity, courage, and intention.

Navigating Feedback Triggers

In their insightful book, *Thanks for the Feedback: The Science and Art of Receiving Feedback Well*, Douglas Stone and Sheila Heen highlight that receiving feedback can be complicated by three types of triggers, each affecting our ability to hear and process feedback effectively.[92]

Truth Triggers: These are activated when the feedback you receive seems off the mark or just plain wrong. You might find yourself reacting defensively, instinctively rejecting the critique. The key to managing these kinds of triggers is to step back and assess the feedback with a lens of objectivity. Try to separate your emotions from the facts and evaluate the feedback on its merits, even if your initial impulse is to reject it. Instead of immediately dismissing the feedback, ask yourself: What could be true here?

Relationship Triggers: Sometimes, who says something matters as much as what they say. If feedback comes from someone you have mixed feelings about, it can skew how you receive their comments. It's helpful to disentangle your feelings about the individual from the feedback itself, allowing you to consider the feedback based on its own merits rather than your personal feelings towards the individual. Ask yourself, Would I react differently if someone else had given this feedback?

Identity Triggers: Feedback that hits a nerve about who you are or how you see yourself can be particularly painful. These triggers can provoke deep-seated fears about our identity and place in the world, often leading to feelings of being threatened or destabilized.

Identity feedback can make us feel as if we are losing our footing, questioning the narrative we've constructed about who we are and what our future might look like. For example, when Beth, a seasoned manager, received feedback that her team found her management style too authoritative and stifling, it contradicted her self-image as an empowering leader.

Feedback that challenges the self-image we hold and have worked hard to build can be disorienting. When our identity feels under attack, our instinctive response is to defend ourselves. This defense can manifest as a mental gearing up for a counterattack, where we might hastily dismiss the feedback or respond with hostility.

Jack, an experienced marketing manager, reacted defensively on receiving criticism that his latest campaign strategies were outdated and not resonating with younger demographics. He asserted that the critics didn't understand the broader strategy and his depth of experience. Perceiving this critical feedback as a threat to his identity as a cutting-edge marketer triggered a defensive posture to protect his professional self-image.

In navigating identity triggers, it's crucial to step back and reflect. Recognize that while the feedback may feel personal, it often reflects specific behaviors or situations, not your entire character or worth. By dissecting the feedback and focusing on actionable items, rather than viewing it as an indictment of your identity, you can transform potentially destabilizing comments into opportunities for genuine growth and self-enhancement. This approach not only helps stabilize your emotional responses but also fosters resilience and adaptability and enriches your professional development journey.

Navigating these triggers involves recognizing them as they happen and consciously choosing to engage with feedback in a way that fosters growth and learning, rather than defensiveness or denial.

Don't Shoot the Messenger

One of the most memorable experiences I've had with identity feedback didn't happen in a professional setting, but in a deeply personal one. Many years ago, when my daughter was young, I received a call from a friend that I'll never forget. "Miki," she said, "I'm calling you because I know you'll tell me the truth." "Of course," I replied, bracing myself. "Is my son, David, difficult?" she asked.

She explained that another friend had reached out to say their child no longer wanted to play with David, he was just too difficult. My friend was looking for honesty, and in that moment, I gave her exactly that. I told her, as gently as I could (or so I thought, though in hindsight I could have probably softened the message), that yes, David could be a challenging playmate. I don't remember all the details of what I said, but I went on to explain why.

What I *do* remember, though, is what happened next. She didn't speak to me for weeks. She shot the messenger. At the time, I felt a little indignant. She asked for the truth, didn't she? But the truth is, I had missed something important.

What I hadn't considered was the impact my words would have on her. She was a devoted, thoughtful mother who took great care in raising her son. Hearing anything negative about him wasn't just feedback about David, it felt like feedback about her as a mother. My honesty, though well-intentioned, had unintentionally rocked her identity.

That day, I learned two things that have stayed with me ever since. First, even when someone explicitly asks for honest feedback, it's crucial to deliver it with care and compassion. Words can land harder than we intend, especially when they touch on something deeply personal.

Second, I learned what it feels like to be the messenger who gets shot. It's not easy being the one to deliver feedback that someone may not want to hear, no matter how kindly you phrase it.

Feedback is powerful. It can help us see blind spots, make meaningful changes, and grow. But it can also sting—especially when it touches a core part of who we are. That's what makes identity feedback so hard to receive. It can feel like a judgment not just of what we did, but of who we are or aspire to be. Understanding this emotional weight is essential if we want to receive feedback with openness. When we recognize our reaction as a natural defense of our identity, we can begin to pause, reflect, and engage more thoughtfully with what's being offered.

Don't Overlook Positive Feedback

Another natural way our mind works, as we discussed in the "Reflect" chapter, is to focus on the negative, an ancient survival mechanism wired to protect us from threats. While it's tempting to zero in on what we need to fix, positive feedback is just as important. It highlights your strengths, the actions and behaviors that are already making a positive impact. When someone tells you what you're doing well, don't brush it off. Pause and consider: What was it about that behavior that worked? How can I do more of it? Positive feedback isn't just affirmation, it's a signal to lean into what's effective. Treat it as a roadmap for growth, not just encouragement.

The Only Response When Receiving Feedback

When you receive feedback, praise or critique, simply listen and express gratitude. As Marshall Goldsmith always says, there is only one response to feedback: Thank you. Thank the giver.

Ask clarifying questions like, "How can I improve?" or "What might be getting in my way?" Make sure you fully grasp the expectations set for you. This moment isn't just about acceptance; it's about active engagement.

Think of the 3 Rs: **Receive, Reflect, Respond.**

- **Receive** the feedback with openness. Try not to interrupt or defend yourself in the moment. Just take it in.

- **Reflect** on it thoughtfully. Sit with the information, separate your emotional response from the substance, and ask yourself what truth might be in it.
- **Respond** with intention. Decide what action, if any, you want to take. This might mean making changes, asking for help, or simply clarifying expectations moving forward.

The Right Source Matters

Feedback is invaluable for personal and professional growth, but its value depends significantly on the source. Not all feedback should carry equal weight.

As organizational psychologist Tasha Eurich points out in her book, *Insight*, what we need most are *loving critics*—people who care about us, want to see us succeed, and are willing to tell us the hard truths. They combine honesty with compassion. Their feedback doesn't come from a place of judgment or superiority, but from genuine care and a desire to help us grow. Because we trust them, we're more likely to take what they say to heart.[93]

Loving critics speak from direct observation, not vague assumptions. They name specific behaviors, not your character. And they've earned your trust over time.

As I began writing this book, I reached out to a mentor, someone I admire, a successful author who had written several books. I was eager to learn from their experience. They were generous with their time and their honesty. They told me, quite bluntly, that writing a book is hard. Most books don't sell. They rarely make money. And then came the real punch: they told me I couldn't write.

They advised that if I really wanted to do this, I should hire a ghostwriter, just as they had done. They hadn't read a single word I'd written, a blog, or even glanced at a draft of my book. Their feedback was based purely on assumptions, their own experiences and not on any observation of my writing or voice. And still, it stung. I had reached out in good faith, and their words rattled me.

I gave myself space to sit with the feedback. And as I processed it, something became clear: while this person cared about me and wanted me to succeed, they didn't meet the full criteria of a loving critic. Yes, they were honest. Yes, they wanted the best for me. But their feedback lacked one essential ingredient—direct observation. They hadn't seen my work. Their assessment came from their own lens, their experience, and perhaps their limitations.

So I took a step back. I shared their comments with a few trusted, loving critics in my life, people who know my writing, my values, and my voice. I listened to their input, and ultimately, I made my own call.

And here we are.

I wrote this book. And not only do I believe it is worth reading, but others, those who've read early drafts, have told me it's thoughtful, well-written, and genuinely helpful. I'm so glad I didn't let one person's assumptions silence my story. Sometimes, while being open to the right mirrors to help us grow, the most important feedback to trust is the quiet confidence within.

Of course, feedback doesn't always come from people we consider loving critics. Sometimes it comes from our bosses. That feedback can be harder to interpret. It might feel loaded, tied to performance reviews, promotions, or organizational politics. Leaders may have good intentions, but they also have their own goals, pressures, and blind spots. Their feedback might be shaped by their priorities as much as your performance. That's why it's especially important to pause, assess the context, and when needed get a second perspective.

Choose your feedback sources wisely. When feedback doesn't quite align with your perspective, seeking a second and third opinion can be an effective way to gain clarity. It's essential to approach this process with an open mind, and resist the urge to dismiss feedback simply because it feels uncomfortable or challenging. At the same time, assess the credibility and intent of the source.

As Dorie Clark emphasized when we spoke, it's important to not only seek feedback from the right people but also discern when feedback should be ignored, or even rebuked. She explained,

> I think the most important piece of advice is just understanding that feedback from the right people should be treasured, and feedback from the wrong people should be ignored. Sometimes, not even

ignored, sometimes rebuked, because some people are giving you feedback you never asked for. It's insulting. Who thinks they have permission to tell you that? Obviously, if someone's your boss or supervising you, it's their job. But if it's a stranger, someone on the internet, or a person with their own ax to grind or agenda, you shouldn't pay attention. In fact, sometimes you need to push back because it's just rude.

That said, the flip side is that we should open our hearts to feedback from people we respect, people we know have our best interests at heart, and people with sufficient expertise to provide accurate, actionable advice. Feedback from the right source, taken in a non-defensive way, is a magnificent opportunity for growth.[94]

This highlights a key principle: feedback is only as valuable as the person providing it. Prioritize insights from those who understand your goals, have your best interests at heart, and possess the expertise to offer constructive input. Conversely, protect your mental energy by disregarding unsolicited or ill-intentioned critiques that serve no purpose in your development.

When choosing whom to ask for additional insights, be intentional. Are you seeking someone who will reflect your views back to you, a supportive mirror, or are you ready to engage with someone who might challenge your assumptions and offer an honest mirror? My friend, who reached out to me for feedback about her son, was looking for an honest mirror. However, as I later realized, she may not have been fully prepared for what she heard.

It's important to strike the right balance. Seek input from your staunchest allies, those who know you well and can cheer you on, and also from those who aren't afraid to challenge your thinking. The people who push back, ask hard questions, or offer a different perspective can often pinpoint areas of potential growth that others might overlook.

By welcoming diverse perspectives, especially from those willing to voice disagreement, you open yourself to deeper insights. This readiness to embrace even uncomfortable feedback can turn defensive moments into powerful opportunities for reflection, development, and meaningful growth.

We all yearn to be accepted for who we are, and feedback can challenge this desire, sometimes stirring strong emotions. Navigating feedback well is not about suppressing these emotions. It is about building the resilience and flexibility to pause, reflect, and respond with intention. Engaging skillfully with feedback, managing emotional triggers, and being open to seeing ourselves through others' eyes helps us deepen self-awareness and strengthen the way we show up for others.

Feedback requires courage—the courage to ask, to hear, and to grow. It also takes courage to give feedback. The most meaningful conversations are often the hardest to start, but they are also the ones that create real change, both for ourselves and for those we lead.

Don't Avoid the Difficult Conversations

Brené Brown's book *Dare to Lead* discusses the cultural norm of using niceness and politeness as strategies to avoid uncomfortable conversations. It highlights how this avoidance can result in a lack of clarity, diminishing trust, and a rise in problematic behaviors within organizations. The reluctance to engage in difficult dialogues often leads to indirect communication methods like gossip or back-channeling, which undermine the integrity of team dynamics. Brown's research reveals that avoiding tough conversations is the top behavior that limits effective leadership. She champions the courage to engage directly, arguing that true leadership involves facing these challenges head-on, thereby fostering a culture of transparency and genuine interaction.[95]

In his book *Hidden Potential*, Adam Grant expands on this idea by distinguishing between being polite and being truly kind, especially in the context of giving feedback. Politeness often involves tempering one's words to avoid upsetting others, resulting in vague and ineffective communication. Kindness, on the other hand, involves a commitment to constructive feedback that supports growth and improvement. This type of feedback, rooted in honesty and empathy, respects the recipient's potential for growth, pushing them toward personal and professional development.[96]

Garry Ridge takes this one step further by reframing feedback as an integral part of leadership's purpose. He asserts:

> Most leaders protect their own comfort zones at the expense of other people's development because they don't want to have

difficult conversations. True leadership is about helping others step into the best version of themselves. Feedback, when given constructively and with care, is one of the most powerful tools to achieve that.[97]

I see this often in my work. In 360° interviews and coaching conversations, leaders will tell me exactly where they think a team member or colleague needs to grow. But when I ask, "Have you shared this with them?" the answer is often, "No." They assume the person either knows already, wouldn't take it well, or that it's not their place. But if we withhold feedback that could help someone improve, we're not being kind, we're playing it safe. Growth starts with awareness, and awareness often starts with a conversation someone had the courage to begin.

People often ask what helps me have these difficult conversations, whether as a coach or when I held leadership roles. My answer is always the same: I remind myself that I'm here to help the other person grow. That this conversation, however hard, is a service. What gives me the courage is knowing that my message might make a difference in their development. It's why I always begin tough feedback conversations with a simple truth: I care about you and your success. That's why I'm sharing this.

Feedback is not about fault-finding. It's about belief. Belief in someone's capacity to grow. When you give feedback from that place, it changes how it's received and how it's felt.

Together, these insights from Brown, Grant, Ridge, and everyday leadership moments underscore a pivotal shift in how we approach feedback. Emphasizing the importance of courage over comfort and kindness over mere politeness, they advocate for a leadership style that not only embraces but also necessitates direct and constructive feedback. Ridge's mantra of leadership as a coaching role, "I'm not here to mark your paper; I'm here to help you get an A," highlights that feedback is a gift of growth, given to empower and uplift others.

Treat feedback as a gift, one that reflects your commitment to someone's success and your belief in their ability to improve. By engaging in these honest, sometimes difficult conversations, you foster trust, drive progress, and create an environment where individuals and teams can evolve, thrive, and deliver their best work.

One of the most effective ways to foster a feedback-rich culture is to start by modeling it yourself. When leaders openly seek feedback, they demonstrate humility, courage, and a genuine commitment to growth. This act of vulnerability invites others to do the same. It sends a clear message: feedback isn't something to be feared, but something to be welcomed. By setting this example, you help build an environment where honest conversations are not just tolerated but encouraged, where growth becomes a shared value and feedback a shared responsibility.

Gain Feedback

The most effective question to ask when seeking feedback is, "How can I do better?" This question is powerful because it is future-oriented and solicits advice rather than criticism.

As Chester Elton emphasized in our interview:

> When you ask someone, 'How can I do better?' you open up a space for trust and clarity. This one question can transform relationships because it shows you care, you're willing to learn, and you're humble enough to make changes.[98]

This practice of asking for feedback isn't just helpful, it's one of the defining habits of the most self-aware people. In her research for *Insight*, Tasha Eurich identified a rare group she calls "self-aware unicorns." These individuals are exceptional not only in understanding themselves (internal self-awareness), but also in understanding how they are perceived by others (external self-awareness). And what sets them apart isn't just insight, it's intention. They don't passively wait for feedback; they actively seek it, especially from those who will tell them the truth with care.

Eurich found that these unicorns share several key behaviors. They ask "What?" instead of "Why?"—as in, "What can I learn from this?" or "What can I do differently?" They treat self-awareness as a skill, not a trait, and they work at it consistently. They invite feedback from loving critics, embrace discomfort, and balance confidence with humility. They're not perfect, but they're persistent.[99]

We may not all be unicorns, but we can adopt the habits that make them special.

By approaching feedback with curiosity rather than defensiveness, you signal to others that you value their perspective and are committed to growth. This mindset not only expands your self-awareness but also deepens trust and strengthens relationships. Ellen's experience, discussed earlier, illustrates this perfectly: without candid feedback, she would have remained unaware of her blind spots, continuing to create unintended perceptions.

Here are some variations of these questions that can be tailored to different contexts:

- How can I be a better _____? (manager, partner, colleague).
- What are the key actions I can take to improve my communication with you/the team?
- In what ways can I better support your work?
- What can I do to enhance our collaboration and drive better results?
- What are one or two things I could do differently to improve my performance?

In a workshop with Marshall Goldsmith, he asked us this question directly. We had to text someone, our partner, manager, or colleague, asking, "How can I be a better ____?" I texted my husband: "How can I be a better partner?" and his response was, "Laugh more." I am quite serious. I promised to work on it.

The husband of the woman next to me said: "Be more affectionate." She looked at me perplexed and said: "But he is so affectionate. He kisses and hugs me all the time." Then she said "Oh," as realization struck: he's the affectionate one, but not so much her. There were funny responses like, "Do you want it in an Excel or PPT format?" But there was one that changed someone's life. The response was, "We need to talk when you get home." This one text opened a much-needed conversation and averted a divorce.

By framing your feedback request with "How can I do better?" or a variation of it, you invite others to focus on constructive, actionable insights. This approach encourages feedback that feels supportive and forward-looking, transforming what could be an uncomfortable moment into a productive and trust-building dialogue. To whom can you direct this question?

You can also use the version mentioned in the "Operationalize" chapter: "What should I stop, start, do more of, or do less of?"

Or try simple alternatives, such as:

- What's one thing I should keep doing?
- What's one thing I should do differently?
- What's one thing you wish I knew?

There is no one right way to ask for feedback. What matters is creating an environment where people feel safe to share honestly. These questions can be asked in one-on-one conversations, or through more structured approaches. Anonymous feedback forms, like Google Forms or Microsoft Forms, can be quick and effective. You can also use feedback walls, physical with sticky notes or digital with tools like Miro or MURAL, inviting people to share what you should start, stop, or continue doing. Another option is to ask a trusted peer to speak with a few colleagues confidentially and summarize common themes. This takes the pressure off individuals while giving you valuable insights. Working with a coach who conducts 360° interviews, simplifies this. As an impartial third party, coaches are able to create a safe and confidential space for people to share their feedback anonymously.

Whichever method you choose, the goal is the same: to make it easier for others to speak up, and for you to hear perspectives you might otherwise miss.

And remember, always receive feedback with openness and curiosity. Even when it's hard to hear, respond with a simple, "Thank you." This signals humility, builds trust, and helps foster a culture of learning and continuous improvement.

→ YOUR TURN: Uncover Your Blind Spots

Be curious about how others see you. Seek to uncover the blind spots that may be holding you back. Feedback is one of the most powerful tools for growth, but only if you stay open to what you hear. Start by identifying your loving critics.

Who are the people in your life who care about you, see you clearly, and are willing to tell you the truth with compassion?

Now, get specific:

- Whom will you reach out to for feedback?
- What questions will you ask? (Consider "How can I do better?" or "What's one thing I should do differently?")
- What approach will you use? (One-on-one conversation, anonymous form, peer-facilitated summary?)
- How will you prepare yourself to truly hear what they say?
- How will you remind yourself that feedback, even when uncomfortable, is a gift?
- What positive feedback did you receive? How can you amplify that strength or apply it more broadly?

Go ahead. Be brave. Seek the feedback. Then take a moment to reflect—what surprised you, what affirmed you, and what will you do next?

From Feedback to Impact

You've received feedback. Maybe you sought it out, or maybe it came unexpectedly. Either way, it takes courage to listen, reflect, and consider what comes next.

Often, employees in organizations are provided with feedback gathered through surveys, shared in performance reviews, or delivered directly by their manager. All too often, they are left wondering, What do I do with this? If you are working with a coach, they can help you identify key insights, highlight where and how to amplify your strengths, and develop clear, actionable steps to address areas for improvement. They can help you move forward with intention and make progress.

Feedback is not helpful merely for the sake of feedback. The real power of feedback lies in its ability to drive change. Insight is only the beginning. Turning it into meaningful action requires clarity and commitment.

Here is a helpful approach you can use, a concept borrowed from business strategy: Pivot or Persist.

Persist

Use this strategy when feedback affirms that something you're doing is working. This is the feedback we're often quick to overlook—positive comments that feel nice in the moment but get dismissed as not needing attention. But this kind of insight holds incredible value. It tells you what to keep doing, and more importantly, what to do more of.

In Chapter 2, "Operationalize," we talked about asking, "What should I do more of?" Feedback can help answer that question. Persisting is how you put that answer into practice. When feedback highlights a strength or an effective behavior, see it as an opportunity to build on what's working. Keep showing up, refining, and reinforcing those behaviors to amplify your impact.

Think of Marc and Joe, from "Operationalize." Marc took his strength in relationship-building within the organization and extended it outside his organization to expand his network. Joe protected time for strategic thinking so he could guide his startup with greater clarity. Persisting means leaning into what's already working—and doing it with greater focus and intention.

Pivot

While Persist is about building on what's working, Pivot is about making a change. Pivot when feedback reveals an undesirable behavior or a gap between your intention and the impact you're having. This doesn't always require a major overhaul. Sometimes, small shifts lead to meaningful results.

A good next step is to identify the specific behavior the feedback is pointing to.

For example, if it's about how you run meetings, what exactly needs attention? Is it that you speak too much and leave little room for others? Is the meeting unfocused? If the feedback is about communication, is your tone coming across as harsh under pressure? Do you over-explain or leave out necessary details? The clearer you are about the behavior, the easier it becomes to take action.

Once you've identified the behavior, pause to reflect.

If you're Persisting:
- What strength was named in the feedback?
- Where else could I apply this strength?
- How could I turn this into a consistent, recognizable behavior?
- How might doubling down here increase my impact or reach?
- Am I being intentional about reinforcing this strength with others?

If you're Pivoting:
- Is this feedback pointing to an outcome I didn't intend?
- Is there a gap between how I see myself and how I'm experienced by others?
- Where else might this behavior be showing up—in other relationships or environments?
- What is the ripple effect of this behavior on my team, my work, or my goals?

In either case:
- How does this feedback align (or conflict) with my values?
- What change would help me show up more like the leader I want to be?

Let's look at three of my clients and how we used the whole CORE process to help them Pivot or Persist. In each case, the journey began with Evaluate, feedback received through 360° interviews, manager input, or team observations. The feedback signaled something could improve or wasn't working as intended. From there, each person moved through Clarify to reconnect with their values, Operationalize to translate intentions into action, and Reflect to examine internal beliefs or assumptions that might be getting in their way. Finally, they returned to Evaluate to check whether their shifts were having the desired impact. Feedback was gathered from key stakeholders throughout the process, reinforcing that growth is not a one-time insight but an ongoing cycle of awareness, adjustment, and alignment.

Andrea: Amplifying a Strength (Persist)

Andrea, a rising star at a tech company, had recently joined the executive leadership team. Her 360° feedback was outstanding—she was well-respected, trusted, and consistently brought valuable insights to the table. What stood out most was how often people said, "I want to hear more from her." When Andrea spoke, others listened. She offered thoughtful, often brilliant contributions. The feedback wasn't about fixing a problem, it was an invitation to build on a strength. Her opportunity was to do more of what was already working.

We started by clarifying her core values. Andrea deeply valued making a positive impact on those around her. Once she connected the feedback she received to this value, something clicked: holding back wasn't humility, it was a missed opportunity to contribute more meaningfully.

Together, we operationalized what stepping up would look like. Andrea identified the key moments when her voice would matter most and practiced specific behaviors to step in with confidence.

Reflecting, Andrea realized that she often held back when more senior leaders were in the room. In those moments, she spoke up less, uncertain about whether her contributions were welcome. But now, knowing that they wanted to hear more from her, she began to see things differently. We identified specific areas where she added clear value, how her insights complemented others' perspectives, and why she was invited into those conversations in the first place. Reframing the reason she was at the table, and the unique lens she brought, gave her the confidence to speak up more often.

Andrea evaluated her impact by checking in with members of the executive leadership team, asking if her presence felt different, more visible, more influential. The result? Andrea's leadership presence expanded, and she became an even more valued member of the executive team.

Rob: A Small Pivot with Big Results

Rob received feedback that he seemed disengaged in cross-functional meetings. His intent was to create space for others, but the impact was that he came across as disinterested.

We began with clarifying. Rob defined the kind of leader he wanted to be—collaborative, engaged, and supportive, without overshadowing others. Once he understood the gap between his intent and how others experienced him, he was ready to make a shift.

Next, we moved to operationalizing. Rob identified a few simple behaviors to help him show up more actively: offering verbal affirmations, asking clarifying questions, and contributing more visibly in discussions.

As he reflected, Rob recognized that he was making assumptions, believing people understood the intent behind his quietness. He realized he needed to redefine what it means to be a collaborative and engaged colleague. Instead of stepping back, he began to envision what it would look like to step in. Together, we crafted a new equation: Showing up = Being seen and heard. It wasn't enough to be present; real engagement required both presence and participation.

To evaluate, Rob gathered informal feedback from his peers. The response was clear. People saw him as more present, more open, and more engaged. A small pivot led to a noticeable shift in how he was perceived.

Leah: Setting Boundaries to Lead with Integrity (Pivot)

Leah, a leader at a fast-paced tech company, was well-liked and highly responsive. But in her 360° feedback, one consistent theme emerged: she was stretched too thin. She had taken on too many commitments, and her tendency to say yes to everything was beginning to affect her follow-through. Leah felt overwhelmed and frustrated, but also guilty at the thought of letting others down.

We began with clarifying. Leah identified what kind of leader she wanted to be: a reliable, values-driven leader who modeled clarity, focus, and follow-through. That vision helped her see that constantly saying yes was getting in the way of her desired impact.

To operationalize her new vision of herself, she started practicing new behaviors: pausing before committing, saying no, setting clearer boundaries around her time, and creating space for higher-priority work. She also created a weekly review ritual to plan and protect time for strategic work.

On reflecting, we uncovered Leah's limiting belief: "If I say no, I'll let people down and they won't respect me." That internal narrative had driven her people-pleasing behavior for years. We reframed it to: "When I set boundaries, I protect my effectiveness and earn respect by being intentional and dependable." That shift helped her quiet the guilt and lead with more clarity.

To evaluate, Leah began checking in with her team, peers, and her manager to assess how the changes were landing. She was surprised to hear that others saw her as more focused, more present, and more effective, not less helpful.

→ YOUR TURN: Turn Feedback into Action

Think of one piece of feedback you've received recently. It could be something that stung or something that felt affirming.

Pause and consider:

- What specific behavior is this feedback pointing to?
- Does this call for a pivot—a meaningful shift in how you show up?
- Or is this a chance to persist—to reinforce and build on a strength?
- How does this feedback align with your values?
- What is one small step you could take to move this insight into action?

And now, who can help you stay on track?

The Role of Stakeholders in Your Growth Journey

Stakeholders play a pivotal role in ensuring the changes you're making create the impact you desire. These are the individuals who will hold you accountable, provide valuable feedback, and offer insights on how your new behaviors are perceived. The concept of stakeholder involvement is central to Marshall Goldsmith's Stakeholder Centered Coaching, a methodology that emphasizes their essential role in leadership development.[100]

Stakeholders are typically those within your work environment, peers, direct reports, managers, and sometimes even clients, who are affected by or can influence your behavior. They provide regular feedback and "feedforward" (future-focused suggestions, advice) to help leaders, like you, achieve your goals. Stakeholders are chosen based on their interactions with you, their connection to your development goal, and their willingness to support your growth.

For example, consider the three executives above:

- Andrea, working on speaking up more in executive meetings, included members of the executive leadership team.
- Leah, working on setting boundaries, included both direct reports and peers as her stakeholders.
- Rob, focused on improving cross-functional communication, engaged peers from other departments.

By actively involving stakeholders and regularly reaching out to them for feedback and feedforward, you ensure that your efforts are grounded in real-world insights, driving meaningful progress.

The involvement of stakeholders enhances leadership development in several ways:

- **Feedback for awareness:** Stakeholders provide insights into how your actions are perceived, allowing you to identify and adjust behaviors to better align with your goals.
- **Feedforward for growth:** Unlike feedback, which focuses on the past, feedforward offers constructive suggestions for future improvement, helping you plan actionable steps.
- **Building relationships:** Regular check-ins strengthen trust and respect, demonstrating your commitment to growth.
- **Changing perceptions:** Consistent engagement with stakeholders allows them to witness and affirm your progress, reshaping outdated or biased views.

This process not only drives your development but also fosters a culture of continuous improvement within your organization.

Changing Perceptions to Cement Change

Leadership change doesn't just require new behaviors, it requires shifting how others perceive you. Stakeholders play a crucial role in this process by observing and affirming your progress over time. By proactively seeking their feedback, you help them notice and appreciate your efforts, even as you navigate setbacks.

For example, if you've been labeled a micromanager in the past, those perceptions may linger despite your progress. Regular, intentional check-ins with stakeholders invite them to reassess these entrenched views, building awareness of your growth and reinforcing your commitment to change.

As Marshall Goldsmith famously says, "Change is a contact sport."[101] It requires active participation, meaningful engagement, and persistence. Leadership development doesn't happen in isolation; it's a collaborative journey involving feedback, accountability, and a willingness to listen and adapt. By fully engaging with your stakeholders and aligning your actions with your core values, you create a dynamic process of growth that benefits not just you but everyone you lead.

→ YOUR TURN: Engage Your Stakeholders

Now that you've identified the change you're working on, who can help you stay accountable and offer perspective along the way?

Whom will you regularly reach out to? Marshall Goldsmith recommends checking in with your stakeholders at least once a month. Think about the people who interact with you on a regular basis, those who are impacted by your behavior or who can observe your growth. Also consider whose perception of you matters most right now and who needs to see your progress.

Stakeholders are not just feedback providers. They are partners in your growth process.

Reflect and take action:

- Whom will you invite to be part of your stakeholder group?
- How will you share the shift you're working on with them?
- What will you ask them to observe or give feedback on?

- How will you invite both feedback ("How did I do this past month?") and feedforward ("What suggestions or advice do you have for how I can keep improving?")?
- How will you thank them and let them know their feedback is helping?

Choose at least two people and take the first step. Reach out, explain what you're working on, and ask for their partnership. Let them know their insight matters and that their observations are helping you grow and increase your impact.

Seeing yourself through others' eyes can be one of the most powerful ways to uncover blind spots and deepen your self-awareness. Ideally, the feedback you've received has helped you understand how your actions are experienced by others, where your intentions may not have matched your impact, and what adjustments could strengthen your leadership.

Don't ignore the positives—what you are doing well, where your impact is aligned with your intentions, and how you can amplify that impact moving forward.

Now it's time to turn inward. Self-evaluation is your chance to pause, take stock of your progress, and consider how far you've come. What changes have you made? What's working? What needs more attention?

In the next section, you'll explore practical ways to assess your growth, and decide what comes next.

Time to Self-Evaluate

You've clarified your values, set intentional actions, reflected on what may hold you back, and gathered feedback. Now, it's time to step back and ask yourself: How am I doing? Have I made meaningful progress? Are my efforts having the impact I hoped for?

Evaluating your progress isn't just a checkbox exercise, it's a practice of conscious leadership. It brings together external insights and internal reflection so you can learn, recalibrate, and continue growing. Here's how to make that reflection practical and actionable:

Start with Alignment

Progress is most fulfilling when it is anchored in what you stand for. Return to the foundation: Clarify. The changes you've made are most meaningful when they reflect who you are and move you closer to the person and leader you want to be.

Ask yourself:

- On a scale of 1–10, how well are my actions reflecting my core values?
- Do my goals still feel aligned with the person and leader I want to become?
- Am I spending energy in ways that support my priorities?
- Has it been a while since I last clarified my values and priorities? Do I need to revisit or refine what those are now?

Realignment is a sign of growth. It means you're checking in and course-correcting, not just moving forward blindly.

Behavior Tracking

Start with your own data, what you're doing day to day.

Track the behaviors you're working on. Use a journal, spreadsheet, or even a quick note on your phone to log how often you're practicing the changes you've committed to. You can also look back at your calendar or schedule. How you spend your time is one of the clearest reflections of your priorities and behaviors in action.

Ask yourself:

- What specific behaviors am I trying to shift or reinforce?
- Am I doing them consistently?
- What new habits have I formed or started to form?
- What adjustments or experiments helped me gain traction?
- When did I show up the way I wanted to, and when did I fall short?
- What patterns or obstacles do I notice?
- Does my calendar reflect the leader I want to be?

This kind of intentional tracking turns awareness into evidence. It helps you recognize progress, spot trends, and adjust your approach to stay on track. Over time, you'll begin to see whether your efforts are turning into habits, and whether those habits are supporting the leader you aspire to become.

Daily or Weekly Self-Questions

As discussed in the "Operationalize" chapter, Marshall Goldsmith's Daily Questions can serve as a powerful accountability anchor. In the Evaluate stage, they also become a meaningful tool for reflection and progress tracking.

Goldsmith's method involves asking yourself a series of questions each day, all beginning with, "Did I do my best to..." and rating your effort on a scale of 1 to 10. These aren't about outcomes, they're about effort. The goal is to track consistency, intention, and personal commitment over time.[102]

If you're not already using this practice, consider trying it. Choose a few questions aligned with your goals and values:

- Did I do my best to empower someone today?
- Did I do my best to stay present in conversations?
- Did I do my best to act in alignment with my values?
- Did I do my best to reflect on feedback and apply what I've learned?
- Did I do my best to manage my energy and attention intentionally?

Rate yourself from 1 to 10 at the end of each day or week, and over time, look for trends. Where are you making progress? Where are you putting in effort but not seeing results yet? What might need to shift?

If you've already picked up the Daily Questions habit during the Operationalize phase, now is the time to go back and reflect on your answers. Are your scores improving? Are your efforts becoming more consistent? What do you notice about your growth?

Outcome Metrics

Your behaviors shape results. While not all impact can be measured in numbers, outcomes still matter. According to your role and the behavior change you are working on, look at a range of indicators to evaluate whether your shifts are making a difference. Look at both formal data (such as KPIs, performance reviews, surveys, or business results) and informal signs (such as more open communication, fewer misunderstandings, or stronger trust). These are all indicators of whether your new approach is making a meaningful difference and creating the ripple effect you intended.

Consider tracking:

- **Quality of relationships and communication:** Notice whether interactions feel more open, trusting, and respectful, and whether difficult conversations are being handled more effectively.
- **Team morale, retention, and engagement survey results:** Monitor whether people are staying longer, expressing greater satisfaction, or feeling more connected to the team or mission.
- **Formal feedback received over time:** Look at trends in 360° feedback or performance reviews. Is feedback revealing that you are making progress toward your goals? Are recurring themes showing signs of improvement or reinforcement?
- **Cross-functional collaboration and partnerships:** Pay attention to how often and how well you're working across teams. Are partnerships smoother, more productive, or more strategic?
- **Consistency and effectiveness of performance:** Track whether your team or personal results are improving—are you meeting goals more reliably, producing higher-quality work, or contributing more value?
- **Client, customer, or external partner feedback:** Review any feedback from outside your team. Are people experiencing you or your work differently? Is trust or satisfaction increasing?

Which one or two of these metrics make the most sense for you to focus on right now? Choose what's most relevant to your role, goals, and the behavior you're working to shift—and check in with it regularly.

→ YOUR TURN: Self Evaluate

You don't need to answer every question or capture every insight perfectly. But don't skip this moment.

It's easy to read through the pages, nod along, and move on. But real growth happens when you pause and do the work. This is your opportunity to step back and self-evaluate, not just in your head, but in a way that makes your progress visible and real.

So take a breath. Make space. Use this time to reflect on where you are right now.

- Where are your actions aligned with who you want to be?
- What are you proud of?
- What habits are starting to take root?
- How is your impact landing, with others and with yourself?
- What have you learned about your mindset, your patterns, your leadership?
- What strengths have you identified, tapped into, or developed?
- What surprised you about this process?
- What feels like the next right step? The next milestone?

Show up with honesty and curiosity. Make this moment count. And remember, this isn't just about what you've achieved. It's about the growth and confidence you've gained along the way. Just like climbing a mountain, the journey itself is as transformative as reaching the summit.

Walking the Talk: Becoming the Person I Wanted to Be

When I set the goal to live a more active life, I decided to take on what felt like an impossible challenge: climbing Mount Kilimanjaro, the highest peak in Africa. As I reflected back, it wasn't just about getting fit. It was about proving to myself that I could achieve something extraordinary. I needed to know I could take on big things—anything I set my mind to.

Reaching the summit gave me more than a sense of accomplishment. It renewed my confidence and reminded me that I could tackle challenges, no matter how daunting. The ripple effects were immediate:

- My husband shared his renewed respect for my determination.
- I felt unstoppable, ready to take on new goals.

And it didn't stop there. After returning home, I took up running. I started completing 5K and 10K races regularly, something I had never imagined myself enjoying. On the toughest runs, I remind myself:

- I can do this.
- I've done way harder things.
- This is thirty minutes, not eighteen hours.

For the first time in my life, running became meditative. I missed it when I couldn't go. I even ran in freezing Boston winters, much to my husband's surprise. "Who is this person?" he asked. I sometimes wondered that too, but in the best way possible. This was me becoming the person I wanted to be.

What started as a challenge became a habit, woven into my days, part of my rhythm. With each run, I wasn't just staying active. I was reinforcing a new identity, a new way of being.

The following year, I set my sights on another adventure: trekking the Manaslu Circuit in Nepal with my son. It was three weeks of breathtaking beauty in the Himalayas. More than the physical challenge, it was an opportunity to live my values, leading an active life, exploring the world, and sharing quality time with my family. I felt so grateful that, at twenty-five, my son wanted to share this journey with me.

This growing confidence didn't just shape my physical habits. It had a ripple effect across other areas of my life. Bit by bit, I began to see myself differently, not only as someone who could tackle physical challenges, but as someone ready to own her voice and her purpose more fully.

It gave me the courage to pursue executive coaching not as a side practice, but as the work I knew I was meant to do. And it gave me the confidence to take on this book, to believe that I have a message worth sharing, and that sharing it might help others. That belief didn't come all at once. It was built, just like the rest of this journey, through effort, reflection, and the willingness to keep showing up.

This was me not only becoming the person I wanted to be, but also the professional I wanted to be.

As I've shared throughout this book, staying fit remains a work in progress, but so does living with intention, growing as a leader, and staying aligned with what I deeply care about. I am still a work in progress, continuing to challenge myself, reflect, and evolve.

I reached for the sky, literally, and climbed to the top of Africa. I keep looking toward new horizons. The question isn't whether I can reach them. It's what mountain I'll climb next.

Summary

Evaluate: Key Takeaways

This chapter helped you assess your progress, uncover blind spots, and see your leadership through the eyes of those you impact.

- **Bridge the intention vs. impact gap:** Your actions don't always create the results you intend. Assess whether your leadership aligns with your values and how others experience you.
- **Gain insights from feedback and self-assessment:** Use external feedback to reveal blind spots and self-evaluation to track personal growth over time.
- **Manage your feedback triggers:** Notice truth, relationship, and identity triggers so you can stay curious rather than defensive and absorb the value in what you hear.
- **Pivot or persist:** When feedback arrives, choose to adjust a misaligned behavior (pivot) or double down on an effective strength (persist).
- **Engage stakeholders and manage perceptions:** Enlist colleagues who see and feel the impact of your leadership; ask them for monthly feedback and feedforward, to help you effectively change your behavior and them to see the change.

- **Track behaviors and outcomes:** Notice shifts in your actions, stakeholder perceptions, and tangible results to measure progress and broaden your influence.

Ask yourself: Are my actions having the impact I intend? Where is there a gap between how I see myself and how others experience me? What small changes will help me realign my leadership with my values?

Bringing It All Together

This chapter, "Evaluate," invited you to step back and ask, How am I truly showing up? It's about uncovering insights that bridge the gap between your intentions and your impact. By seeking feedback and embracing self-assessment, you've taken an honest look at how others perceive you and how your behaviors align, or misalign, with the outcomes you aim to achieve.

You've likely learned that feedback, while often uncomfortable, is a powerful gift. It can challenge your assumptions, reveal blind spots, and help you see yourself more clearly. But it can also feel overwhelming, especially when it's unexpected, conflicting, or hits a nerve. When that happens, pause. Check your emotional triggers. Consider the credibility and intent of the feedback giver. If needed, seek a second and third opinion. Then, come back to your values. Let them guide your next step, helping you discern whether the feedback aligns with the kind of leader and person you want to become. When you meet this discomfort with curiosity instead of defensiveness, feedback becomes a catalyst for growth.

You've also discovered that self-evaluation is most powerful when it brings together insight, intention, and action. It helps you connect the dots between how you're showing up, what is truly important to you, and the progress you're making.

The true power of self-evaluation lies in what it unlocks: clarity, confidence, and commitment. And it's not just about looking back. It's about looking inward and using what you discover to move forward—more aware, more intentional, and more aligned with the person you aspire to be.

Connecting feedback to your values makes it more meaningful and ensures that the changes you make aren't surface-level adjustments but lasting, purposeful transformations.

That's what the CORE framework is ultimately about. Clarifying what truly matters to you. Operationalizing it through intentional action. Reflecting on what gets in your way. Evaluating whether your efforts are working, so you can keep growing.

Sometimes this process creates subtle shifts. Other times, it leads to something bigger. A moment of realignment. A decision to act. A new story about who you are and what's possible.

These insights are invaluable. They highlight not just areas for improvement but also your capacity for growth and resilience. By acknowledging both the uncomfortable truths and the affirming discoveries, you gain a clearer picture of who you are today, and who you have the potential to become.

Keep asking the questions. Keep noticing the shifts. Keep choosing the next small step.

This is how you turn growth into a habit and intention into influence and impact. Keep asking yourself: Am I truly becoming the person and leader I aspire to be?

As you move forward, commit to this ongoing practice: seek honest mirrors, stay open to growth, and make time to celebrate.

Take a moment to appreciate the effort, the reflection, and the intentional steps you've taken. Not just the outcomes, but the courage it took to show up. Whether the shifts are big or small, they matter. You've done the work. You've moved forward with clarity and purpose. That is worth celebrating.

Let this be your reminder: Transformation doesn't come from insight alone, but from what you choose to do next.

So pause once more and ask yourself:

What's the most powerful insight you've gained about yourself?
What will you do with it?
Who are you becoming?

What's Next: CORE's Ripple Effect

This work doesn't stop with you. As your inner clarity deepens, your outer impact expands. The more grounded and intentional you become, the more you influence everything you touch. The next section explores how your growth creates a ripple effect far beyond yourself.

THE RIPPLE EFFECT OF CORE

Just as ripples spread out when a single pebble is dropped into water, the actions of individuals can have a far-reaching effect.

The Dalai Lama

A Path to Greater Fulfillment

As you've moved through this book, you haven't just learned to lead yourself more effectively. You've equipped yourself with tools to live more deliberately, more fully, and with deeper meaning.

The CORE framework isn't just a leadership strategy. It's a life strategy.

Each part of the process supports the foundational elements of well-being: strong relationships, a sense of purpose, the ability to grow and adapt, and the daily habits that shape how you feel and show up in the world.

Let's look at the impact more clearly:

Clarity strengthens purpose and direction. When you clarify your values, strengths, and priorities, you create an internal compass. You begin to define success on your own terms. This gives your actions a sense of purpose and helps you move with intention. A clear sense of purpose is one of the strongest predictors of long-term happiness.

Operationalizing builds habits that support a meaningful life. When you turn your values into consistent action, you create habits that align with what matters most to you. These daily choices, however small, reinforce your identity, fuel progress, and support your goals. These habits build your character and become the scaffolding for lasting change.

Reflection deepens self-awareness and emotional resilience. When you reflect, you create the space to notice how you're thinking, feeling, and reacting. You become more mindful. You learn to pause instead of just powering through or reacting automatically. That pause is powerful. It gives you the ability to respond deliberately, which strengthens relationships, increases emotional intelligence, and helps you stay aligned with your values, even under pressure.

Evaluation connects insight with impact. It helps you stay connected to your purpose and course-correct when needed. When you step back to ask, Am I doing what I said I would do? Am I having the impact I intended? you assess how others experience you, identify gaps, repair misunderstandings, and strengthen trust. This is the foundation of meaningful connection.

And when these pieces come together, they shape how you feel day to day.

You become more present.

You feel more confident in who you are and your direction.

You respond more intentionally.

You experience stronger relationships.

You build a life that feels aligned on the inside and impactful on the outside.

As a result, CORE isn't just about individual growth. It's about creating a ripple effect that starts with you and touches everyone around you.

The CORE of a Happier Life

You've been shaping the way you live, connect, and lead, both within yourself and in your relationships with others. In doing so, you create the conditions for greater happiness and well-being for yourself and those around you.

Happiness grows when we feel aligned with who we are, when our actions reflect our values, and when we experience progress, even in small ways. Each time you live with greater alignment, you contribute to the happiness of those around you.

While genetics play a role in baseline well-being, research consistently shows that how we live, our habits, mindset, and relationships, have a far greater impact on long-term happiness. From the Harvard Study of Adult Development[103] to research published by Calm,[104] Buffer,[105] and others, the message is clear: Happiness and fulfillment are shaped less by circumstances and more by how we choose to show up in our lives.

The tools in this book are not just leadership tools. They are life tools. They help you feel more connected, more grounded, and more capable of building a life that feels good from the inside out.

You may have started this journey to become a stronger leader. But along the way, you've also equipped yourself with the tools to become a happier, more whole version of yourself.

Happiness is not a static trait. It's shaped by how we live, connect, and grow. And the CORE framework gives you the tools to cultivate it, intentionally, consistently, and in ways that ripple far beyond yourself.

When you live with clarity, act with purpose, reflect with honesty, and evaluate with courage, you create a life that feels more grounded, meaningful, and fulfilling.

And when you lead with clarity, purpose, and authenticity, you not only impact your own life, you influence the lives of others; you create a ripple effect. As Garry Ridge reminds us, "Happy people create happy families. Happy families create happy communities. Happy communities create a happy world."[106]

Your growth doesn't end with you. By showing up with greater intention and alignment, you help create the conditions for others to thrive, too. You help create a better, more connected world.

That's how real change happens. It starts from within and ripples outward. And that's the true power of CORE.

What's Next?

Moving Forward with Clarity and Purpose

As we reach the end of our journey together through the CORE framework, pause to take it all in. You've explored the depths of "Clarity," "Operationalize," "Reflect," and "Evaluate," each step guiding you closer to a more intentional focused and fulfilled life.

What have you discovered about yourself through this process?

How have you grown?

Perhaps you've uncovered patterns or perspectives you hadn't fully seen before, or limiting beliefs you didn't know were holding you back. Maybe you've reconnected with values you had forgotten or found the courage to make changes you once thought were impossible. This journey has invited you to deepen your understanding of yourself and supported your commitment to living in alignment with your aspirations.

Pause to consider what you've learned and how you can build on it. Think about the insights you've gained, the challenges you've navigated, the effort you've invested, and the strengths you've uncovered or refined along the way.

Growth doesn't just come from outcomes, it comes from awareness, reflection, and the willingness to keep learning. Let these lessons guide your next steps.

I hope you've found meaning in this journey and growth in the process. You've gained new tools, deeper insights, and a renewed sense of what is possible when you lead with clarity and intention. Let those insights stay with you, not just for today, but as a lasting guide to help you navigate life's twists and turns with purpose and resilience.

Stay grounded in the belief that change is possible and worth pursuing.

Build Your Community

I've often found that the path to personal transformation becomes more enriching and less daunting when shared with others. Growth doesn't have to be a solo journey. Some of the most meaningful insights and changes come from conversations, reflections, and shared experiences.

Start a discussion group. Join a circle of trusted peers. Create space in your workplace, community, or circle of friends to explore these ideas together. Even a single conversation can spark new awareness and reinforce the work you're doing. Talk about the challenges you've faced and the tools that helped. Celebrate the small wins. Ask the hard questions. Support each other in staying accountable to the changes you want to make.

There's power in learning together. And strength in knowing you're not alone. When you create space for honest conversations, shared learning, and mutual encouragement, you help build communities that are stronger, more open, and more resilient.

Embrace Lifelong Learning

Growth doesn't stop with the last page of this book. In fact, this is just the beginning. I encourage you to keep this conversation with yourself alive. Continue to seek out new experiences, read voraciously, and challenge your preconceptions. As you evolve, so will your understanding of these core principles.

Reflect on what you've achieved, celebrate your progress, and turn your gaze forward.

There will always be new layers to uncover, more wisdom to gain, and further clarity to achieve. Make it a goal to revisit your CORE framework regularly; let it be a living guide, adapting as you do. Ask yourself:

- How have I continued to grow?
- What new insights have emerged as I apply these tools in my life?
- What transformations am I most proud of?

Define Your Next Kilimanjaro

So, here you stand, stronger and more self-aware than when you started. But this isn't the end, it's the beginning of the next chapter.

What will be your next Kilimanjaro? What bold, ambitious challenge will you take on to continue stretching, growing, and becoming the person you aspire to be? Keep reaching for new heights and new skies.

Remember, the work you do for yourself has the power to uplift those around you, your teams, your family, and your communities. As you lead with purpose and integrity, you contribute to a world where happiness and fulfillment can grow and thrive.

Let your journey inspire you, your values ground you, and your aspirations drive you.

Your next summit awaits. Keep climbing.

A Personal Note From Miki

This book is my heart laid bare, a culmination of years of learning, stumbling, and triumphing. Each word penned in these pages has been a step in my own path of clarity and purpose. I wrote this book to connect with you, to share what I've learned in the hope that it might light your way, as it has mine. From challenging the limiting beliefs instilled in me to embracing my capacity for leadership and self-growth, every step has been worth it.

Your journey might be different from mine, but the essence of discovery remains the same. As you close this book, don't see it as the end. It's a new beginning, a first step on your own unique path to leading a more conscious, purpose-driven life. Remember, leadership starts with you, from the quiet moments of self-reflection to the bold steps you take towards your dreams. Keep moving forward, keep leading by example, and let your life be your message.

Acknowledgments

FIRST AND FOREMOST, I want to express my deepest gratitude to my husband, Bart. Our supportive relationship has enabled me to pursue my passions and forge my career path. Your unwavering support over the past thirty-five years has been my anchor. Thank you for loving me for who I am and who I aspire to be. Your belief in my message and our cross-country adventures with our dogs in a camper van, just so I could find my idyllic writing space, mean more to me than words can convey. Thank you for understanding and supporting those late nights and weekends when I was lost in my writing flow.

To my best friend, Michal Ramon, thank you for embodying what it means to live by your values. Your constant inspiration and belief in me have been invaluable.

To my children, Arden and Sean, this book is dedicated to you. I've learned so much from you, and I hope the messages within these pages guide you to lead happy, fulfilled lives.

My deepest appreciation to my beta readers, Chris Fenning, Josh Brand, and Anne Bazel, and to my editor, Ruth-Anne Eisler. Your edits, critiques and support have been instrumental in shaping this book. A big thank you to Jenny Lisk, my go-to guide throughout the publishing journey. Your sharp eye and practical guidance—catching mistakes, refining text, and helping me navigate the ins and outs of the process—made this book stronger. Just as importantly, your support preserved my sanity along the way. Thank you to Andrew Welyczko, my cover designer and layout formatter, for bringing creativity and patience to the many iterations, and for your dedication to making this book the best it can be.

I'd like to thank the incredible individuals I interviewed for this book: Garry Ridge, Ayse Birsel, Chester Elton, Rhett Power, Carol Kauffman, and a special thank you to Dorie Clark. Your insights and the Recognized Expert community you've created have been pivotal in honing my message and the CORE framework.

A heartfelt thanks to my mentor, Liz Kislik, for her invaluable guidance. I also want to acknowledge Ron Carucci, who, along with Liz, chose me to be part of the first cohort of the Forefront program. This program has enriched my life, propelling my career and leadership to where I am today.

And finally, to Marshall Goldsmith—your guidance, conversations, and the Forefront program have been a beacon on my journey. Thank you for everything.

Notes

Chapter 1

1. Dorie Clark, interview by Miki Feldman Simon, https://coreleadershipbook.com/resources.
2. Clark, interview.
3. Frances Hesselbein, Frances Hesselbein Oral History Interviews, https://tobiascenter.iu.edu/research/oral-history/audio-transcripts/hesselbein-frances.html.
4. Adam Grant, *Think Again: The Power of Knowing What You Don't Know* (Viking, 2021).
5. Grant, *Think Again*.
6. Chester Elton and Adrian Gostick, *Leading with Gratitude: Eight Leadership Practices for Extraordinary Business Results* (Harper Business, 2020).
7. Andrew Molinsky et al, "Avoiding the Pitfalls of Identity Conflict: Psychological and Behavioral Consequences of Identity Integration," *Organizational Behavior and Human Decision Processes* 109, no. 1 (2009): 104–116. https://doi.org/10.1016/j.obhdp.2009.03.002.
8. Marshall Goldsmith, *Triggers: Creating Behavior That Lasts—Becoming the Person You Want to Be* (Crown Business, 2015).
9. Carol Kauffman, interview by Miki Feldman Simon, https://coreleadershipbook/com/resources.
10. Gallup, "U.S. Employee Engagement Sinks to 10-Year Low," Gallup Workplace Insights, January 13, 2025. This report notes that "employee engagement in the U.S. fell to its lowest level in a decade in 2024, with only 31% of employees engaged."
11. Garry Ridge, interview by Miki Feldman Simon, https://coreleadershipbook/com/resources.
12. Warren Buffett et al, *The Tao of Warren Buffett: Warren Buffett's Words of Wisdom* (New York: Scribner, 2006).
13. Ayse Birsel, interview by Miki Feldman Simon, https://coreleadershipbook/com/resources.
14. Ayse Birsel, *Design the Life You Love: A Step-by-Step Guide to Building a Meaningful Future* (Ten Speed Press, 2015).
15. Karen Kimsey-House et al, *Co-Active Coaching* (Quercus, 2018).

16. Martin Seligman, *Flourish: A Visionary New Understanding of Happiness and Well-being* (Free Press, 2011).
17. Clark, interview.
18. Take the VIA Character Strengths assessment: https://www.viacharacter.org/.
19. Take the Clifton Strengths Assessment: https://www.gallup.com/cliftonstrengths/en/home.aspx.
20. Take The 6 Types of Working Genius Assessment: https://www.workinggenius.com/.
21. Patrick Lencioni, *The 6 Types of Working Genius* (Table Group, 2022).
22. Rhett Power, interview by Miki Feldman Simon, https://coreleadershipbook.com/resources.
23. Power, interview.
24. Toyota, "The 5 Whys Problem-Solving Method," 2025, https://www.toyota.com/usa/5whys.
25. Simon Sinek, *Start with Why: How Great Leaders Inspire Everyone to Take Action* (Portfolio, 2009).
26. Adam Grant, *Originals: How Non-Conformists Move the World* (Viking, 2016).
27. Grant, *Originals*.
28. Ridge, interview.
29. Gail Matthews, "Goal Research Summary," (paper presented at the International Conference on Personal and Professional Coaching, Dominican University of California, 2007).

Chapter 2

30. Birsel, interview.
31. Birsel, interview.
32. Clayton Christensen, *How Will You Measure Your Life?* (Harvard Business Review Press, 2012).
33. Clark, interview.
34. Clark, interview.
35. Greg McKeown, *Essentialism: The Disciplined Pursuit of Less* (Crown Business, 2014).
36. McKeown, *Essentialism*.
37. Phillippa Lally et al, "How Are Habits Formed: Modelling Habit Formation in the Real World," *European Journal of Social Psychology* 40, no. 6 (2010): 998–1009.
38. James Clear, *Atomic Habits: An Easy & Proven Way to Build Good Habits & Break Bad Ones* (Avery, 2018).
39. Power, interview.
40. Power, interview.
41. Goldsmith, *Triggers*.
42. Goldsmith, *Triggers*.
43. Goldsmith, *Triggers*.

44. Robert Emmons, *Thanks! How the New Science of Gratitude Can Make You Happier* (Houghton Mifflin Harcourt, 2007).
45. Elton and Gostick, *Leading with Gratitude.*
46. Chester Elton, interview by Miki Feldman Simon, https://coreleadershipbook.com/resources.
47. Elton, interview
48. Seth Godin, *The Dip: A Little Book That Teaches You When to Quit (and When to Stick)* (Portfolio, 2007).
49. Ridge, interview.
50. Ridge, interview.
51. Carol Kauffman, interview by Miki Feldman Simon, https://coreleadershipbook.com/resources.
52. Kauffman, interview.
53. Kauffman, interview.

Chapter 3

54. Marcus Aurelius, *Meditations*, trans. Gregory Hays (Modern Library, 2002).
55. Viktor E. Frankl, *Man's Search For Meaning* (Boston: Beacon Press, 2006).
56. Steven Covey, *The 7 Habits of Highly Effective People* (Free Press, 1989).
57. Daniel Kahneman, *Thinking, Fast and Slow* (Farrar, Straus and Giroux, 2011).
58. Kahneman, *Thinking.*
59. Malcolm Gladwell, *Blink: The Power of Thinking Without Thinking* (Little, Brown and Company, 2005).
60. Kahneman, *Thinking.*
61. Shirzad Chamine, *Positive Intelligence: Why Only 20% of Teams and Individuals Achieve Their True Potential and How You Can Achieve Yours* (Greenleaf Book Group Press, 2012).
62. Chamine, *Positive Intelligence.*
63. Chamine, *Positive Intelligence.*
64. Take Shirzad Chamine's Saboteur Assessment: https://www.positiveintelligence.com/saboteurs/
65. Chamine, *Positive Intelligence.*
66. Chamine, *Positive Intelligence.*
67. Paula Davis, *Beating Burnout at Work: Why Teams Hold the Secret to Well-Being and Resilience* (Philadelphia: Wharton School Press, 2021). Davis outlines the "4 Ps" (Pause, Process, Plan, Proceed) as a micro-strategy for stress management and intentional action.
68. Kauffman, interview.
69. Kauffman, interview. Learn more about the 5 Cs in Carol Kauffman and David Noble's book: *Real-Time Leadership: Find Your Winning Moves When the Stakes Are High* (Harvard Business Review Press, 2023)

70. Peter Senge, *The Fifth Discipline: The Art and Practice of the Learning Organization* (Doubleday, 1990).
71. Daniel J. Simons and Christopher F. Chabris, "Gorillas in Our Midst: Sustained Inattentional Blindness for Dynamic Events," *Perception* 28, no. 9 (1999): 1059–1074. About half of participants failed to notice the gorilla.
72. Quote Investigator, "Watch Your Thoughts, They Become Words," May 9, 2013, https://quoteinvestigator.com/2013/05/09/watch-your-thoughts/. Commonly attributed to Lao Tzu, though not found in the *Tao Te Ching*. The earliest documented version appears in the early 20th century and is considered a modern proverb.
73. David Bayer, *A Changed Mind: Go Beyond Self Awareness, Rewire Your Brain & Reengineer Your Reality* (Self-published, 2023).
74. Bayer, *A Changed Mind*.
75. Bruce Lipton, *The Biology of Belief: Unleashing the Power of Consciousness, Matter and Miracles* (Hay House, 2005).
76. Christian van Nieuwerburgh, *An Introduction to Coaching Skills: A Practical Guide*, 2nd ed. (London: SAGE, 2017). Exact figures vary across sources, but the consistent finding is that most of our thoughts are repetitive and a large portion lean negative.
77. Richard L. Gregory, Eye and Brain: *The Psychology of Seeing*, 5th ed. (Princeton, NJ: Princeton University Press, 1997).
78. Edward Titchener, *Experimental Psychology: A Manual of Laboratory Practice* (Macmillan, 1901).
79. Daniel Wegner et al, "Paradoxical Effects of Thought Suppression," *Journal of Personality and Social Psychology* 53, no. 1 (1987): 5–13.
80. Olga Khazan, "Can Three Words Turn Anxiety Into Success?" *The Atlantic*, March 23, 2016, https://www.theatlantic.com/health/archive/2016/03/can-three-words-turn-anxiety-into-success/474909/.
81. Eric Barker, "5 Questions That Will Make You Emotionally Strong," *Barking Up the Wrong Tree* (blog), n.d., https://bakadesuyo.com/2017/03/emotionally-strong/
82. Barker, 5 Questions.
83. Barker, 5 Questions.
84. NHS Foundation Trust, *Catch it, Check it, Change it: A Guide to Thinking Differently*, (National Health Service, 2014).
85. James Clear, *Atomic Habits: An Easy & Proven Way to Build Good Habits & Break Bad Ones* (Avery, 2018).
86. Carol Dweck, *Mindset: The New Psychology of Success* (Random House, 2006).
87. Dweck, *Mindset*.
88. Dweck, *Mindset*.
89. Malcolm Gladwell, *Outliers: The Story of Success* (Little, Brown and Company, 2008).

Chapter 4

90. Joseph Luft and Harrington Ingham, "The Johari Window: A Graphic Model of Awareness in Interpersonal Relations," *Proceedings of the Western Training Laboratory in Group Development* (University of California, 1955).

91. Elton, interview.

92. Douglas Stone and Sheila Heen, *Thanks for the Feedback: The Science and Art of Receiving Feedback Well* (Viking, 2014).

93. Tasha Eurich, *Insight: Why We're Not as Self-Aware as We Think, and How Seeing Ourselves Clearly Helps Us Succeed at Work and in Life* (Crown Business, 2017).

94. Clark, interview.

95. Brené Brown, *Dare to Lead: Brave Work. Tough Conversations. Whole Hearts* (Random House, 2018).

96. Adam Grant, *Hidden Potential: The Science of Achieving Greater Things* (Viking, 2023).

97. Ridge, interview.

98. Elton, interview.

99. Eurich, *Insight*.

100. Marshall Goldsmith, "Stakeholder Centered Coaching," Marshall Goldsmith, Accessed August 15, 2025, https://www.marshallgoldsmith.com/post/stakeholder-centered-coaching.

101. Marshall Goldsmith, "Leadership is a Contact Sport," Marshall Goldsmith, Accessed August 15, 2025, https://www.marshallgoldsmith.com/post/leadership-is-a-contact-sport.

102. Goldsmith, *Triggers*.

Chapter 5

103. Robert Waldinger, "Good Genes Are Nice, but Joy Is Better," *Harvard Gazette*, April 11, 2017, https://news.harvard.edu/gazette/story/2017/04/over-nearly-80-years-harvard-study-has-been-showing-how-to-live-a-healthy-and-happy-life/ p. 172.

104. Calm, "What Makes People Happy? Here's What Research Says," Accessed 2025, https://www.calm.com/blog/what-makes-people-happy.

105. Buffer, "11 Simple Things That Will Make You Happier, Backed by Science," Accessed 2025, https://buffer.com/resources/happiness-habits-backed-by-science.

106. Ridge, interview.

Index

Numbers
3 Rs (Receive, Reflect, Respond) 199–200
4 Ps heuristic (Pause, Process, Plan, Proceed) 123–125
5 Primary Drivers 141
The 6 Types of Working Genius 40–41
"10,000-hour rule" 176
360° interviews 5, 34, 68, 187–188, 204, 212, 219

A
above the line 193–194
acceptance 156
accountability 61, 92–97
    daily questions 94–97
actions, from values 63–64
adaptability, leveraging strengths 88
affect labeling 163–165
Alex's story 118–119
aligning
    actions with values and priorities 59–66
    values with actions 24–26
Andrea's story 211, 214
Angelou, Maya 47
anxiety 157–158
appreciation 99
Argyris, Chris 135–136
assessing your alignment 65–66
assumptions, Ladder of Inference 136–138
attention, redirecting 159–161
Aurelius, Marcus 112
authentic self, living your values 19–20
Avoiders 120
awareness, reframing toolbox 155

B
Barker, Eric 160
Bayer, David 139, 141
behavior tracking, self-evaluate 217–218
behaviors that align with your values 61–63
being the person I want to be 103–105
being versus doing 50–51
beliefs
    limiting 142–148
    thoughts become reality 140–142
Beth's story 197
Birsel, Ayse 29, 47, 58
blind spots
    identifying your strengths 190–192
    uncovering 207–208
body scanning 121
boundaries, setting 21
Brown, Brené 203
Buffett, Warren 28
building habits and routines 77–87

C
celebrating progress 100–101
Chamine, Shirzad 120
changing perceptions to cement change 215
character 11
childhood echoes, shaping your values 16–18
childhood values 28
Christensen, Clayton 59
Clarify 4–6, 11–12
    clarity 12–15
    defining success 46–52
    defining your values *see* values
    identifying your strengths 31–42
    mission statements 51–52
    navigating priorities 42–46
clarity 21, 227
    as a key to success 12–15
    moving forward with 231–233
    reflecting on your values 23–24
Clark, Dorie 12–13, 38–39, 47, 75, 201–202

Clear, James 82, 168
Cognitive Behavioral Therapy, Three Cs (Catching, Checking, and Changing) 166–167
cognitive loop, habits 80
collaboration, leveraging strengths 88
commitment to quality 62
community, building 232
compassion 21, 126–127
compliments 36–38
consistency 177
Controllers 120
CORE framework 4–6
  Clarify *see* Clarify
  Evaluate *see* Evaluate
  Operationalize *see* Operationalize
  Reflect *see* Reflect
Covey, Stephen R. 114
COVID pandemic 17, 69–70
cue-routine-reward sequence 79
cue/triggers
  habit stacking 82
  habits 78, 81
  see also triggers
cultural values 18–19

D
daily questions 94–97, 218
daily reflection, power of 112
David's story 44–45, 67, 96
decisions, re-evaluating 138–139
decisiveness, leveraging strengths 88
deconstruction 58
difficult conversations, feedback 203–205
directing your attention 161
discipline 21
do less of, living your values through action 66, 68–69, 73
do more of, living your values through action 67, 69–71, 73
doing, versus being 50–51
Dweck, Carol 168, 170–171
  "power of yet" 172–173

E
Ebbinghaus illusion 152–153
effective communication, leveraging strengths 88
Einstein, Albert 47
Ellen's story 187–188, 195, 206
Elton, Chester 47, 99, 192, 205

emotion
  affect labeling 163–165
  as insight 165–166
  and language 161–163
  see also feelings
emotional contagion 174
empathy 62
  leveraging strengths 88–89
energy, nurturing a growth mindset 174–176
environment, setting up for success 90–91
Eurich, Tasha 200, 205
Evaluate 5–6, 188
  mind the gap *see* mind the gap
  persist 209–211
  pivot 209–213
  self-evaluate 216–220
  turning feedback into impact 208–216
evaluation 228

F
family comes first, behaviors that align with your values 62–63
feedback 188, 192
  above the line 193–194
  below the line 193–196
  gaining 205–208
  having difficult conversations 203–205
  navigating feedback triggers 196–200
  pivot 211–213
  positive feedback 199
  receiving 192–196
  reframing 206–207
  role of stakeholders in your growth journey 213–215
  sources for 200–203
  turning into impact 208–216
feedback loops 177
feedforward 214
feelings
  naming 167
  see also emotion
Fiona's story 36
firm no 76
Five Cs (Calm, Clear, Curious, Compassionate, and Courageous) 125–128
The Five Whys 48–50
fixed mindset 170–172
focused breathing 121
Frankl, Viktor 114
"friers" 18

G

Gabriela's story 157–158
Gavin's story 36
generosity 63
George's story 68, 90
gift of compliments 36–38
Ginsburg, Ruth Bader 28–29
"The Glad Game" 98–99
Gladwell, Malcolm 117, 176
goals 57, 177
Godin, Seth 102
Goldsmith, Marshall 20, 24, 47, 92, 94–95, 145, 178, 199, 206, 215, 218
Gostick, Adrian 99
Grant, Adam 18–19, 50, 203
grateful no 76
gratitude 97–100, 157
growth
    having the difficult conversations 204–205
    personal and professional 32–33
    stakeholders in your growth journey 213–215
growth mindset, nurturing 170–177, 181

H

habit loop 79, 81–82
habit stacking 82–87
habits
    designing 82
    how long before they form 80–81
    how they work 77–82
    transferring across domains 85–87
happiness 228–229
heroes 28–29
Heroes Exercise 29
Hesselbein, Frances 13
high identity integration 20
high-performance teams, leveraging strengths to build 33–34
Huffington, Arianna 47
Hyper-Achiever 120

I

"I am" statement 51–52
identifying
    blind spots 190–192
    your strengths, trail of excellence 31–32
    your triggers 131
    your values 27–31
identity, being versus doing, 50–51
identity integration, living your values 20
identity triggers 197
impact 208–209
    persist 209–211
    pivot 209–213
improving new things every day 176–177
incremental learning 176
Ingham, Harrington 190
innovation 61–62
integrating the pause 129–130
integrity 61
intention 174
    clarity 12
intention vs. impact gap 188–190
    identifying blind spots and expanding self-awareness 190–192
internal dialogues, rewriting 150
interviews, getting people to open up 37
intuition 117
Invisible Gorilla Experiment 138

J

Jack's story 197
Jake's story 71–72, 194–195
Jane's story 131
Janice's story 86–87
Joe's story 70, 209
John's story 144–145
Johari Window 190–191
Jordan, Michael 47, 171
Judge 120

K

Kahneman, Daniel 115
Kauffman, Carol 22, 47, 104, 114, 125–126
Ken's story 85
Kilimanjaro 3, 32, 64, 172, 178
    trekking up 179–181
Kislik, Liz 146
Kurzweil Education 33

L

Ladder of Inference 135–138
language 161–163, 167–170
language shift 156
leadership, behaviors that align with your values 62
Leah's story 212–214
learning
    incremental learning 176
    lifelong learning 232

learning dip, navigating 101–103
learning from what already works 70–71
Lencioni, Patrick 40
letting go 177–178
leveraging strengths
    to build high-performance teams 33–34
    Operationalize 87–91
    see also strengths
limiting beliefs 141–148
Linda's story 162–163
Lipton, Bruce 142
Lisa's story 194–195
living your mandate 22–23
living your values
    aligning values with actions 24–26
    living your mandate 22–23
    one authentic self 19–20
    reflecting on your values 23–24
    ripple effect 20–21
living your values through action
    do less of 66, 68–69, 73
    do more of 67, 69–71, 73
    learning from what already works 70–71
    saying no 73–77
    start 66–67, 73
    stop 66–68, 72
low identity integration 20
Luft, Joseph 190

M

mandates, living 22–23
Mandela, Nelson 47
mapping triggers 133
Marc's story 70–71, 209
Mark's story 123–125
Martin's story 130–132
Mary's story 193–194
meaning-making 133
mind the gap 188–190
    above the line 193–194
    below the line 193–196
    feedback *see* feedback
    identifying blind spots and expanding self-awareness 190–192
    receiving feedback 192–196
mind tricks 151–154
mindfulness 156
mindset 177
    see also growth mindset
mission statements 51–52
Mom's story 134–135

motivation *see* staying motivated
moving forward with clarity and purpose 231–233
Müller-Lyer illusion 151–152

N

naming feelings 167
negative self-talk 149, 169
negative thoughts 150–151
    challenging 155
no with a rain check 76
nurturing a growth mindset 170–177
    energy 174–176
    improving new things every day 176–177
    "power of yet" 172–173

O

Obama, Michelle 47
Operationalize 5–6
    accountability 92–97
    aligning actions with values and priorities 59–66
    building habits and routines 77–87
    gratitude 97–100
    leveraging strengths 87–91
    living your values through action 66–77
    staying motivated 97–105
operationalizing 227–228
optical illusions 151–153
optimism, "The Glad Game" 98–99
organizational values 26–31
outcome metrics, self-evaluate 218–219

P

Pam's story 137–138
Paul's story 24–26
path to greater fulfillment 227–229
pause
    4 Ps heuristic (Pause, Process, Plan, Proceed) 123–125
    Five Cs (Calm, Clear, Curious, Compassionate, and Courageous) 125–128
    integrating 129–130
    physiological impacts of 114–115
    Positive Intelligence 120–123
    power of 114–115
    System 1 and System 2 Thinking 115–119
perception
    changing to cement change 215

INDEX

and language 161–163
persist 209–211
personal growth 32–33
   see also growth
perspective-taking 156
Phonetic Systems 22–23
physiological impacts of a pause 114–115
pivot 209–213
polite no 75
positive feedback 199
positive intelligence 120–123
Positive Intelligence repetitions (PQ reps) 120–123
Positive Psychology 31, 69
positive self-talk 150
Power, Rhett 44, 92–93
power of a pause 114–115
power of daily reflection 112
power of words 168–169
"power of yet" 172–173
PQ reps (Positive Intelligence repetitions) 120–123
priorities
   aligning with actions 59–66
   navigating 42–46
professional growth 32–33
purpose, moving forward with 231–233

R
receiving feedback 192–196
recognition, staying motivated 101
reconstruction 58
redirecting your attention 159–161
re-evaluating decisions 138–139
Reflect 5–6
   letting go 177–178
   nurturing a growth mindset 170–177
   power of daily reflection 112
   slowing down to speed up *see* slowing down to speed up
   stories we tell ourselves 134–139
   triggers 130–133
   What we think, we become *see* What we think, we become
reflecting 228
   on your values 21, 23–24
   power of daily reflection 112
   through self-assessments 40–41
reframing 154–159
   feedback 206–207
reframing toolbox 155–157
relationship triggers 197

repetition and reinforcement, habits 79
resilience
   building to triggers 132–133
   leveraging strengths 88
respect 61
reward/outcome, habits 78, 81
rewriting internal dialogues 150
Ridge, Garry 26–27, 47, 51, 103, 203–204
ripple effect 227–229
   living your values 20–21
Rob's story 211–212, 214
role-model balance 21
routine/behavior, habits 78, 81

S
saboteurs 120–121
Samantha's story 123–125
Sandy's story 77
Sarah's story 34–35
saying no 73–77
seeing ourselves through others' eyes 39
self-assessments
   aligning actions with values and priorities 66
   structured reflections on strength 40–41
self-awareness 117
   expanding 190–192
self-awareness unicorns 205–206
self-discovery, gift of compliments 36–38
self-evaluate
   alignment 217
   behavior tracking 217–218
   daily questions 218
   outcome metrics 218–219
   see also Evaluate
self-leadership 1–2
self-reflection 34, 84, 92, 104, 137
self-talk 148–150
   upgrading 169–170
Seligman, Martin 31
sensory awareness 121
shaping your values, childhood echoes 16–18
Sharon's story 81–82
Shelley's story 67, 90, 96
shifting your perspective, reframing toolbox 155–157
silent counting 121
slowing down to speed up 113–115
   4 Ps heuristic (Pause, Process, Plan, Proceed) 123–125

Five Cs (Calm, Clear, Curoius,
    Compassionate, and Courageous)
    125–128
  integrating the pause 129–130
  pause 114–119
  positive intelligence 120–123
  see also pause
Sofia's story 140–141, 163–165
sources for feedback 200–203
stakeholders in your growth journey
    213–215
  engaging 215–216
start, living your values through action
    66–67, 73
staying motivated
  am I the person I want to be 103–105
  celebrating progress 100–101
  gratitude 97–100
  navigating the Learning Dip 101–103
Steve's story 101
stop, living your values through action
    66–68, 72
stories we tell ourselves, Reflect 134–139
strategic thinking, leveraging strengths
    87
strengths
  accountability 92–97
  discovering 36–39
  leveraging 87–91
  leveraging to build high-performance
    teams 33–34
  personal and professional growth
    32–33
  playing to 31–32
  seeing ourselves through other's eyes
    39
  uncovering what sets you apart 34–35
  unleashing talents 36
structured reflections through, self-
    assessments 40–41
success
  defining 46–52
  harnessing strengths for 88–89
  setting up your environment for 90–91
support 157
System 1 and System 2 Thinking 115–119

T

talents, unleashing 36
thoughts, negative thoughts 151
thoughts become reality 140–142

Three Cs (Catching, Checking, and
    Changing) 166–167
time 73–77
  aligning actions with values and
    priorities 59–60
Titchener, Edward B. 152
Titchener circles 152–153
triggers 130–133
  feedback triggers 196–200
  mapping 133
  truth triggers 196–197
  see cue/triggers
Tzu, Lao 140

V

value pantheon 29–31
values 15–16
  aligning with actions 24–26, 59–66
  childhood values 28
  cultural values 18–19
  defining behaviors that align with
    values 61–63
  identifying 27–31
  living 19–26
  organizational values 26–31
  reflecting on 23–24
  shaping 16–19
  turning into actions 63–64
  value pantheon 29–31
values clarification exercise 25
visionary leaders, definitions of success
    46–48

W

WD-40 26–27
weekly self-questions 218
What we think, we become
  attention 159–161
  emotions as insight 165–166
  language 167–170
  limiting beliefs 142–148
  mind tricks 151–154
  negative thoughts 150–151
  reframing 154–159
  self-talk 148–150
  thoughts become reality 140–142
  Three Cs (Catching, Checking, and
    Changing) 166–167
  you are not what you feel 161–165
working genius 40–41

About the Author

MIKI FELDMAN SIMON is an executive coach, successful business leader, and dynamic public speaker. Over her thirty-year career, she has worked globally—in the United States, Israel, and Australia—holding leadership roles in marketing, operations, and human resources across multiple industries. She has led organizations through growth and successful acquisitions, including Profitect and Phonetic Systems, and brings a deep understanding of the challenges executives face.

Whether through this book, working one-on-one, or on stage in keynotes and workshops, Miki's enthusiasm and insights inspire action and lasting impact. Known for her positive energy, humor, and authenticity, she blends personal and professional experience with practical, research-based tools that audiences can apply immediately. Her contagious passion for growth motivates leaders and teams to push past barriers, overcome obstacles, and discover new possibilities.

As an executive coach, Miki partners with seasoned leaders to broaden their impact and supports newly promoted executives to succeed in their roles. She meets her clients where they are in their leadership journey. Using the CORE Leadership framework she has created—Clarify, Operationalize, Reflect, Evaluate—she helps them better align personally and professionally, and lead with authenticity and impact. Miki brings to her clients practical tools and strategies, rooted in science and behavioral psychology, enabling them to achieve and sustain meaningful change. Her clients describe her as a "straight shooter" with a rare combination of warmth, intelligence, and honesty—collaborative, empathetic, and unafraid to provide candid feedback. She has worked with leaders in small startups as well as thriving unicorns in a variety of industries. Many of their stories are in this book.

Passionate about equality in leadership, Miki has helped organizations achieve meaningful change, including leading Profitect to gender parity across all levels—with a 50 percent female management team heading the company's finance, marketing, program management, human resources, and customer success departments. She also founded *IamBackatWork*, a platform that has helped thousands of women regain their confidence and reenter the workforce.

Miki holds a BA in psychology and educational counseling, an MS in organizational behavior, is a certified executive coach (ICF PCC), certified in Marshall Goldsmith's Stakeholder Centered Coaching and Applied Critical Thinking, and is a member of the inaugural Forefront cohort powered by Marshall Goldsmith and 100 Coaches.

Miki is an avid traveler and a global citizen. She enjoys a good challenge, whether reinventing her career multiple times or getting fit at fifty to summit Mount Kilimanjaro. Her greatest fulfillment comes from her thirty-two-year marriage, her two children, and the relationships she's built along the way. She calls Lexington, Massachusetts home, where she lives with her husband and two dogs. Her son works as an avalanche forecaster in Missoula, Montana, and her daughter as an event planner in Boston, Massachusetts.

Miki's work and insights have been featured in the *Boston Globe*, *HuffPost*, *Society for Human Resource Management*, *Business News Daily*, *Knox News*, and more. She writes and coaches in a voice that is clear, practical, and deeply human—blending strategic insight with empathy and always inviting people to see what's possible when they choose to lead themselves first.

www.ingramcontent.com/pod-product-compliance
Lightning Source LLC
Chambersburg PA
CBHW030453100526
44580CB00009B/119/J